Praise for *How Words Get Good*

'An engaging little eye-opener about the publishing business, full of tasty nuggets about books, writers and their editors' *Sunday Times*

'A revelatory account of how books get made, and a delightful hymn to human collaboration. No really: you'll be entertained on every page!' Rebecca Gowers, author of *Horrible Words: A Guide to the Misuse of English*

'Bibliophiles will really enjoy this ... Rebecca Lee takes you on a journey – a book's journey – and there's never a dull moment. She moves skilfully back and forth between fascinating book-making history to delightful modern-day anecdotes from both her own experience and other experts in the book-publishing profession' Hana Videen, author of *The Wordhord: Daily Life in Old English*

'Everything you could want to know, and a whole lot more you didn't even know you wanted, about the history and process of writing. Fascinating stories, secrets and nuggets of advice from inside the belly of the publishing beast. You'll finish this book wanting to get started on your own, and knowing exactly how to go about it' Edward Brooke-Hitching, author of *The Madman's Library: The Greatest Curiosities of Literature*

'A book full of good words about how words get good. Drawing on wide reading and long experience, Rebecca Lee shines a light on the talented people who work behind the scenes to bring the best possible version of a book to its readers. Revealing, readable and fun' Tom Mole, author of *The Secret Life of Books: W*

T0020557

Join Rebecca Lee, professional text-improver, as she embarks on a fascinating journey to find out how words get from author's brain to printed book. She'll reveal the dark arts of ghostwriters, explore the secret world of literary agents and uncover the hidden beauty of typesetting. Along the way, her quest will be punctuated by a litany of little-known considerations that make a big impact: ellipses, indexes, hyphens, esoteric points of grammar and juicy post-publication corrections. After all, the best stories happen when it all goes wrong.

From foot-and-note disease to the town of Index, Missouri – turn the page to discover how books get made and words get good.*

About the author

Rebecca Lee is a senior editorial manager at Penguin Press, where she has spent twenty years wrangling hundreds of high-profile books to print.

Her knowledge and experience cover the whole of publishing, from the physical nuts and bolts (and plates) of printing to the abstract world of ellipses, Oxford commas and gerunds. Along the way, she's absorbed the delicate art of author management and how to behave at launch parties. From coordinating manuscripts covertly despatched by MI5 to triple-checking the minutiae of a chef's secret sauce, she's curated her own storied career from the thousands of pages that have passed through her hands.

Her days are spent turning raw manuscripts into reader-ready books, making sure the words have got good before they're set free.

---

* Or, at least, better.

HOW WORDS GET GOOD

The Story of Making a Book

REBECCA LEE

P

PROFILE BOOKS

This paperback edition first published in 2023

First published in Great Britain in 2022 by
Profile Books Ltd
29 Cloth Fair
London
ECIA 7JQ
www.profilebooks.com

10 9 8 7 6 5 4 3 2 1

Printed and bound in Great Britain by
CPI Group (UK) Ltd, Croydon CR0 4YY

A CIP catalogue record for this book is available from the British Library.

ISBN 978 1 78816 638 6
eISBN 978 1 78283 759 6

In memory of Patricia Mary Lee,
who taught me my first words

'A book is a version of the world. If you do not like it, ignore it; or offer your own version in return.'
Salman Rushdie

Contents

INTRODUCTION: WELCOME TO
THE GUTENBERG GALAXY

'There is no frigate like a book.'
Emily Dickinson

In 1962 Canadian philosopher Marshall McLuhan published a book called *The Gutenberg Galaxy: The Making of Typographic Man*. In it, McLuhan explored the role of mass media (and especially the printing press) in human society, and its impact on human consciousness. *The Gutenberg Galaxy* divided history into four epochs: oral tribe culture, manuscript culture, the Gutenberg Galaxy – the name McLuhan chose for the era of movable type and mass printing – and, finally, the era to come, the electronic age.*

McLuhan's concept of the Gutenberg Galaxy took its name from Johannes Gutenberg, the German printer who changed the world with the invention of movable type and mechanical mass-produced printing in Renaissance Europe. The phrase 'Gutenberg Galaxy' reminds us that, in whatever

---

*McLuhan's final chapter, 'The Galaxy Reconfigured', predicted a decline in individualistic print culture and a shift towards the 'global village' (a phrase he coined) of electronic media. Although he died in 1980, he would presumably not have been at all astonished to see his work now available in hardback, paperback and ebook.

format they appear, every word is part of a vast and dynamic universe of all those that have ever been recorded – whether on clay, papyrus, paper or silicon – and all those still to be born.

That's a lot of words. So many, in fact, that if we are to engage meaningfully with written culture, we need a way to sort and categorise all the words swirling round the Gutenberg Galaxy, to separate what we find to be good from what we find to be not-so-good. There simply isn't time for us to deal with all the words that are out there. We take on this monumental task in a variety of ways – every book group, word-of-mouth recommendation, book review or book discussing another book is part of the human instinct to sort the good words from the bad.

We might decide that a collection of words bound together in a book or displayed on a digital screen is 'good' because we find them readable, entertaining, inspiring, life-changing, informative, opinionated or profitable. Because they report history, change history or give a voice to those who might otherwise not be heard.

And the boundaries of 'good' are wide and blurry. Some words are critically acclaimed, studied, analysed and disseminated across borders and across centuries. Others are airily dismissed by the literati, yet wildly popular with readers, who hold them to very different standards: those of comfort, titillation, humour, terror, familiarity, escape, melancholy and every other form of emotional resonance in the vast pantheon of the human experience. A book only needs to succeed on its own terms – a brilliant whodunnit has different aims to a magisterial academic treatise on EU law.

So, every time a reader alights in a new corner of the Gutenberg Galaxy and starts to read, the pleasure and privilege of deciding which books are *good* is theirs. But 'book' is just a name for a collection of words, and we can make those words *better* by what we choose to do with them. All collections of words (from sentences to entire books) can be improved, and in lots of different ways. This book is for anyone who's ever wondered just how words navigate from one side of the Gutenberg Galaxy to the other – from the mind of the author to the eyes of the reader.

How do the words that we eventually hold in our hands in a book come to be? What are their stories? And how do those raw words coalesce into readable, recognisable phrases, sentences, paragraphs, pages and chapters? Finally, and in some ways most importantly, what frees those words to make the last step of their journey – to leave their author behind and find their audience?

In between looking at how words get good, better and free, this book will shed light on the practical process of how the insides and outsides of books come together and demystify the alchemy that transforms raw unedited text to smooth readable prose. Every book has a parallel story: that of how it was created. There is the story that the words tell us, and then the journey behind how those particular words came to be on a page. We'll meet the supporting cast needed for words to fulfil their potential, and hear from the people who make it happen; who make it their business and call it their passion to help words get good.

Oh, and every now and then we'll encounter some – if not objectively, then at least arguably – 'bad' words, with which we'll no doubt have a good time. Life, literature and human nature being what they are, we can find real pleasure, interest and humour in reading words that are, by any reasonable consensus, *bad*. Bad words are the junk food of the literary world – we know we shouldn't, but just sometimes, we do. We'll also have close encounters with some lost words – those we know once existed but that have disappeared from our view; and then those that were lost (and in some cases perhaps should have stayed that way) but have made their way back to new audiences.

Your (largely) reliable narrator

What qualifies me to know anything about how words get good? Over the course of twenty years working in the editorial department of one of the world's largest publishers I've signed off millions and millions of words for print. Words in every conceivable combination, language, tone, style and typeface. I've edited, proofread, fact-checked, copy-checked, rewritten, edited again, indexed, re-indexed, checked corrections, dealt with authors, commissioned freelancers, calmed down commissioning editors, cooperated with typesetters and printers, and, finally, sent words to print.

Have I read all these words? No. Have I understood all those I *have*? Not entirely. Have I experienced the occasional slip along the path to making them good? Yes, indeed. Have I had an author email me (very politely, under the circumstances) to point out I'd misspelt their name on the title page of their proofs? Mea culpa. Have I been part of a team that managed to print 20,000 copies of *The Importance of Being Ernest*? Speaking earnestly, I absolutely have.

As this might suggest, my job is at least as terrifying as it is satisfying. The longer I do it, the closer I must surely be edging towards a truly irrecoverable cock-up. In my worst moments – the 3 a.m. ones, followed by the even worse 4 a.m. ones – I wonder if I can carry on at all. Because I *know* that one day soon 40,000 copies of a high-profile hardback will have to be pulped because of something I did or didn't do. (Which is worse? Both!)

As well as the words I approve and send to print, I spend my days arguing over how to present ellipses. Trying to convince authors to follow our standard endnote style.

Wondering why I'm working on a book with 2,000 cross references that need to be cross-checked – or matching 60 trivia questions on one side of a jacket with 60 answers on the other. Everything that is put in front of me – cover, index, text, images, maps, diagrams – must be interrogated, made sense of, checked and re-checked to help make it good.

Before I worked in the world of books, I gave very little thought to the integrity of the printed word. If it was in print, it must be correct. Ipso facto. Doubly (ip)so if it was printed in gold foil on the jacket. It didn't occur to me that authors and publishers sometimes got things *wrong*. If I thought about editing or editors at all, it was to assume they might tidy up some grammar and spot the occasional typo. In my mind, manuscripts arrived on publishers' desks in an almost fully formed state. A quick once-over, and off to the printer you go. This was not a view that survived first contact with a manuscript. It was only when I was responsible for producing a book from start to finish that I began to grasp just how complicated the whole business really was.

Initially, it all seemed simple enough. There were rules, you see. Rules for making words good. Copy-editing rules, typesetting rules, house style, style sheets, dictionaries. Authors would send me their art and I, by God, was going to science the sh*t out of it for them.

But gradually I came to understand that the rules weren't the problem; it was the exceptions. And the exceptions were *everywhere*. On top of that, the closer I got to a piece of text the more ephemeral it seemed. No line, paragraph or book was the same as another; no author had the same tone, style or intent. Each book had to be built from scratch from the raw material supplied. Even the rulebook had to be rewritten. Or heavily edited, at the very least.

The liberation of words

> 'Homer on parchment pages!
> The Iliad and all the adventures
> Of Ulysses, foe of Priam's kingdom!
> All locked within a piece of skin
> Folded into several little sheets!'
>
> Martial, *Epigrammata*, XIV

In *The Gutenberg Galaxy*, McLuhan argued that the development of the printing press led eventually to rationalism, nationalism, dualism, the automatisation of scientific research, the standardisation of culture across the globe, and the alienation of individual men and women. This is what happens when you allow words their freedom: the printing press, then, has been radically accelerating change since it was first invented.

If the *way* we get words onto the page has been a driver of change, then the format we encounter them in has an effect, too. This was a theme that McLuhan explored through his axiom 'The medium is the message'.* Our response to words can be altered by how we physically encounter them, and the way we record words has meaning, too.

Before the book, there was the scroll. And before that there was the clay tablet, used by speakers of more than fifteen different languages and for over three thousand years. The clay tablet may have held sway in ancient Western civilisations, but in South America (and China) things were recorded in a very different way – on knotted strings. Called *quipu*, these

---

*When proofs of McLuhan's 1967 book – which he originally planned to call *The Medium is the Message* – were sent back from the typesetters, he realised that they had incorrectly set the title as *The Medium is the Massage*. According to McLuhan's official website, 'After McLuhan saw the typo, he exclaimed, "Leave it alone! It's great, and right on target!"'

strings were used for storing census data, keeping records, and even monitoring how and when people paid their tax. The scroll had many advantages over the clay tablet (and the *quipu*) – it was editable and portable, and once humans had worked out how to make paper, it was much more convenient, especially for long documents.

But although scrolls were the dominant way of presenting written information in the ancient world, by the sixth century they had almost completely disappeared, having been replaced by the codex, which means 'trunk of a tree', or 'book'. Codices looked just as books look today, with the pages stacked on top of each other and fixed to a spine made of slightly thicker material. The arrival of the codex was the most important advance in bookmaking until Gutenberg's printing press changed the world – and the world of words.

The Romans* were the first to use the codex, and in the same way that the scroll was superior to the tablet, the codex had plenty of advantages over the scroll. The Roman poet Martial wrote some lines to go with gifts of books exchanged during the festival of Saturnalia, demonstrating the benefits of the codex form, as well as sticking in a quick advert for where you could buy his own writings:

> You who long for my little books to be with you every-where and want to have companions for a long journey, buy these ones which parchment confines within small pages: give your scroll-cases to the great authors – one hand can hold me. So that you are not ignorant of where I am on sale, and don't wander aimlessly through the whole city, I will be your guide and you will be certain:

---

*And not just any old Roman. Apparently, Julius Caesar was an early adopter of the codex, and would write to his troops on pages bound together like a book.

look for Secundus, the freedman of learned Lucensis, behind the threshold of the Temple of Peace and the Forum of Pallas.

As Martial describes, the codex was an efficient way of travelling with your favourite reading material. Unlike the scroll, the codex was small enough to hold in one hand (it was also easy to conceal among your clothes, which meant that 'forbidden' texts could be hidden), robust owing to its covers, and economic – both sides of the parchment could be used. One of the drawbacks of the scroll was that it was sequential access – like a cassette tape, you could only access the work in the order it was 'stored'. A codex is random access, more like a CD.* By the second century the codex was the preferred form of presenting written material in the Western world, and was used particularly by Christians†; the Bible was presented in codex format, for example, rather than scroll.

The codex was actually an evolution of the scroll rather than an entirely new technology – some scrolls (the Dead Sea Scrolls are a famous example) were unrolled horizontally, which meant that they could be folded up like an accordion. Then someone had the idea of cutting the pages and sewing or gluing them at the centre. Inside, the parchment was folded. One fold to a piece of parchment was a folio. Two and it was a quarto. And if you folded it again, you had an octavo.

---

*Will future readers even know what a CD or cassette is?

†The random access nature of the codex is part of the story of St Augustine's conversion to Christianity. When Augustine picked up his copy of St Paul's Epistles, he records in his *Confessions* that 'I took hold of it and opened it, and in silence I read the first section on which my eyes fell'. The passage that Augustine read was from Romans 13, and at the end of it 'the darkness of doubt' disappears from his mind and he embraces Christianity.

Of course, although a codex is recognisable to us as a precursor to the book, producing even one was a time-consuming effort. Before the printing press, manuscripts were copied out by monks. And inevitably this method of producing text led to many errors and variations in each version. Punctuation, spelling and grammar weren't standardised, and in classical manuscripts *scriptio continua* was used – which meant that there were no spaces between words.* The time it took to create written material meant that codices, and hence the ideas, knowledge and opinions that the words inside could pass on, were confined to the elite: monasteries, the universities and the well off. It was the invention of printing in the mid-fifteenth century that changed all this, and more.

From scroll to codex to bound book, the people who have written, edited, crafted and produced them have faced similar issues: how to make sure the information is correct, how to reduce errors, how to entice readers to stay with the story, and crucially, to stay with the story until the very end. The story of *How Words Get Good* is the story of how these problems have been solved.

An odyssey from front to back

Something that remains a source of awe even to these jaded eyes is the sheer distance it is possible to travel between the covers of every book. One of the joys of reading is the ability to bridge time and cultures in just a sentence. That's the

---

*As a reader this might sound challenging, but it was nothing compared to trying to read something written in Boustrophedon. This excellent word means 'in the manner of oxen turning in ploughing' and is a bi-directional text – alternate lines are read in opposite directions. As if that weren't enough, the individual characters are also reversed. It was often used to carve on stone in ancient Greece.

remarkable power of words. But, every line of printed matter demands huge quantities of energy, time, imagination and expertise from those involved in the world of words to successfully construct that bridge.

These expeditions are undertaken by the editorial team I'm part of: the section of publishing I fell into and a career that's always been fairly opaque to my family and friends. There are lots of things that I *don't* do to words: I don't find them in the first place, or commission them, and I don't get to be their first readers. That unmarked trail is broken for us by agents and commissioning editors, who between them do the initial exploring and scouting for words across the Gutenberg Galaxy. But once those words have been captured, they are fed in at one end to our department to emerge from the other in a form that can be safely released to the reading public. The words that were 'good' at the start should have been made 'better' by the time they leave us; what happens in the intervening months is between me, the author and a set of shadowy professional wordsmiths – copy-editors, indexers and proofreaders – each with their own arcane specialisms, interests and quirks.

While a manuscript arriving with me is the start of its journey, before that the words have already been thought about, edited, re-edited, drafted and revised by the author, their agent (if they have one) and their commissioning editor in a process that always takes months and often takes years. And after the words leave us, they continue to be refined by designers, typesetters and printers, all of whom have their own complex and fascinating sub-worlds (which we will dip a toe into), with their own history, foibles, stories and traditions.

Just as every book has its own unique genesis in the mind of its author, it has its own unique journey into the hands of its readers. To help words get good, I need to scurry back and forth between these two points to make sure we never lose sight of either the author's vision and intent or the reader's ability and willingness to receive it.

The Prime Directive of Publishing

'The first sentence you write will be the most important sentence in your life, and so will the second, and the third. This is because, although you – an employee, an apostle or an apologist – may feel obliged to write, nobody has ever felt obliged to read.'

This is from a *Guardian* article by Tim Radford called 'A manifesto for the simple scribe – my 25 commandments for journalists'. But true to form, I might as well have edited this more expansive erudition down into the blunter form preferred by American copywriter, screenwriter and novelist Steven Pressfield for his guide to professional writing: *Nobody Wants to Read Your Sh*t*.

So this book is really all about you: the reader. The simple single truth – the Prime Directive of Publishing, if you prefer – is that all the work that goes into making words good is for nought if it doesn't ultimately persuade someone to *read* them. Because the only real, true and meaningful way to measure how good words are is by liberating them from the publishing process and disseminating them in their most accessible form, so readers everywhere can encounter and respond to them in the way the author imagined when they were writing them.

Well, we've come this far together. That's an encouraging start. I hope you'll keep turning the pages as we explore how words get good.

HOW WORDS GET BORN

'Times are bad. Children no longer obey their parents, and everyone is writing a book.'

Cicero

When you work in publishing, it can feel as if everyone you meet is writing a book. And if they aren't writing one, they are asking your advice on how to write one, how to make one better, or if you're thinking about writing one yourself. But this is what feeds the Gutenberg Galaxy. F. Scott Fitzgerald wrote that 'Writers aren't people exactly. Or, if they're any good, they're a whole lot of people trying so hard to be one person.' And that 'one person' can only come to us through what a writer allows us to see. But every word, and the story behind its birth, is a clue.

Ernest Hemingway described the process of writing in *A Moveable Feast* in these terms: 'The story was writing itself and I was having a hard time keeping up with it.' E. L. Doctorow's take was slightly different: 'I have found one explanation that seems to satisfy people. I tell them it's like driving a car at night: you never see further than your headlights, but you can make the whole trip that way.' I like to think these explanations demonstrate the spectrum of how words get born. From the enviable animus of a story that is 'writing itself' to one that's gradually revealed like the next few metres of tarmac on a late-night car journey, how does being an author *work*?

Many books attempt to tackle the question of what writing is, and how it happens. It's a vast topic: on Amazon, searching 'how to write' throws up more than 60,000 titles on the subject. Since the dawn of time, humans have enjoyed telling stories – and those stories have followed predictable patterns. In fact, the pattern of the story – its structure – was sometimes more important than the author. For a long time, authors were generally anonymous – they retold and embellished classical stories rather than inventing new ones (a process that still happens today), and it didn't matter who was doing the telling – only that the story was absorbing.

One of the earliest and most enduring story structures was the epic: a long narrative poem in a time set outside the author's own, which described the extraordinary lives and events of humans encountering gods or superhuman forces. Epics evolved into poems of courtly love and romance, then into travel literature and stories about conquests, with the same themes and structures appearing again and again, and laying down the foundations of what eventually became the novel as they did so. That's why, in this section, I have chosen to focus on a few key ways of telling stories: these recurring structures and ways of writing tell us a lot about how words get good.

THE BEAUTIFUL SHAPE OF
STORIES: AUTHORS

Man in hole: what to write

In his autobiography *Palm Sunday*, American novelist Kurt Vonnegut explained that his 'prettiest contribution to culture' had been his master's thesis in anthropology, 'which was rejected because it was so simple and looked like too much fun'. So simple was it that Vonnegut was able to explain the concept of the thesis in one sentence: 'The fundamental idea is that stories have shapes which can be drawn on graph paper, and the shape of a given society's stories is at least as interesting as the shape of its pots or spearheads.'

Stories, as Vonnegut says, have simple shapes, which can be plotted on a graph *(overleaf)* by humans – or computers. If you search on YouTube for 'The Shape of Stories' (the title of his thesis), you'll be able to watch just over four minutes of him drawing (and explaining) some of these story shapes on a blackboard.

Vonnegut uses one axis to represent fortune, good and bad – the y-axis – and the x-axis represents the progression of a story from beginning to end. If you're wondering what the ∞ in the 'Cinderella' graph means, it's there to show unending good fortune.

'I have tried to bring scientific thinking to literary criticism and there has been very little gratitude for this,' said Vonnegut in a lecture on the topic. But we should be grateful. Who could resist the simple but elegant story shape described by the line on the graph labelled 'Man in hole'? As

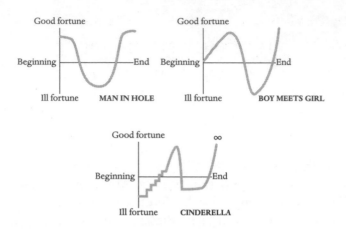

The shape of stories

Vonnegut says in 'The Shape of Stories', it doesn't necessarily need to be a man, and he doesn't have to be in a hole – but we can all relate to and follow the structure of a story where the protagonist loses his good fortune by encountering some sort of depression (literal or figurative), and then against the odds finds a way to escape it. The plot is as old as storytelling, and structure is what provides the shape of that descent and escape, using words as the scaffolding.

Sentences and paragraphs in a book arrange the author's meaning for the reader. The patterns that words follow once they are born, and the way we organise them, help them to convey something useful, interesting or emotionally involving.

When we begin the adventure of reading, we do so immersed in a cultural and sociological context – we experience how stories work as we learn to read when we are young. If the structure that we intuitively expect is not there we have to work hard to follow the story – or the argument – and we start to feel lost. Without structure, there would be no logical direction of travel, no plot for a reader, and no sense of adventure or suspense. Words would be scattered about with no shape to them at all: structure is what helps a writer guide a reader along the path of their words.

In *The Seven Basic Plots: Why We Tell Stories*, Christopher Booker analyses and breaks down stories into . . . well, seven basic plots. They are: 'Overcoming the monster', 'Rags to riches', 'The quest', 'Voyage and return', 'Comedy', 'Tragedy' and 'Rebirth'. The book took him thirty-four years to write, which means his own story might fit into 'The quest', or perhaps by the end, 'Overcoming the monster'. What these seven plots have in common is that they present a dramatic turning point which creates a conflict that must be resolved, which gives them a beginning, middle and end that we can follow and understand, with a sense of satisfaction. We set out on a journey, are presented with a problem, and then there is resolution. What could be more pleasing than that?

Some genres of writing have even more specific rules: during the golden age of detective fiction (broadly, the 1920s and 1930s in England), mysteries were considered to be games that the reader could play along with, and hope to solve. In this way, the reader was an active participant in the plot, and writers of these types of stories understood that part of their job as author was to fulfil this expectation.

As Ronald Knox,* author of a number of detective stories, wrote, 'A detective story must have as its main interest the unravelling of a mystery; a mystery whose elements are clearly presented to the reader at an early stage in the proceedings, and whose nature is such as to arouse curiosity, a curiosity which is gratified at the end.' If the author didn't

---

*Knox also came up with a 'Decalogue' of commandments for detective fiction; my favourite is the very specific no. 3, which states that no more than one secret room or passage is allowable in a story.

play by the rules, then the mystery couldn't be solved by the reader, and dissatisfaction with the storyline would ensue. The book would, in some important way, have failed.

Telling the story backwards

But, of course, rules – literary or otherwise – are there to be broken. This chapter started by looking at Kurt Vonnegut's ideas about predictable story structures. But Vonnegut often played with and subverted those very notions. In *Slaughterhouse-Five*, part of the plot is viewed backwards by Billy Pilgrim, the unreliable narrator:

> It was a movie about American bombers in World War II and the gallant men who flew them. Seen backwards by Billy, the story went like this: American planes, full of holes and wounded men and corpses took off backwards from an airfield in England. Over France, a few German fighter planes flew at them backwards, sucked bullets and shell fragments from some of the planes and crewmen. They did the same for wrecked American bombers on the ground, and those planes flew up backwards to join the formation.
>
> The formation flew backwards over a German city that was in flames. The bombers opened their bomb bay doors, exerted a miraculous magnetism which shrunk the fires, gathered them into cylindrical steel containers, and lifted the containers into the bellies of the planes. The containers were stored neatly in racks. The Germans below had miraculous devices of their own, which were long steel tubes. They used them to suck more fragments from the crewmen and planes. But there were still a few wounded Americans though and some of the bombers were in bad repair. Over France though,

German fighters came up again, made everything and everybody as good as new.

When the bombers got back to their base, the steel cylinders were taken from the racks and shipped back to the United States of America, where factories were operating night and day, dismantling the cylinders, separating the dangerous contents into minerals. Touchingly, it was mainly women who did this work. The minerals were then shipped to specialists in remote areas. It was their business to put them into the ground, to hide them cleverly, so they would never hurt anybody ever again.

Despite these words being used to describe the exact reverse of the story we might be expecting, there is still a structure to them which allows us to follow along. It's simply 'Man in hole' flipped upside down in order to make a point about the madness of war. Pleasingly, it manages to do so while also being rather uplifting. And as Vonnegut explained in his lectures on the topic of structure in stories: 'The story is "Man in hole" . . . somebody gets into trouble, gets out of it again. It is not accidental that the line ends up higher than where it began. This is encouraging to readers.'

Below the waterline: How to write

One of the difficulties in storytelling is how and when you reveal things. Most fiction depends at some point on suspense – will our hero ever escape from the hole? – or the reader finding out something about the characters, or a situation being revealed. When you write fiction, you often suffer from the curse of knowledge: *you* know what's going to happen next, but your reader doesn't. The clues you leave, what you show, and when, can't be too oblique – or too obvious. To structure fiction successfully you may have to do the opposite of structuring for non-fiction – by leaving things out and respecting that the reader will, through careful attention to your words, be able to work out what is happening. That's why fiction writers will often rely on ambiguity, an unreliable narrator, inference and metaphor to conceal elements of a story – and to allow the reader to make their own leaps in understanding what is happening.

William Thackeray wrote of *Vanity Fair* that:

> There are things we do and know perfectly well in *Vanity Fair*, though we never speak them . . . In describing this syren [Becky Sharp], singing and smiling, coaxing and cajoling, the author, with modest pride, asks his readers all around, has he once forgotten the laws of politeness, and showed the monster's hideous tail above water? No! Those who like may peep down under waves that are pretty transparent, and see it writhing and twirling, diabolically hideous and slimy, flapping amongst bones, or curling round corpses; but above the water-line, I ask, has not everything been proper, agreeable, and decorous?

Thackeray's idea of what is hidden below the waterline – that we know to be true, even without the words there to tell us – is echoed by Ernest Hemingway. In *Death in the Afternoon*, Hemingway elaborated on his own theory of literary omission – known as the iceberg theory:

> If a writer of prose knows enough of what he is writing about he may omit things that he knows and the reader, if the writer is writing truly enough, will have a feeling of those things as strongly as though the writer had stated them. The dignity of movement of an ice-berg is due to only one-eighth of it being above water. A writer

who omits things because he does not know them only makes hollow places in his writing.

Words must be conceived thoughtfully and birthed precisely for maximum narrative impact. The writing must be strong and true enough that even without saying what is happening, the reader *knows*. 'A few things I have found to be true. If you leave out important things or events that you know about, the story is strengthened. If you leave or skip something because you do not know it, the story will be worthless. The test of any story is how very good the stuff that you, not your editors, omit,' explained Hemingway in 'The Art of the Short Story'. This is the essence of how words get good: knowing which to leave out.

Five write a book in five days

In *Bookworm: A Memoir of Childhood Reading*, Lucy Mangan writes that 'When you are young, even if you like it and are good at it, reading is hard. It is important to have somewhere you can go and know that your efforts are guaranteed to be rewarded. You need a satisfying story and an unbroken contract of delivery from your author.' That's why, particularly when we are children, we love series of books that create a familiar, comfortable world that we can retreat to time and time again – the knowledge that what we expect to happen *will* happen adds greatly to the pleasure of these word-worlds. Familiar characters and themes are what we crave – and writers know this. They too probably enjoy returning to these familiar and comforting anchors when they sit down to write.

'I shut my eyes for a few minutes, with my portable type-writer on my knee – I make my mind a blank and wait – and then, as clearly as I would see real children, my characters stand before me in my mind's eye . . . The first sentence comes straight into my mind, I don't have to think of it – I don't have to think of anything.'

This was Enid Blyton describing her creative process. Blyton is estimated to have written 760 books over the course of a fifty-year career. She believed she could tap into what she called her 'under-mind' to find inspiration for her copious output (which does sound enticing), but as her biographer Barbara Stoney suggests, this method had its drawbacks. Blyton told her husband that 'While her characters were being established . . . they would "walk about" in her head, take over her dreams and give her little rest until she had got back to her typewriter the following day.' In addition to her characters invading her headspace, this stream-of-consciousness way of writing, and the volume of her output, meant that, unsurprisingly, she often plagiarised her own work. She was also troubled by persistent rumours that she employed a stable of ghostwriters to work for her, and in 1956 she sued a librarian for saying that not all the books with her name on the cover were written by her.

Enid Blyton usually wrote between 6,000 and 10,000 words a day. Those who have never picked up and read a *Famous Five* or *Secret Seven* adventure would still probably recognise the Blyton formula: fast-paced, action-driven, with complete moral certainty (her heroes and villains are clearly signposted), excitement and escapism, without loss of life or real jeopardy.

This use of formula is why Blyton was able to be so prolific, and possibly why she is so open to parody, in forms such as *Five Go Gluten Free*, *Five on Brexit Island* and *Five Go On A Strategy Away Day*. The covers of these spin-offs, like her own books, feature her official signature – Blyton was an early, and devoted, proponent of presenting herself as a brand. Not everyone was a fan: Blyton was banned by the

BBC for almost thirty years (from 1936 until 1963, when she finally appeared on *Woman's Hour*), with one BBC employee writing: 'It really is odd to think that this woman is a best-seller. It is all such very small beer.' In 'The Blyton Line', psychologist Michael Woods gives his rather damning view on her methods of writing:

> Enid Blyton has no moral dilemmas and her books satisfy children because they present things clearly in black and white with no confusing intermediate shades of grey. For the adult of course this is what makes life interesting; for the child ambiguity is untenable. The reason Enid Blyton was able to write so much . . . was because she did not have to make any effort to think herself back into childhood or wrestle with her conscience.

Yet the scaffolding of an expected structure is a reassuring handhold when we set out across the Gutenberg Galaxy, and surely part of the reason Blyton's books remain bestsellers today. For children learning to read, formulaic storytelling is a comfort and an encouragement – we may read to discover new worlds, but having found one we like, we want to explore it further. We stick with what we know. And having taken up the habit and comfort of familiar plots, we often carry it with us into adulthood.

oo Secret 7: Formulas

'I write for about three hours in the morning. . . and I do another hour's work between six and seven in the evening. I never correct anything and I never go back to see what I have written . . . By following my formula, you write 2,000 words a day.'

Ian Fleming used our natural love of formulaic writing to his advantage. As we have seen, be it romance or detective fiction, there are rules for the writer to follow, and sticking to them forms the unbroken contract of delivery between reader and author. And they can also help authors get on with the business of actually writing.

Fleming had enormous success with his James Bond stories, which he described as 'thrillers designed to be read as literature'. He wrote them using a formula which applied not just to *how* he wrote, but to *what* he wrote. Writing your book at GoldenEye* in 'the gorgeous vacuum of a Jamaican holiday', as Fleming described his three-hours-a-day writing life, is surely authorial nirvana. Stick to the formula, 2,000 words a day, don't trouble yourself with corrections, sell 30 million copies of your books while you're alive, and double that after your death.† Simple.

In his 2012 introduction to *Live and Let Die*, Andrew Taylor writes that 'It's the first of Fleming's books to use what was to become his classic formula. Bond is sent to an exotic location to deal with an amoral and physically unusual villain with limitless wealth and a superhuman lust for power. A beautiful woman serves as both plot device and trophy.' As well as being physically unusual, the way Fleming chose to name his villains was also out of the ordinary. Auric Goldfinger was named after modernist architect Ernö Goldfinger, whose work Fleming hated (Goldfinger took legal advice

---

*Yes, you too can stay at GoldenEye. According to its website: 'Without the slightest experience but with the greatest self-confidence, Fleming designed the house himself. As a typically dogmatic Englishman, he decided there would be no windows – just customary Jamaican jalousie blinds to let in the air and sun. And of course, he was right: The breezes at GoldenEye are a delight, all hours of the day, all times of the year.'

†Fleming's last words after what would prove his final fatal heart attack in 1964 were to the ambulance crew that came out to him: 'I am sorry to trouble you chaps. I don't know how you get along so fast with the traffic on the roads these days.'

upon the publication of *Goldfinger*, which prompted Fleming to threaten to rename the character 'Goldprick'), while Hugo Drax, the villain in *Moonraker*, was named after the excessively monikered Admiral Sir Reginald Aylmer Ranfurly Plunkett-Ernle-Erle-Drax, an acquaintance of Fleming's.

In 1966 Umberto Eco wrote an essay titled 'Narrative Structures in Fleming', which outlined how the novels were 'fixed as a sequence of "moves" inspired by the code and constituted according to a perfectly rearranged scheme'. What were those moves?

1. M moves and gives a task to Bond
2. Villain moves and appears to Bond (perhaps in vicarious form)
3. Bond moves and gives a first check to Villain or Villain gives first check to Bond
4. Woman moves and shows herself
5. Bond takes Woman (possesses her or begins her seduction)
6. Villain captures Bond (with or without Woman, or at different moments)
7. Villain tortures Bond (with or without Woman)
8. Bond beats Villain (kills him, or kills his representative or helps at their killing)
9. Bond, convalescing, enjoys Woman, whom he then loses

This formulaic style of writing words, though, is what has made the Bond brand and Fleming's work both enduring and durable. In a 1964 interview Fleming said:

'I'm too interested in surface things, and I'm too interested in maintaining a fast pace, in writing at speed.* I'm afraid I shouldn't have the patience to delve into the necessary psychological introspection and historical background. But in the end, I must say, I'm very happy writing as I do. And I greatly enjoy knowing that other people, quite intelligent people, find my books amusing and entertaining. But I'm not really surprised, because they entertain and amuse me too.'

As well as amusement and entertainment, Fleming's formula presumably also meant that he only had to spend a few hours a day doing the heavy lifting of writing, and rather more enjoying the cool breeze flowing through his jalousie blinds.

While Fleming aimed for 2,000 words a day, his formula has had a substantial afterlife, too – so far, new adventures for Bond have been provided by Kingsley Amis (writing as Robert Markham), John Gardner, Raymond Benson, Jeffrey Deaver, William Boyd, Sebastian Faulks and Anthony Horowitz, all benefiting from the proven success of the 007 formula.

Even as Bond puts himself in the way of mortal danger on every outing, we know that eventually we'll reach 'Bond, convalescing, enjoys Woman, whom he then loses'. Because it is only once Bond has convalesced and lost the woman that the adventure can begin again.

─────────────

*Talking of writing at speed, here is John Self on Georges Simenon, creator of the legendary sleuth Maigret and author of more than five hundred novels: 'Simenon's productivity is legendary: he wrote one chapter a day, without interruption, and if he had to stop working on a book for more than 48 hours, for example through illness, he threw it away. He completed most of his novels in ten or eleven days, editing them only to "cut, cut, cut" anything that he deemed too "literary". It's reported that Alfred Hitchcock once telephoned him only to be told that Simenon was incommunicado as he had just begun a new novel. "That's all right," said Hitchcock, "I'll wait."'

The Secret of the Stratemeyer Syndicate

Does this subheading sound a bit Blytonesque? She may have been a one-woman writing machine, but Enid Blyton had nothing on Edward Stratemeyer. When he died in 1930 the *New York Times* reported that his *Rover Boys* series had sold more than 5 million copies. But Stratemeyer was also responsible for even more millions of book sales: as well as *The Rover Boys*, he dreamt up *The Bobbsey Twins*, *Tom Swift*, *Baseball Joe*, *The Hardy Boys*, *Nancy Drew* and *The Dana Girls*. The *Nancy Drew* series alone has sold over 80 million books.

How did Stratemeyer do it? He discovered, as an article about him in *Fortune* magazine published four years after his death pointed out, that 'the reading capacity of the American adolescent was limitless'. He began his career at a magazine publisher's called Smith & Smith, where he was asked to finish the incomplete manuscripts of Horatio Alger* after he died. Stratemeyer completed from Alger's notes, or invented himself, eleven volumes of stories published under Alger's name. This success led to him establishing a number of series of books for adolescent readers, which he initially wrote himself. One man could not keep up with the limitless demand he had identified, however, and Stratemeyer realised that to satisfy his readers he would have to draft in help. Although the series Stratemeyer established had an 'author' named on the cover, they were in fact the work of a syndicate.

We are programmed to think of the author as a lone genius, tapping away in isolation and channelling a vision

---

*Horatio Alger (1832–1899) had published roughly a hundred 'rags-to-riches' stories by the time he died. Alger scholar Gary Scharnhorst describes Alger's writing style as 'often laughable' and 'anachronistic', but more than half his books contain references to Shakespeare, as well as allusions to John Milton and Cicero.

that is solely theirs, but Stratemeyer's books show that's not the only model of authorship: the formula can be so effective it doesn't much matter who the author *is*, as long as the book conforms to its own terms of reference.

By 1910 Stratemeyer's syndicate was officially incorporated, and had a streamlined system: he would think up a new series, then for each volume would develop an outline that was passed on to a contracted writer, who would turn it into a 200-page book. This is a system still used today: James Patterson, a prodigious literary figure and the world's bestselling author (at least 114 *New York Times* bestsellers), manages to sustain his output year after year by working with a stable of co-authors. His name looms large on his covers, but Patterson doesn't actually write his books. Instead, he provides a detailed outline, then hires someone else to do the actual writing, while providing feedback for them.

Stratemeyer would carefully schedule appointments at his office so that his writers would never meet, and once the book was written he would revise and proofread each one, and then send it on to a publisher. Crucially, the syndicate, not the writer, owned the copyright of each volume. One Stratemeyer writer called Albert Svenson described the formula that syndicate writers were expected to follow: 'A low death rate but plenty of plot. Verbs of action, and polka-dotted with exclamation points and provocative questions. No use of guns by the hero. No smooching. The main character introduced on page one and a slambang mystery or peril set up. Page one used to be fifteen lines, and now it's eighteen.'

In *Nabokov's Favourite Word is Mauve*, Ben Blatt analyses the final sentence of each chapter in a sample of *The Hardy Boys* and *Nancy Drew* titles. In *The Hardy Boys*, 71 per cent of chapter-ending sentences finish with what Blatt calls marks of 'obvious excitement (!)' or 'obvious mystery (?)'. These cliffhanger chapter endings,* supplied to a formula by a syndicate, are what have kept readers turning the pages for nearly a hundred years. (If you looked at the publishing output of Carolyn Keene, the 'author' of the *Nancy Drew* books, you'd see that she was active as a writer from 1930 until the present day, and that Nancy has evolved from the *Nancy Drew Mystery Stories* via *The Nancy Drew Files*, *Nancy Drew on Campus*, *Girl Detective* to finally a series of graphic novels in which Nancy appears in manga-style illustrations and drives a hybrid car.)

While we might think that good words are all about originality, creativity and groundbreaking new literary devices (indeed, literary fiction is reviewed, praised and awarded prizes for its stylistic experimentation and originality), much of our enjoyment of reading comes from words that provide the balm of the familiar, the comforting, and that meet our expectations – and that keep us turning the pages with obvious excitements and mysteries. Readers know what they are getting, and that's just how they like it. Not only is it satisfying when we are reading, Patterson, Blyton, Fleming and Stratemeyer show us how commercially successful this kind of literary factory farming can also be.

---

*According to Blatt, Enid Blyton's 'obvious cliffhanger mark' rating is 83 per cent.

'SINGERS OF STITCHED
WORDS': GHOSTWRITERS

Did Homer exist? This is one strand of the Homeric Question – an academic discipline that attempts to answer the question of who Homer was, who really composed the *Iliad* and the *Odyssey*, and how and when they were written.

If he did exist, was he one individual or should 'Homeric' refer to an entire group and culture of oral storytelling? Although we don't know for sure that Homer existed as a person, we do know that a society of poets called the Homeridae did. Some scholars believe that the name Homer was back-extracted from the name of this society – they claimed to be 'children of Homer', hence the name. Homeridae means 'sons of hostages', so some have theorised that they were the descendants of prisoners of war. As their loyalty was suspect, they weren't sent into battle; instead, their job was to commit to memory the epic oral poetry of the area so that in a time before literacy it would be preserved. The Greek poet Pindar referred to the Homeridae as the 'singers of stitched words' – a quite beautiful description.

It's likely the poems attributed to Homer are based on oral culture – they consist of repeated phrases and verses that would have been memorised – the telltale formula of singer-poets throughout history. It wasn't until the eighth century BC that these pieces were refined and standardised, possibly by one man called Homer. But does it matter *who* is telling us a story – do we need to know who an author is? Does it add to our enjoyment of the words, or does it skew our view of them before we have even turned a page?

'Anonymous was a woman'

From the Pauline Epistles in the New Testament (fourteen books are explicitly stated to be written by Paul the Apostle, but claims have been made from Eusebius onwards that Paul was not the author of the Epistle to the Hebrews) to *Primary Colors*, a 1996 book based on Bill Clinton's 1992 presidential campaign, deliberately withholding the name of the author can help generate publicity, let writers speak more candidly, and, in some cases, just allow them to enjoy creating one giant literary mystery. It's actually far more difficult than it used to be to conceal your identity: the author of *Primary Colors* wasn't able to stay anonymous for long, as the book was subjected to stylometric analysis by a professor of linguistic style and then handwriting analysis by the *Washington Post*, which forced the columnist Joe Klein to admit he was the 'Anonymous' of the cover.

Hidden identities have been around for a long time in writing. For some, setting down their words, and finding an audience, was an act of social transgression, or positively unsafe.

'For most of history, anonymous was a woman,' wrote Virginia Woolf in her 1929 essay *A Room of One's Own*. Charlotte, Emily and Anne Brontë all wrote under male pseudonyms,* with Charlotte explaining that 'we did not like to declare ourselves women, because – without at that time suspecting that our mode of writing and thinking was not what is called "feminine" – we had a vague impression that authoresses are liable to be looked on with prejudice'.

---

*Currer, Ellis and Acton Bell.

Membership of the Gutenberg Galaxy has not always been open to all, and some writers know they can only have access if they obscure their identity, or present themselves as someone else.*

Mary Ann Evans (George Eliot), Karen Blixen (Isak Dinesen) and Louisa May Alcott (A. M. Barnard) all chose to write under male names for some or all of their careers, because they knew that they would be taken more seriously as writers if they did so. Conversely, the biggest growth area in male/female name swapping in recent years has been in crime fiction. Women account for between 60 and 80 per cent of sales in that market, and authors like Gillian Flynn, Paula Hawkins and Karin Slaughter have sold millions of books. So it should be no surprise that male writers are now using women's names (or at least ambiguous, gender-neutral ones) to sell their work. Authors A. J. Finn, S. J. Watson and S. K. Tremayne are all men.

Writers have been using pseudonyms for centuries. The fourteenth-century Persian poet known as Hafez ('the memoriser') was one, as was the name of the Japanese haiku poet Matsuo Bashō (*Bashō* means banana plant). More recently, Elena Ferrante, the bestselling author of *My Brilliant Friend* and the other books in the 'Neapolitan Novels' series, has chosen not to reveal her identity – 'Elena Ferrante' is a pseudonym. In a letter that Ferrante sent to her publisher in 1991 when her first novel was about to be published, she wrote: 'I believe that books, once they are written, have no need of

---

*Even when an author chooses to hide, they often leave clues for us in plain sight. In *Why Not Catch-21? The Stories Behind the Titles*, Gary Dexter explains in detail how the Brontës may have come to choose their pseudonyms, noting that each sister chose a name that would still give them the same initial as their real name. Dexter also points out that 'Branwell' – their mother's maiden name and that of their brother – becomes 'Bell' if you remove 'ranw'.

their authors. If they have something to say, they will sooner or later find readers; if not, they won't . . . I very much love those mysterious volumes, both ancient and modern, that have no definite author but have had and continue to have an intense life of their own. They seem to me a sort of night-time miracle . . .'

The truth of who Ferrante is has been speculated about, commented on, investigated and probed for the last thirty years. An Italian journalist, Claudio Gatti, has used a forensic analysis of the financial transactions of the person he believes is Ferrante to try to unmask them. But as Alexandra Schwartz writes in a piece in the *New Yorker*, shouldn't we continue to respect Ferrante's decision to conceal herself?

> To fall in love with a book, in that way that I and so many others have fallen in love with Ferrante's, is to feel a special kinship with its author, a profound sort of mutual receptivity and comprehension. The author knows nothing about you, and yet you feel that your most intimate self has been understood. The fact that Ferrante has chosen to be anonymous has become part of this contract, and has put readers and writer on a rare, equal plane. Ferrante doesn't know the details of our lives, and doesn't care to. We don't know those of hers. We meet on an imaginative neutral ground, open to all.

This 'imaginative neutral ground' can be found only through a writer's anonymity. If we don't know their gender, age, background and history, we approach their work with no preconceptions to colour our reading, and all we have are the words on the page. As Virginia Woolf wrote, 'Obscurity rids the mind of the irk of envy and spite; [it] sets running in the veins the free waters of generosity and magnanimity; and allows giving and taking without thanks offered or praise given.'

'The delight of having no name'

Virginia Woolf described 'the delight of having no name . . . being like a wave which returns to the dark body of the sea'. Some authors, like crime writer Josephine Tey, delight in having several authorial names* to write under, to conceal themselves. 'Strange as it may seem,' a school friend of Tey's said, 'few of us had ever known the real person. We had rubbed shoulders with her in our busy streets; admired her pretty home and picturesque garden – and some had even shared schooldays with her – yet no one enjoyed her companionship, for Gordon Daviot was, and wished to be what she herself termed herself, "a lone wolf", discouraging any attempts at fraternisation.'

Given Tey's predilection (or perhaps need) for privacy and secrecy, it shouldn't be a surprise that her novels focus on similar themes. *The Franchise Affair* (1948), *Brat Farrar* (1949) and *To Love and Be Wise* (1950) are all stories of concealment, disputed identity and double lives.† Even when Tey's characters have a name, it is often not their own – and neither is their background, history or, in one case, gender. Anonymity is one way of disguising an author, and ghostwriting is another – and both have a long history.

In recent times, the term 'ghostwritten' is often used

---

*Gordon Daviot's death was recorded in *The Times* on 13 February 1952. Daviot had written a number of successful plays in the 1920s and 30s, the best-known of which was *Richard of Bordeaux*, directed by and starring John Gielgud. But Gordon Daviot existed only as an author, not as a person. 'He' was Elizabeth MacKintosh. And she had yet another identity, as the crime writer Josephine Tey, author of *The Franchise Affair* and others.

†*The Franchise Affair* and *Brat Farrar* are based on two infamous British legal cases: that of Elizabeth Canning (a kidnap allegation) and the Tichborne Claimant (the case of a man who claimed he was the missing heir to the Tichborne baronetcy).

negatively. There's a suspicion that the words inside a ghost-written book are inauthentic, and that ghostwriting is, somehow, cheating. But the ghostwriter has a distinguished and intriguing history. Almost as vast as the output of Shakespeare is that of discussion about whether he really existed, and who wrote his plays. Christopher Marlowe, Sir Francis Bacon and the 17th Earl of Oxford are frontrunners in a field of more than eighty candidates.

Harper Lee's childhood friend Truman Capote has occasionally been mooted as the author of her 1960 best-seller *To Kill a Mockingbird* – in part because until *Go Set a Watchman* appeared in 2015 she never published another a book. It might, however, be more accurate to say that Lee was Capote's ghostwriter – she was his researcher on his 1966 non-fiction book *In Cold Blood*, the second bestselling* true-crime book in history. Lee spent six months in Kansas winning over locals and doing background research to help Capote with the story; he probably couldn't have written it without her help.

Crime has remained a fertile territory for the ghostwriter: former jockey Dick Francis sold millions of copies of his thrillers after he retired from racing, but a 1999 biography of him claimed that much of the writing was done by his wife Mary. 'It's much better for everyone, including the readers, to think that he writes them because they're taut, masculine books that might otherwise lose their credibility,' she said in an interview with Graham Lord, who wrote her husband's biography, *A Racing Life*. Mary Francis here puts her finger on one of the key truths about the ghostwriting relationship: one party brings the credibility (in whatever field the book

---

*The first? It's *Helter Skelter: The True Story of the Manson Murders*, by Vincent Bugliosi and Curt Gentry. Originally published in 1974, it has gone on to sell more than 7 million copies.

is about), the other the way with words. The whole business of ghostwriting tells us something about how we view words. We make assumptions, draw conclusions, and decide whether we will embrace them, based not just on the story or insight they promise, but on where they come from. If the source seems suspect – or perhaps even simply unknown to us – we might choose not to eat from the tree of knowledge.

In 1924 the pulp magazine *Weird Tales* published a story by Harry Houdini, called 'Imprisoned with the Pharaohs'. The story was actually written by H. P. Lovecraft,* who was paid $100 to write it. It was the 'true' account of Houdini's kidnap by a tour guide in Egypt, followed by being thrown into a hole near the Great Sphinx of Gaza, and, while attempting his escape, encountering the god that inspired the building of the Sphinx. Would any reader believe that this 'true', if unlikely, story had happened to Lovecraft? *Weird Tales* presumably felt not, but that readers *might* believe that Harry Houdini led the kind of lifestyle that culminated in such adventures.

Sometimes this sleight of hand can seem less like a fairly innocent attempt to provide the reader with something both enjoyable and credible, and more like a fraud on the reader. John F. Kennedy won a Pulitzer Prize for his 1956 book *Profiles in Courage*, but the book was mostly written by Ted Sorensen, one of his speechwriters. This deception was known as early as 1957 when journalist Drew Pearson commented on television that 'John F. Kennedy is the only man in history that I know who won a Pulitzer Prize for

---

*H. P. Lovecraft only had one book of fiction published while he was alive. It was called *The Shadow over Innsmouth*, and Lovecraft wrote to a friend that 'My *Shadow over Innsmouth* is now out – but as a first clothbound book it doesn't awake any enthusiasm in me. Indeed, it is one of the lousiest jobs I've ever seen – 30 misprints, slovenly format, & loose, slipshod binding.' An errata slip was printed, but that too contained errors.

a book that was ghostwritten for him.' Charles de Gaulle was both ghostwriter and ghostwritten. He wrote Marshal Pétain's history of the French army, and his own memoirs were probably ghostwritten by André Malraux, his long-time Minister for Culture. When it comes to words, the ghosts are everywhere, just hidden in the shadows. One such agreed to answer my questions on the ghostwriting life from beneath their shroud of mystery.

'Most ghosts I know are fascinated by stories and are driven by the desire to get them out into the world in the most compelling way they can. The accusation that "authors", the people for whom we're working, are cheating, somehow, by not doing it themselves is usually slightly undermined by the fact that we spend quite a lot of time with them. For one book I wrote a few years ago I must have clocked up about three months' face time – including a week-long trip to India, one week in Verbier, about ten trips to Sweden of various lengths, and one amazing four-day stay in Portugal. More in hope than expectation, I wish people would focus on the story, rather than how it arrived on the page.'

Like most things to do with words, ghosts and ghostwriting can work in many ways. Some ghosts come up with ideas for a book themselves: they stumble upon a story they think needs telling, write an outline, and approach a publisher or editor to pitch the idea. In the opposite direction, the publisher or editor might have the spark of an idea, has found the person or the story, but knows that the 'owner' of the story has neither the time nor skills to actually write it. That's when a ghost is ushered in and commissioned.

'The ghost usually goes through an interview process to land the job. Finding the right fit between ghost and author is one of the most important stages of any project. Ask any ghost and they'll tell you of books they've turned down because the chemistry isn't right. Like dating, there has to be a connection between ghost and author for the collaboration to work. I recently turned down a very well-paid offer because I just couldn't see how we'd work successfully together – nothing wrong with the person (or me, I hope!) but it wasn't the right fit. It's arguably the most important decision in any ghosting project, and to be able to walk away or pass the book on to other collaborators is essential if the book is to be as good as it can be.'

Ghostwriters have also benefited from the boom in self-publishing. If someone wants to tell a story but doesn't feel they have the skills to do so, they can commission their own ghost. It's faster than traditional publishing, and allows individuals to quickly and lucratively get their story out, especially if they have an existing social media or professional following.

'This is where ghosting has got even more interesting. I can be involved from helping shape what the book will be – before I write one word – to writing, editing, commissioning designers and copy-editors, all the way to sending books to print. Everyone I know who ghosts has made their own way to the job. For me, I was a publisher turned author who was asked to help with a book on a ridiculous deadline. It worked and I was asked to write another and then another – it just grew naturally.

'For others that I know (I belong to a little collective of ghostwriters)* the route has been through journalism, their own writing, and sometimes their profession (particularly those coming from a business background). I don't think any of us set out with the intention of becoming a ghost, but all of us love it now we're doing it.

'To build reputation it's probably like any other business:

---

*Apparently (please let it be true) the collective noun for a gathering of ghosts is a 'fright'.

you have to get out and sell yourself a bit, make connections, talk to publishers and agents, approach people you think will have an interesting story to tell. Basically, make some noise, probably take some low-paid work to build a portfolio and keep at it. Some ghosts – a lot probably – specialise to make their presence in a particular category pool bigger. And some have close relationships with particular publishers and editors and agents.'

So many people believe they have a story to tell, and that there is an audience out there. And the internet has changed everything about how those stories find an audience. Sometimes, a little help is needed to convert those stories into words with structure, sense and meaning. Most ghosts have their own website, so it's the work of a moment to begin, and Zoom, Skype and FaceTime mean that ghosts and their subjects don't actually have to meet unless they choose to.

'Someone with extraordinary experiences to recount (preferably ones that are not libellous in any way!) and can remember details are the easiest and most fun. I've even worked with a few people who can talk in complete joined-up paragraphs. That is a joy, obviously. And then, yes, there are several who have no interest, no memory, or no storytelling ability. They're the ones where you really earn your fee.

'One person I worked with spent twenty years injecting himself with the most mind-bending assortment of drugs and ended up physically and mentally broken. He was on the road to recovery and doing some wonderful things to "give back" to society but he could remember hardly any details of those two decades of extreme abuse. Dragging stories out of him was very painful. These kinds of books though are often the most satisfying – to write 70–80,000 words from a broad story arc and a handful of major events but few specifics and to manage to stay true to the spirit, emotion and facts of the story is something that a ghost can genuinely feel proud of.'

But the singers of stitched words can sometimes come into conflict with their Homer. Of course, trying to piece together a story that is someone else's can lead to frustration, as my ghost explained.

'The one that drives me mad is the phrase "Is that enough?" I worked with one person – very well known – who afforded me precious little time but was constantly asking whether I'd finished asking him questions. He just wanted the book "done". I ended up chasing him all round the world to try to get interview time. His assistant called me once and suggested that I fly to Korea where my author was going to fly from to go to a conference in LA. We could have eight hours on the flight and then I could fly directly back to London from LA. That was one of the few times I have refused a meeting. Instead I went directly to LA where I waited for five days for a meeting and managed, on the final morning, to get three hours with him. Bookended of course with "Is that enough? Are we done?" In fact, we weren't done, and the final session took place in the Far East on the top floor of his penthouse . . . in the sauna. My iPhone nearly died.

'It's also not unusual for an author to lose it a bit the first time they see some sample material. It's all very well talking in abstract about how the book is going to look, sound and read, but when it comes to seeing their words finally on the page, some authors baulk and you hear the cry, "That's not how I sound! That's not my voice!" That can be down to any number of reasons, but it's essential at that point to have a conversation that allows you to understand why the author is complaining. Writing a book (particularly autobiography or memoir) forces people to confront a lot of things. The process is very hard – every single one of the subjects of the autobiographies and memoirs I've written has ended up in tears at one or more interviews – and it's best to establish parameters from the outset. If they say their family is off limits, for example, I push a little to try to find out why. Usually there is a way of talking about partners or children that allows mention without being intrusive.

'It gets tricky when you realise that some of the important facts about a person's life – facts that are out in the public domain – simply aren't true. And that's when you have to get creative with the way you talk about them. For obvious reasons, I can't go into detail about this, but it can be problematic. When a "fact" becomes public early in the career of a celebrity, they feel it's too late to correct it and decades later it's part of their public story despite being a fabrication – something that they may have only nodded along to when a journalist mentioned it to them years earlier is now cemented into the narrative.'

'It needs to be more like Ayn Rand'*

In March 2014 Andrew O'Hagan[†] wrote an article for the *London Review of Books* describing his experience of being Julian Assange's ghostwriter. O'Hagan explains how at the start of the project he felt that the job would be 'consistent with my instinct to walk the unstable border between fiction and non-fiction, to see how porous the parameters between invention and personality are'. Assange apparently hoped for a book

---

*Russian-American philosopher Ayn Rand described her theory of Objectivism as 'the concept of man as a heroic being, with his own happiness as the moral purpose of his life, with productive achievement as his noblest activity, and reason as his only absolute', which she explored in her two best-known books, *The Fountainhead* (1943) and *Atlas Shrugged* (1957).

[†]O'Hagan is the author of a number of successful fiction and non-fiction books, including *The Secret Life: Three True Stories*, which goes into the background of the birth of the Assange book in a chapter called 'Ghosting'.

that would 'read like Hemingway'. O'Hagan spends weeks attempting to get Assange to focus on the book from his location in Norfolk, all while dealing with his subject's paranoia, narcissism, legal wrangles, daily police station visits (part of the bail conditions he was then living under), disorganisation, lack of focus and vendettas against various parts of the media. At one point, Assange suggests that the book could be 'experimental' – 'like chapter one has one word; chapter two has two words . . .'; at another, that 'the book should contain "parables", and . . . the paragraphs should be numbered, like verses'.

Gradually, it becomes clear that Assange has no intention of working with him on the book, or indeed allowing it to be published at all.

'For months, Julian thought he was in control of his relationship with his publishers, agent, lawyers and writer, but he was demonstrating every day in a hundred ways that he couldn't face the book. He'd signed up for it, he was pretending to work on it, but, even before the lies, he was dignifying his denial with higher appointments and legal struggles. The book became his evil "other", his nightmare "autobiography", and rather than being haunted by me, his ghost, he decided to convert me into a quietly ineffective follower.'

In perhaps the only flash of self-awareness that Assange shows during the whole project, he comments to O'Hagan: 'People think you're helping me write my book, but actually I'm helping you write your novel.' O'Hagan tries to keep him committed by reminding him that his UK publisher, Canongate, had paid £600,000 for the book, then sold the rights to more than forty secondary publishers, meaning that worldwide over £2 million had now been advanced on the book's proposal. Assange refuses to contribute meaningfully to the draft that O'Hagan has managed to assemble, or even to read it. As the weeks tick by, Assange moves on from trying to channel Hemingway, deciding that the book needs to be 'more like Ayn Rand'.

'I would have fired him myself if I hadn't been there merely to help him straighten out his sentences,' writes O'Hagan. 'But his sentences too were infected with his habits of self-regard and truth-manipulation. The man who put himself in charge of disclosing the world's secrets simply couldn't bear his own. The story of his life mortified him and sent him scurrying for excuses. He didn't want to do the book. He hadn't from the beginning.'

Eventually, after Assange tries to persuade O'Hagan to fly with him to the Hay literary festival to promote a book that hasn't been written and will never be published, the contract is cancelled. Canongate then decide to publish O'Hagan's first draft of the book as an incomplete, unauthorised biography of Assange. Inevitably, 'lawyers' letters were exchanged', but Canongate went ahead and published. At the end of the *LRB* piece, O'Hagan describes being given the first copy of the printed book: 'Holding it, I realised I felt nothing. I didn't feel it was by me, and the ghost's prerogative, to live a half-life in a house that wasn't mine, was all I had.'

In fact, O'Hagan's relationship with Assange always remained amicable, even while the book deal was collapsing about them. But as he points out, in using a ghostwriter, 'He thought I was his creature and he forgot what a writer is, someone with a tendency to write things down and perhaps seek the truth and aim for transparency.'

Herein lies the tension of ghostwritten words. We like to think that we use words to tell the truth about something: but who owns that truth, and what is owed to the reader, and what to the subject? If Homer did exist, would he have been happy with the interpretations of the Homeridae – happy enough to put his name to them?

Ghostwriters must walk a fine line between being true to what they are told, and pleasing the person ultimately paying their fee. It is a business transaction: at its most base level, either the publisher or the person with their name on the cover is paying someone else to write the words attributed to them. But at least for most ghosts, the deal is an ethical one: the author ultimately retains the rights to the ghostwritten words, and ghost and subject work collaboratively to stitch together a story that will appeal to a reader.

Of course, there are always exceptions to this – perhaps if there is a mismatch between ghost and author, where the ghost is creatively 'filling in' topics that the author has not engaged with, or where the author doesn't carefully check that what has been written in their voice is in fact accurate and true. And what if it turns out that you end up as the voice of an unstable narcissist, who just happens to become leader of the free world?

Trump fiction

In 1985 journalist Mark Schwartz agreed to ghostwrite a business book for Donald Trump. In a *New Yorker* article reflecting on his role decades later, Schwartz notes that in writing *The Art of the Deal*, 'I created a character far more winning than Trump actually is.' The *New Yorker* article explains how: 'In his journal, Schwartz describes the process of trying to make Trump's voice palatable in the book. It was kind of "a trick," he writes, to mimic Trump's blunt, staccato, no-apologies delivery while making him seem almost boyishly appealing.'

That doesn't seem to be the biggest crime for a ghost-writer, but *The Art of the Deal* led directly to *The Apprentice*, and thus became part of the origin story of the myths that Trump would peddle about himself during his ultimately successful 2016 campaign* to run for president. 'I wrote the book. I wrote the book. It was my book. And was a No. 1 bestseller, and one of the best-selling business books of all time. Some say it was the best-selling business book ever,' Trump would claim, with dubious veracity. This makes Schwartz's concerns about his role in Trump's rise seem reasonable. 'I feel a deep sense of remorse that I contributed to presenting Trump in a way that brought him wider attention and made him more appealing than he is . . . I genuinely believe that if Trump wins and gets the nuclear codes there is an excellent possibility it will lead to the end of civilization.' In 2016, Schwartz announced he would donate the royalties he receives from *The Art of the Deal* to several charities, including Human Rights Watch and the National Immigration Forum.

So there you have it. You take on a well-remunerated† but unpleasant ghostwriting gig, and next thing you know you're potentially responsible for the end of the world. That's the thing about words: once freed, they can sometimes head off in directions you could never anticipate.

---

*'We need a leader that wrote *The Art of the Deal*,' said Trump when he declared his presidency.

†'I knew I was selling out,' said Schwartz. 'Literally, the term was invented to describe what I did.' After publication Trump asked Schwartz to cover half the cost of the book's launch party, on the grounds that as Schwartz received half of the advance and royalties of the book, he should also cover half the costs of promoting it. 'He wanted me to split the cost of entertaining his list of nine hundred second-rate celebrities?' exclaimed Schwartz.

Lifting the mask

In November 2019, *The Times* wrote up Tyson Fury's response to being asked by a journalist in an interview about his ghost-written memoir:

> His memoir is called *Behind the Mask* . . . For the past three years he has said he has a type of bipolar disorder, but now he says, 'I don't have bipolar. That's something you don't know.' But I just read about the diagnosis again in his own book, I point out. He shoots me a triumphant 'gotcha!' look. 'Well, I don't have a book out, so you can't have.' I have to remind him that his book is the whole reason why we're here.

Was this the sign of the ultimate ghost? If your subject isn't even aware that you've written their life story, can you disappear back behind your curtain with ghostly satisfaction? I couldn't resist putting this story to my pet ghost.

'Ha ha – yes! And some of course conveniently forget or rather airbrush us out of history. I had one author I worked with on an adventure story. When I saw the page proofs – before publication – he had written a gracious paragraph about our work together. When it came to the final printed book, the paragraph had gone altogether. He had taken it out at the final moment. Who knows why? As a ghost, you just have to move on to the next project.'

THE SECRETS OF AGENTS

The job title 'agent' can evoke something really quite different depending on the modifier you place before it. 'Estate', say, might conjure hair gel and a shiny suit. Whereas 'intelligence' might give you more of a slick Bondian vibe. 'Hollywood'? I'm getting dense cigar smoke and avarice. But how about 'literary'? Maybe something a little more refined and intellectual? A whiff of Earl Grey and eccentric socks, perhaps? Let's embark on this chapter with the firm conviction that we can do better than these lazy stereotypes. After all, for the millions of aspiring authors out there, a literary agent is someone they would very much like to meet. But what's the background on how this singular role in the Gutenberg Galaxy came to be?

Intermedias res

Whether it's harnessing good writers to meet the latest reader demands or surfacing stories and voices people would never otherwise have known they wanted to read, the fundamentals of the literary agent's role have changed little since they first ambled onto the publishing scene in the latter half of the nineteenth century: find good writers, find them a willing publisher and find them a paying audience – for a fixed percentage.

For a long time after the big bang that led to the creation of the Gutenberg Galaxy, agents simply didn't exist. Neither did publishers; your printer *was* your publisher. But gradually it became apparent that the skills necessary to run a big oily noisy mechanical printing press were not, in fact, the same skills required to cultivate a stable of real human authors and a portfolio of literary intellectual property.

As a result, publishers divorced themselves from the means of production and instead positioned themselves as the gatekeepers between writers and printers, providing – for a fee, of course – editorial support in the service of the author. Shortly thereafter, in another epiphany of inter-mediation, it must have occurred to some bright spark that – similar to the printer/agent bifurcation above – the cre-ativity, erudition and bottomless self-doubt of your average author did not make them the best or most hard-nosed repre-sentatives of their own commercial interests. It's not easy to be objective about your own art. Literary agents stepped into the breach to protect their clients' financial (and emotional) well-being. Praise be to the middleman or woman.

That said, the book agent's position in the publishing eco-system is not without controversy. Their efficacy at inflating the advances and royalties of their most marketable clients has arguably had an unintended consequence: the con-centration of publishing opportunities into the hands of a decreasing number of book-shifting stalwarts as publishers become more risk-averse owing to the size of the bets they are now forced to place. This potentially limits access to new and unknown authors, especially those with unfamiliar voices or different perspectives.

But, having mentioned a process of historical inter-mediation above, it's worth remembering that today we live in a golden age of the reverse: disintermediation. In other words, as digital democratisation removes barriers to entry and connects producers directly with consumers, there's never been a greater proliferation of publishing. Whether this will herald a transformative shift towards genuine inclusivity and creative equity remains to be seen. But it's possible the internet will prove to be the ultimate agent of literary change.

I talked to Karolina Sutton, an agent for leading literary and talent agency Curtis Brown, about what being an agent means. Adding to her already not inconsiderable workload, I started by asking her what agents really do. She, demonstrating a facility with an intriguing hook that no doubt makes her very good at her job, summarised it thus: 'Agents are the first filters – they keep a lot of secrets, and some of those secrets are bad words. Our job is to keep those words away from editors, and only let them see the good ones.'

I really liked this idea. Imagine as an author having someone on your side who will work tirelessly to shine a light on your best words while being just as rigorous about stopping any of your bad words from escaping into the wider world. But what that takes can be . . . almost anything, it seems, from talent-spotting to financial advice. What makes a good agent? I asked.

'Time management. You have to be very disciplined. You need to carve out thinking time, and time to read and edit as well as everything else – you have to learn not to be available 24/7, while still providing client care when it is needed. And the work is changing. For example, there are now some that don't deal with the printed word at all – they specialise in taking on clients who write podcasts or are only writing for audio. And increasingly agents also need to be able to deal with digital marketing, metadata, and occasionally become experts in IT.'

That sounds like . . . a lot. 'It's an unusual combination of skills. You need to be literate, numerate, have excellent taste, be a business person, and you have a pastoral role, too. It's self-defining – you make it what it is – and you need to serve an apprenticeship. Essentially, you are a salesperson on behalf of each writer that you represent.'

Yes, agents are salespeople – that's how they make money for themselves and their authors – but an agent is also the person who helps the author get what they want out of the process long after the deal has been done. Authors tend to involve their agents to help state their case and back them up if they are in disagreement with their publisher about any number of issues. No detail is too small for a good agent to care about, as Karolina described: 'You have no idea what the day ahead might bring. You might have a plan for it, but one email can derail it all. For each of your clients, you are chasing up every tiny detail for their work: is the metadata on Amazon correct? Is the audiobook available in Ireland? If not, why not? About 80 per cent of the role is admin: royalties need paying, contracts sorting. You have to be advocating for your client constantly – about publication dates, covers, publicity – you are the bridge between your client and their publisher. You must be assertive and prepared to ask difficult questions.'

This is true. It's my experience that agents don't tend to get involved when things are going well. Rather, they are the crack problem-solvers of publishing, deployed only when the author feels their publisher is not listening to them, or when things have reached such an impasse that they need a third party to negotiate. As a writer, you want to spend your time *writing* – not wondering why your metadata isn't accurate on Amazon or why the gold foil on the cover of your latest bestseller is peeling off. Or, indeed, worrying if your precious IP address is being hacked from your publisher's IP address.

Karolina told me that recently Curtis Brown came under cyberattack – she described the campaign to the *Bookseller* as 'carefully orchestrated' and that it 'carried on daily for months'. The cybercriminals were attempting to get hold of a copy of *The Testaments* by Margaret Atwood in advance of its publication (they should have joined forces with Amazon in the US, who managed to send out copies of the book to readers a week in advance of its strict release date). I think this is what Karolina means when she says that as an agent you have no idea what each day will bring.

But perhaps to focus on the agent's role as the bridge between author and publisher is to jump the gun a bit, because one of the most – if not *the* most – important roles that agents fulfil is to keep the pipeline of literary talent that publishers increasingly rely on flowing. Karolina reminds me that agents need to go out and hunt down words to sell to publishers in the first place.

'You go out and find ideas and authors anywhere and everywhere.* For example, I often engage with people who have come through creative writing classes. There is an idea that agents are gatekeepers who are always saying no, but actually, they are facilitators who want to say *yes*. When looking at a submission we won't read all of it, just the proposal. There isn't time to read every word and there is a physical limit to how many manuscripts you can look at, so I work in a team with my assistants. I'm looking for potential – when you know exactly which commissioning editor it should go to for consideration is when you are excited.'

But if you know what you're looking for, what publishers want and what is likely to sell, why not just help authors write a proposal that fits?

'Being an agent is *not* about rewriting proposals. A proposal should be an honest reflection of an author's style. You should never sell what you – well, the author! – can't deliver. Lots of people think they have an idea for a book, but a

---

*There is a special agent code which means that approaching someone else's authors is strictly frowned upon (although apparently it still happens). You're meant to wait for an author to approach you if they want to switch agent.

proposal should reflect that they can maintain that idea over 80,000 words. You need to have an instinct to see something in it, and that only comes with experience.'

If agents are sometimes disparaged among aspiring authors for being overly picky or difficult to impress, there's a simple reason for this: they are and they have to be. As Karolina puts it, 'The one thing you have as an agent is your reputation – which means that when you send a proposal over to an editor, they will pay attention and move you to the top of the pile, because they know that you will only send over solid proposals. I am always looking for excellent writing, which means I can sell books and sell rights to be able to look after my authors.'

WLTM via #MSWL

Members of the popular sub-sect (sub-genre?) of techno-bibliophiles out there may have stumbled across this Twitter hashtag used by literary agents to distribute their personal shopping lists of writing and writers to represent: #MSWL. A quick search for #MSWL – 'manuscript wish list' – turned up some intriguing results. I found agents hankering for manuscripts featuring 'romance involving unique races', specifically 'shamans, fae, nymphs, mermaids, satyrs, sirens, werecats, werebears, or other under-represented paranormals'. There was also a plaintive request for 'some 1920s/1950s upmarket fiction with vivid historical settings', not to mention a more open-to-interpretation invitation for 'a super cute and hilarious small-town romance that's also got a lot of sexy times in it'. Oh, and a *lot* of #MSWL posts for vampire novels, upmarket vampire novels, young adult vampire comedies and a toxic vampire bromance. That whole vampire trend? Very much trending.

I'd never considered that Twitter might have so many

agents hunting for such specific manuscripts to read and potentially publish. Of course, surfing a proven pop culture trend is a perfectly sensible and respectable element of publishing – give the people what they want! – but then so too is giving an auteur or subject-matter expert the freedom to express their vision or expertise free of social-media-based suggestions. You *could* try tweeting Donna Tartt* with a request for a zombie slash superhero redux of *Romeo and Juliet*. I wouldn't necessarily recommend it.

#amquerying, therefore I am

What I was glimpsing through the lens of the Twitter telescope was a tiny corner of the protean Gutenberg Galaxy; a snapshot of the nurseries where good words might be born, delivered unto the wider literary universe by one of a circling flock of eager midwives.

As well as being full of agents requesting made-to-order submissions, Twitter had poster after poster using the hashtag #amquerying in their posts. What did it mean? I'd never heard anyone say this before (with or without the hashtag). But there they were, a plethora of writers merrily am-querying away. From the context, I deduced its meaning: that a writer is approaching an agent with a submission, and 'querying' them to find out if they would be interested in representing them and their words.

You can understand why this phrase has evolved – it sounds polite but hopeful, professional yet creative. There were even people offering 'querying kits': template letters

---

* 'There's an expectation these days that novels – like any other consumer product – should be made on a production line, with one dropping from the conveyor belt every couple of years,' said the enigmatic author of *The Secret History*, *The Little Friend* and *The Goldfinch*.

you could personalise for your submissions to help you query agents without reinventing the wheel – or, indeed, rewriting the spiel – every time. They often included a submission tracker spreadsheet, which hints at the sheer volume of queries some writers are sending out – and the number of agents available to receive them. In fact, the deeper I delved into the #writingcommunity, the more it seemed as if there were almost as many agents out there as writers, each whirling through cyberspace in search of their perfect literary match.

Decoding Dan Brown

Of course, digital innovation is already an integral part of publishing in the same way as it pervades all parts of twenty-first-century life. Agents didn't exist in 1850. Will they still exist in 2050? You can't fire up YouTube without catching a TED Talk espousing the 'game-changing' (sigh) impact of big data, machine learning and AI. With all the technology and data points now available in the publishing industry, surely some maverick digital visionary could science the heck out of the art of identifying potential bestsellers, thereby making a large part of the agent's role redundant?

In *The Bestseller Code*, authors Jodie Archer and Matthew L. Jockers run data through a computer algorithm designed to reveal which books *should* be successful, and which less so. Having used their algorithm to analyse a selection of *New York Times* bestseller lists, they claim that those books that earn a place on it are not as arbitrary and chaotic as it might seem to the casual observer. Their algorithm obviously didn't know what was on the bestseller lists, but nonetheless, it showed a surprising degree of correlation with them. When presented with text written by Dan Brown, the computer came up with a 95.7 per cent likelihood of bestselling success, giving a gentle spanking to E. L. James's *Fifty Shades of Grey*, which only achieved 90 per cent.

The algorithm is aware of nothing more than the words it is presented with: it has no knowledge of the author's age, background, race, gender or previous publishing history. Nor does it know or care if there is a big, small or non-existent publicity and marketing campaign planned, or if it is about to be made into a film or get picked for a sales promotion. 'Five years of study suggests that bestselling is largely dependent upon having just the right words in just the right order, and the most intriguing thing about the *NYT* list is about nothing more or less than the author's manuscript, black ink on white paper, unadorned.'

The algorithm took thousands of data points from each manuscript to give it an aggregate score of potential success. These data points included the topic of the book ('The computer revealed that the most frequently occurring and important theme is one that involves human closeness, a theme that is all about characters relating emotionally'), plotlines (according to the algorithm symmetrical plotlines with a three-act structure were the hallmarks of a bestseller), style (which trends towards an author with a mastery of 'everyday', rather than particularly 'literary' language), and finally the verbs used to describe the actions of the characters.

After all this analysis, the algorithm was able to use the data it had received to rank the manuscripts that had been fed to it. Its favourite book – the one it most wanted to take on holiday and thought most likely to be a bestseller – was Dave Eggers's 2014 novel *The Circle* – ironically, a novel about the use and misuse of data. The authors of *The Bestseller Code* didn't miss the irony.* 'It's a little awkward . . . The algorithm appears to have winked at us all. We weren't sure whether we should take a sledgehammer to it, or buy it dinner.'

---

*Adding to the irony, *The Circle* never appeared in any bestseller charts.

A million (code) monkeys

Of course, the worth of a literary endeavour is not defined by its presence or otherwise on a bestseller list. An algorithm might be able to identify works that will be popular, but can lines of code ever really separate the infinite shades of subtlety and nuance that lie between the good words and the bad? We're familiar with the idea that everyone has a book in them, but it's not always a good idea to let those books out into the world. Indeed, they may even end up destabilising the very concept of a 'book'.

In the world of bad words, even a book titled *The 2009– 2014 World Outlook for 60-milligram Containers of Fromage Frais* can pick up an award. In this case, the Diagram Prize for Oddest Book Title of the Year, a showcase of the most ingeniously mundane and bafflingly esoteric since 1978, originally developed as a way to keep visitors to the Frankfurt Book Fair entertained. Previous worthy winners include 2004's *Bombproof Your Horse*, 2005's *Too Naked for the Nazis* and *How to Avoid Huge Ships*, buoyed to victory by a huge swell of support in 1992. Since 2000, the winner has been voted for by readers of the *Bookseller* magazine, who clearly enjoy being on to a bad thing.

So far so weird. But the aforementioned *Containers of Fromage Frais* was even odder than its title might suggest. While its cover presented its author as Phillip M. Parker, *Fromage Frais* was actually written by a computer. Parker may take the plaudits – and, indeed, he does so for this and the other 200,000 books on Amazon credited to him. From *The 2007–2012 Outlook for Tufted Washable Scatter Rugs, Bathmats and Sets That Measure 6-Feet by 9-Feet or Smaller in India** to *Ehlers-Danlos Syndrome: A Bibliography and Dictionary for Physicians,*

---

*A copy costs £795 and it is for 'global strategic planners who cannot be content with traditional methods of segmenting world markets'.

Patients and Genome Researchers,* Parker and his machines are prolific, as an article in the *New York Times* explains:

> Mr. Parker . . . has developed computer algorithms that collect publicly available information on a subject broad or obscure and, aided by his 60 to 70 computers and six or seven programmers, he turns the results into books in a range of genres, many of them in the range of 150 pages and printed only when a customer buys one.
>
> If this sounds like cheating to the layman's ear, it does not to Mr. Parker, who holds some provocative and apparently profitable ideas on what constitutes a book. While the most popular of his books may sell hundreds of copies, he said, many have sales in the dozens, often to medical libraries collecting nearly everything he produces. He has extended his technique to crossword puzzles, rudimentary poetry and even to scripts for animated game shows. And he is laying the groundwork for romance novels generated by new algorithms. 'I've already set it up,' he said. 'There are only so many body parts.'

Is this imaginative variation on the apocryphal million monkeys on a million typewriters the (il)logical endpoint of algorithmic writing? While the idea that we can create a formula that will provide a manuscript full of words in a combination that we can guarantee will sell is seductive, we should also recognise that this is not how words and our response to them work in the real world. A computer cannot spot new trends, break new literary ground, understand word-of-mouth recommendations or how a book can perhaps suddenly or unexpectedly find its moment against the

---

*Two reviews on Amazon. One of which says: 'Wasn't an easy read by any means.'

odds. For that, we still rely on the people out there whose job it is to constantly scan the galaxy, searching for those magic combinations of words that can unite an author's ideas with a reader's imagination. I can see how a book that combines much of the written information on fromage frais could be useful – if you work in the dairy industry, say – but it seems vanishingly unlikely to produce anything that will touch the human heart.

No Thanks To . . .

Having explored some of the ways in which the modern world is challenging and changing agents' role in identifying good books and the good words they comprise, it's worth remembering that this process is the means; not the end. Let us not forget the literary agents' Prime Directive: get it published. And achieving this can be a lot more trying than you might think.

In 1935, E. E. Cummings* borrowed $300 from his mother and self-published a book of poetry called *No Thanks*. Originally, he had planned to call it *70 Poems*, but after receiving 'no thanks' letters from fourteen publishers, he changed the title and dedicated the book to those who had turned him down. And, to make sure they really got the message, he arranged their names on the dedication page into the shape of a funeral urn:

---

*e e or E. E.? Although often styled as e e, *The Chicago Manual of Style* states that: 'E. E. Cummings can be safely capitalized; it was one of his publishers, not he himself, who lowercased his name.' Cummings legally changed his name to e e cummings (according to his biographer), but his widow claimed that the biographer was incorrect. In short: you can use either variation as long as you use it consistently and are prepared to pick a side to justify your decision. Much as I love the lower-case style I'm with his widow; I feel she would have known him best.

NO
THANKS
TO
Farrar & Rinehart
Simon & Schuster
Coward-McCann
Limited Editions
Harcourt, Brace
Random House
Equinox Press
Smith & Haas
Viking Press
Knopf
Dutton
Harper's
Scribner's
Covici-Friede

While we can't truly see inside the mind of E. E. Cummings at this point in his writing career, I think it's reasonable to suggest he might have benefited from the emotional buffer provided by an agent.

Though, to be fair, he was in good company. Manuscripts turned down repeatedly by publishers include *The Diary of Anne Frank*, *Carrie*, *Harry Potter and the Philosopher's Stone*, *The Spy Who Came in from the Cold*,* *Anne of Green Gables*, *Lord of the Flies*, *The Help* and *Gone with the Wind*. It seems there are occasions when you can't judge a book by its contents.

Even printers sometimes get in on the act. James Joyce

---

*One editor who turned down *Spy* advised John le Carré that he had 'no future as a writer'. Le Carré earned his living as a writer for almost sixty years, with his final novel *Silverview* being published posthumously in 2021.

first submitted the manuscript of *Dubliners* to publishers in 1905, and it quickly found one called Grant Richards. But their printer refused to set one of the stories ('Two Gallants'), claiming it was obscene. Ultimately, Grant Richards sided with the printer and it had to be resubmitted to other publishers. Maunsel & Roberts picked it up in 1909 only for the same thing to happen. This time, Joyce asked if he could have the printed sheets returned to him. The printers, accommodating to the last, refused and promptly burnt them. Joyce managed to save a set and, in 1914, Grant Richards agreed to use these page proofs to finally publish the book. Which printers actually stamped ink on paper is not recorded, but Joyce can only have been grateful that in this instance they chose not to revert to type(face).

What this shows us is that the path to publication can be long and arduous – far more so than you might think – and having an expert Sherpa at your side can be of huge support. It's easy with hindsight to criticise the editors and publishing houses that rejected what turned out to be bestsellers, but publishing budgets are not limitless and perhaps they simply got a better pitch from some other author's agent? But, if Cummings and Joyce had had an agent acting on their behalf, they might have been able to spend more time writing and less time devising obscure revenge-based typography or wrangling with prudish printers. It's no wonder that – even at a time of prodigious growth in self-publishing – getting a good agent is number two on every aspiring author's to-do list, just after 'Write the damn book'. They're close to indispensable.

Lord of the slush pile

Type in 'slush pile' and Google will tellingly expand your query with suggestions including: 'How to avoid . . .', 'How to get out of . . .' and, most dramatically, 'How to escape'. For an aspiring author, being trapped forever in the slush pile is the worst outcome of all. A slush pile is the collective noun for the various unsolicited query letters and manuscripts a publisher receives directly from writers. Hilary Mantel made a successful escape from the slush pile. So did Stephenie Meyer.

For many years, publishers employed readers to look through manuscripts in the slush pile and make an assessment as to whether any of them should go forward to be looked at by a living, breathing editor. But as time went on, publishers realised it was more economical to get rid of these salaried readers and simply rely on agents to do the initial vetting. These days, the biggest publishers will not accept any unsolicited manuscripts. You might say they have escaped the slush pile themselves.

Where the slush pile does still live on, however, is with smaller independent publishers and agents that might be more inclined to invest time and resources in using it as a way to find new talent.* And inevitably the slush pile has been outsourced to the hive mind of the internet, to websites like Youwriteon, which allows new writers to gain initial feedback on their work from their peers, and then – for those with the highest ratings – from a group of publishing

---

*Or not. 'It's the hope that kills you,' said one editor at a small press when she was faced with a slush pile. 'You approach each time convinced you'll find a diamond in the rough, that you will be the person who has the perspicacity and taste to spot the raw talent that everyone else has missed. It will make your career! And then you're met with a slew of manuscripts that range between the unpublishably dull and the genuinely disturbing. I once looked up the author of a mildly promising slush-pile find about French politics and discovered they were in prison for strangling their girlfriend. I think these days everyone sensible knows you really need an agent, and they probably concentrate their energy there.'

professionals. Eventually a Book of the Year is chosen, many of which have gone on to be successfully published.

'Time: the Future. Absurd & uninteresting fantasy about the explosion of an atom bomb on the Colonies. A group of children who land in jungle-country near New Guinea. Rubbish & dull. Pointless.'

This less-than-impressive summary was scribbled by Faber & Faber's professional slush-pile reader on the corner of a manuscript sent to them for consideration. The manuscript was titled *Strangers from Within*, and apparently included a long and boring Prologue about a nuclear war that featured no characters at all (I'd still like to read it, though. Just me?). It's perhaps not surprising that the reader summed it up as 'Absurd & uninteresting'.

What saved the manuscript was that Charles Monteith, a new arrival to Faber, was about to head to Oxford on a train. By chance, he picked up the pages from the slush pile to read on the journey. By the end of his trip, he was convinced he wanted to publish the book. He persuaded the author William Golding to ditch the prologue, make a number of other improvements and change the title. The original prologue that Golding wrote is lost, so none of us can know what bad words Monteith had to endure on that train journey before he got to the heart of the story that eventually became *Lord of the Flies*. It has now sold more than 10 million copies and twice been made into a film. Simon and Piggy never made it off the island, but at least their story made a successful escape from the slush pile.

The #amquerying continues

Like all in the #writingcommunity, I needed to query more than one agent. So I did. Chris Wellbelove is a director at an agency called Aitken Alexander, and he represents (among others) Man Booker shortlist author Daisy Johnson and the Secret Barrister. I asked Chris to tell me a bit about how he spent his days.

'The great thing about being an agent is the variety of the work. A lot of time is spent talking to the authors I represent about the projects they're working on or about various aspects of the publishing process – from editorial notes they may have received to marketing and publicity plans and sales figures. We're also in regular touch with editors and publishing teams, though the level of contact tends to depend on where in the publishing process we are; it's much more intensive around publication. There's also time spent talking to colleagues internally about books I might have coming up, or that we are in the process of selling. I will be meeting potential new clients, and then there are the meetings with editors, who are the people we sell to. I sell to publishers in the UK and US, and so keep up to date on what is working well in each territory and what particular editors are looking for.'

'Variety' seems like something of an understatement. Much like my conversation with Karolina, I got the sense of a lot of plates spinning on a lot of poles with not the least bit of difficulty. Come on, Chris. There must be something that impinges into an agent's Zen-like calm?

'The trickiest part of my job is around managing expectations – both my authors' and my own. At the start of any project, ambitions on all sides (author, agent and publisher) are high, but of course some books do better than others, and a part of the agent's job is breaking bad news. The other thing I find challenging is the juggling – I have a list of fiction and non-fiction writers, and will at any one time be working on a number of different books and having to switch between the two.'

Ah, those plates then. But what sort of words was Chris looking for? The amount of #amquerying going on out there felt like it would make it difficult for an agent to cut through all the noise and be able to focus on the words that they might be interested in.

'I started out with very specific ideas about what I'd represent, but soon discovered that not many of those books come along and so needed to find a way to expand my areas of interest without taking on projects cynically. What I am interested in definitely moves around, though mostly influenced by things I have been reading or watching, world events and the market. Often there will be ideas that I'm chewing over and I'll look for writers or experts to discuss those with, but I try to stay as open as possible – within my very general areas of interest. And I think, as an agent whose list has more non-fiction on it than fiction, the internet has offered lots of opportunities. That said, I don't tend to represent books that come directly from the internet – the Secret Barrister is the client of mine with the biggest online profile, but I approached them with a specific idea on the strength of a couple of early blog posts when they only had about 3,000 Twitter followers.'

The Secret Barrister: Stories of the Law and How It's Broken was published in 2018 and is a non-fiction sensation. It has sold more than 400,000 copies and the author of the books and blogs remains unknown. There is speculation that the Secret Barrister is Keir Starmer, but a reference in an early blog entry to a moustache suggests that this is unlikely. In a 2019 interview about the book's success the masked author commented: 'It was weird not to be able to celebrate the success of my book publicly – criminal barristers are wild egotists and my other half finds it amusing that the greatest success I've had is something no one will find out about.'

'For me,' said Chris, 'the internet is mostly a resource, and I'll spend a lot of time looking for people who have interesting ideas, or are working on interesting things. I suppose I feel that in non-fiction a big part of my job is helping people who know a lot more on a topic than me translate their ideas for a general reader. I am interested in lots of subjects, but expert in none, and that makes me a good stand-in for the people who go into Waterstones at the weekend and buy a couple of the latest big non-fiction books.

'In fiction a lot of what I take on comes through creative writing courses or recommendation, but the internet has certainly opened things up. A record of publishing in journals or online can help put a submission towards the top of an editor's pile. What I'm mostly looking for in fiction submissions is an energy in the writing, a distinctiveness to the voice and a sense of ambition. It's the closest I get to a kind of purity – I am reading initially without thinking about the market, prepared to be bowled over. In non-fiction I tend to be more interested in the person, their expertise and their ideas. With non-fiction writers I find that the writing often needs most work when the book idea isn't quite right, so I like to build proposals from the ground up, trying to find the way into their subject that will carry the general reader through ideas that can be complicated. One of the strange things about this job is that we spend most of our time working on books that are years away from being published.'

Chris is right there. One thing you should know about publishing is that it moves about as fast as a glacier. Add up the time an author spends on their manuscript, the months and often years it takes to go through the cycle of idea development, proposal, selling to a publishing house, book being written, rewritten, written again, edited, copy-edited, typeset, proofread, finalised, printed, bound and finally shipped to retailers, and you can see that publishing really is a long game. It took Margaret Mitchell ten years just to write *Gone with the Wind*. Imagine the patience required of her agent, had she had one.

STET AND ECHT: EDITORS

'Just get it down on paper, and then
we'll see what to do with it.'
Maxwell Perkins

As a first-time author, I can confirm that the advice in the epigraph above from Maxwell Perkins, who spent thirty-six years as an editor at Scribner in the United States, still rings true. I don't know if all writers feel as I do, but what I've learned from writing this book is that the only way to make any progress is just to *write*. Get the words down on paper, and only then can you see what to do with them – how to make your words better, and fit to send out to readers.

But after you've got your words down, then what? They need editing. 'Edit' comes from the Latin word *edere*, and means 'to bring out', or to 'put forth'. And if you only had two (or three) words to sum up what an editor does, those might be the ones you would choose to get to the heart of the matter. According to Perkins, 'An editor does not add to a book. At best he serves as a handmaiden to an author. Don't ever get to feeling important about yourself, because an editor at most releases energy. He creates nothing.'

'Releases energy' fits, I think, with the idea that an editor 'brings out' a collection of words and aids in putting it together and then presenting it to the people who matter most: the readers. It's worth bearing in mind that 'editor' is one of those publishing words that can mean a multitude of different things: 'editing' can mean anything from compiling an anthology to taking a manuscript, tearing apart its structure and putting it together again, to copy-editing, where each sentence is interrogated for typos and sense. Then there are commissioning editors, the hunter-gatherers of the literary world: their job is to stay abreast of current trends and sales, know what the market is doing, and ferret out voices to publish that will find an audience.

The commissioning editor is the crucial bridge between the author and their audience, going out to find proposals with potential before acquiring them (probably from an agent) and then overseeing their publication. Kenneth McCormick, an editor-in-chief at Doubleday, described the job of commissioning editor as 'to know what to publish, how to get it, and what to do to help it achieve the largest readership'. Simple.

Max Perkins began his career by discovering, championing and editing F. Scott Fitzgerald, then moved on successfully to argue the case for Scribner publishing Ernest Hemingway. Not content with that, he also managed to persuade Thomas Wolfe* to actually cut text from his novels. Wolfe was famously attached to each sentence he wrote; one manuscript he submitted consisted of over a million words, and although Wolfe and Perkins eventually fell out over Wolfe's resentment that much of his success became

---

*Not to be confused with Tom Wolfe (author of *The Bonfire of the Vanities*), Thomas Wolfe was an influential American novelist of the early twentieth century. His first novel, *Look Homeward, Angel* (1929), chronicled the lives of many of his family and friends in his hometown of Asheville, North Carolina. Such was the reaction to the novel that Wolfe chose not to return there for eight years. His next novel, *Of Time and the River* (1935), was also met with disapproval on publication by the inhabitants of Asheville: this time they were upset at not being featured.

attributed to Perkins's efforts as his editor, Wolfe wrote to him on his deathbed acknowledging the role he had played in making publication of his work possible.

By the time of his own death in 1947, Perkins was the most famous editor of American literature, in what was considered to be the golden age of American editors. As McCormick said, Perkins supported his authors in numerous ways: 'He helped them structure their books, if help was needed; thought up titles, invented plots; he served as psychologist, lovelorn advisor, marriage counsellor, career manager, money-lender. Few editors before him had done so much work on manuscripts, yet he was always faithful to his credo: "The book belongs to the author."'

Perkins was a contemporary of Ezra Pound. Described by *Time* magazine in 1933 as 'a cat that walks by himself, tenaciously unhousebroken and very unsafe for children' (this was in reference to his Fascist views), Pound assisted in the serialisation of James Joyce's* *The Portrait of An Artist as a Young Man* in 1914, and in 1915 persuaded *Poetry* magazine to publish T. S. Eliot's 'The Love Song of J. Alfred Prufrock'. His best-known contribution to Eliot's work was as editor and reviser of the text that eventually became *The Waste Land*, published in 1922.

According to the poetry critic Marjorie Perloff, 'Pound and Eliot worked on the poem [*The Waste Land*] page by page, piecemeal, not trying to salvage a structure but to reclaim the authentic lines and passages from the contrived.' Eliot himself said: 'I have sometimes tried to perform the same sort of maieutic† task; and I knew that one of the

---

*Joyce described Pound as 'a miracle of ebullience, gusto and help'; Gertrude Stein was less impressed and described him as 'a village explainer, excellent if you were a village, but if you were not, not'.

†This word (new to me, when I encountered this quote) was coined by

temptations against which I have to be on guard, is trying to re-write somebody's poem in the way that I should have written it myself if I had wanted to write that poem. Pound never did that: he tried first to understand what one was attempting to do, and then tried to help one do it in one's own way.' When asked if editors were just failed writers, Eliot responded: 'Perhaps – but so are most writers.' Ouch.

The original version of *The Waste Land* that Pound and Eliot worked on was roughly eight hundred lines and together they reduced it by half. For many years the original was thought to be lost to history. 'Well, the fate of that manuscript or typescript with his blue-pencillings on it is one of the permanent – so far as I know – minor mysteries of literature,' said Eliot, unaware that the manuscript was actually among the papers of his friend John Quinn. In 1968 the manuscript was rediscovered, festooned in the handwritten notes of Pound, Eliot, and Eliot's first wife, Vivienne Haigh-Wood Eliot.

The pencil notes that Pound most often made on the manuscript were the Latin word *'stet'*,* which means 'let it stand', and *'echt'*, which is German for something that is true and genuine. Pound's work as an editor was to identify those words that were 'true'– the echt that should be stet – and excise the ones that rang false; to decide between what should stand and what not. Brutally, this meant that some words needed to be extirpated – something all good editors must be happy to do, especially when an author can't bear to.

Socrates, and means to bring forth new ideas by the use of reasoning and dialogue. Socrates' mother was a midwife, and the word comes from the Greek word for midwifery: *maieutikos*. Socrates was right: editors serve as midwives to the birth of words.

*'Stet' is what's known as an obelism. That's the word for annotating manuscripts with marks in the margin. We'll encounter more obelisms later on in this book.

'Editors *love* to cut,' my editor gleefully explained, even as I added to my word count with every re-draft.

Salvaging a structure

All texts need to have a structure, or they are meaningless. Structure can apply to a clause, a sentence, a paragraph, or an entire book. Does each section of the book follow on from the previous in a logical way? Can a reader follow the argument without having to stop, double back, look something up or simply give up in confusion and frustration? The same questions need to be asked of the sentences and paragraphs, too – a logical structure needs to overlay every unit of how words are grouped together.

If your words are fiction, does the plot have a structure that allows the story to be followed? Does it deliver suspense and surprises when necessary? As a writer, you might feel that your structure and arguments are perfectly reasoned – but nearly always, you need someone else to examine your text with a fresh eye. It's very hard to *see* a structure through the words when you are so close to them and you know what you are writing about so intimately.

This is where structural editing – of the kind that Max Perkins was renowned for – comes in. I asked Luke Brown – an author and structural editor – to talk me through how it works.

'There is an inherent tension between what the writer thinks they are doing, and what you, the reader, think they are doing. My job is to make things measurably better for the reader and to protect the writer from reviewers. What does the reader want to know about? Does the plot follow a narrative arc? Does conflict intensify in a way that is satisfying? Is there resolution (either change / no change on the part of the protagonist) – and if not, why not? There is a tendency with inexperienced writers to fill up space for its own sake. One of the most important things to recognise is that in the world of words, concision is generosity.' As G. K. Chesterton said: 'Art consists of limitation. The most beautiful part of every picture is the frame.'

'Some of the issues I come up against over and over again,' Luke continued, 'are a lack of clarity, where a writer doesn't know what they are trying to say, and a lack of imagination about what a reader really *wants*. Less experienced writers often have an ideal reader in their heads, but of course, that person doesn't exist. There needs to be a pact of communication between the reader and the writer. Working as a structural or line editor you develop a series of rules over time: you work on your eye for language and clarity. Part of the joy of editing is listening to how the music of the text works – you need to be sensitive to the language. There should be no wastage of words: every one should have meaning.'

I love the idea that the reader and writer make a pact together – on the writer's side, that they will strive to use the best words to evoke an emotional response and structure them in a way that makes sense, and on the reader's that they will open their minds to allow that response to happen. Here's what my editor said about how she thought of her part: 'I often think of myself as a kind of "first reader" of the book – your role as editor is to help the author tell the story (or deliver the message) that they want to, in a way that will help them reach their audience best. You need to be able to stand in both sets of shoes at once, and see both what the author wants to say and what the reader needs to hear to be charmed and informed by the book.'

That's how words get good: when both sides – author and reader – are able to play their part. The broker in the middle is the person who can see the structure lurking in the undergrowth, and clear the way to make it easy for the reader to follow the path of the story.

Asking the right questions

'I got my first job working as an assistant to one of the pre-eminent literary agents in London. She was a maverick in all kinds of ways. Rather than providing detailed notes to her authors, she would invite them to sit on one of the ancient armchairs in her office, and spend hours talking to them about their manuscripts – what she felt worked and why, what she thought didn't work and why this might be – and in a way she was summoning the characters into the room, treating them like the complete human beings the author wanted them to be, and showing up any flaws or gaps for them to see. So, my first lessons in editing were really about talking, not writing. Asking the right questions in a support-ive way, listening to the answers, and then asking more questions. To summarise: when you edit, you don't have the answer, and if the author doesn't either, don't try to suggest solutions, just ask the right questions so they can find it for themselves.'

This description is from Hannah, a fiction editor, explain-ing how she approaches structural editing at the start of a manuscript's journey. What she touches on here – 'showing up any flaws or gaps for them to see' – is the essence of editing. When you are so close to your words it becomes almost impossible to put yourself into the mind of the reader: what is obvious to you might be completely opaque to the people you are writing for.

'My first step after these types of conversations might be to follow up with a "structural" edit – which for me is usually a letter outlining broadly the areas of the manuscript that I think need attention – again framed as questions that invite the writer to seek the solution for themselves. This might result in a new draft that still requires some back-and-forth questions, and then finally working through a line edit, essentially picking up instances where the prose works less well, or any tics the author might be prone to.'

From over-view to line-by-line

In all this talk about how editing works, it's quite difficult to pin down what it actually *means* in practice. My colleague Simon explained to me how he works on his non-fiction manuscripts.

'Like all editors, when I'm reading, I'm trying to think constantly about clarity, about expectation in the potential reader and about the level of previous knowledge required. Our authors are generally chosen for their articulacy and originality, but it is surprising how sometimes they can get in a terrible muddle nonetheless.'

What jumped out at me here was how at the forefront of Simon's mind was the *reader*. It makes sense – what's the point of writing something that only satisfies you, the author? Words live to find their reading audience, and a good editor knows what the reader might want, and how it can be achieved. There was an echo here of how Luke described trying to help his writers to imagine what their readers wanted – and to help them realise that the ideal reader simply didn't exist.

Speaking with another editor, Shoaib, about how he went about working with his authors, he let me see a letter he had written to one of them in response to their first draft. As well as being a detailed breakdown of each chapter of the book and what refinement it might need, he had pointed out overarching structural themes that needed working on: expanding the storytelling; interrogating bias and building urgency that will ultimately lead to a resolution in a way that a reader will find satisfying.

All the editors I spoke to were concerned about high-lighting times when their writers assumed a certain level of knowledge on the part of the reader. That ultimately runs the risk of frustrating and disappointing your audience. The writer is the guide, and has to provide safe handholds; make it easy for your reader to travel through the text with you.

Components with vision

For Shoaib, a structural edit is 'about harmonising the narrative to marry its constituent components – voice, exposition, rhythm, style, etc. – with the writer's core vision'. This concise explanation sounds straightforward – but I think it's difficult as a writer to be able to successfully marry these two ideas together when it's your book. Your closeness to the text, your all-consuming immersion in whatever it is you're writing about, means that to objectively be able to stand back and assess whether you have managed to unify the book's components with the core vision is probably impossible. Writers sweat over deciding which words they will allow to live – that can do the job of conveying their meaning to a reader – and the thought of extinguishing their kindling spark before they have had a chance to journey from one side of the Gutenberg Galaxy to the other is painful. That's why all writers, no matter how successful or experienced, benefit from working with an editor.

Looking at some of Shoaib's line-by-line edits, I began to understand how close non-fiction editing is really about interrogating the argument to make sure it bears scrutiny. 'I don't understand this sentence!' (I had this from my editor, too); 'Make this more specific'; 'We need an example here';

'This is a generalisation'; 'My mind is blown' (I *didn't* have this from my editor, sadly). I could go on, but let's just say that every word, sentence, paragraph and argument was thoroughly tested from every angle, and where it was found wanting, it was flagged for the author to improve.

What makes the process of editing even more demanding, of course, is that every author, and every manuscript, is different. Shannon, a commissioning editor in children's publishing, explained that 'Manuscripts need variable amounts of work, but as a commissioning editor you're prepared to work with the author on as many drafts as is necessary. Some authors might like you to make suggestions on how to resolve a plotting problem, and others prefer you to highlight the challenge and let them work it out. Then you may need to do a line-edit, which is literally a line-by-line process of checking for repeated words, the flow of the prose, continuity. Even though this is also the role of a copy-editor, a good commissioning editor does that, too.'

So, enter yet another type of editor: the copy-editor.

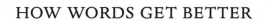

HOW WORDS GET BETTER

When Agatha Christie's play *The Mousetrap* was reviewed by the *Manchester Guardian* in 1952 the critic commented that 'Coincidence is stretched unreasonably' in the plot; and indeed, *The Mousetrap* is known for a number of plot holes, most notably that instead of arresting the murderer once he knows his identity, Detective Sergeant Trotter allows him to carry on killing. There are plot holes in *Harry Potter*, *Fifty Shades of Grey*, *The Lord of the Rings*, *I Am Pilgrim* and *The Adventures of Huckleberry Finn* – and many other well-known stories.

Even though most fiction writers will take great care to outline their plot carefully before they start writing, it's tricky to hold multiple characters, scenarios and timelines in your head and reveal them at the right point in the story and in a way that makes sense and maintains the suspense for a reader. That's where structural editing and copy-editing can really make a difference to the power of words.

As Shannon noted in the previous section, a commissioning editor will be concerned to check that the broad arc of a manuscript makes sense, and they will then rely on a copy-editor to go through the words meticulously to ensure that there are no gaping holes in the structure of the story. A good copy-editor does a belt-and-braces check that it all hangs together when someone with no prior knowledge enters your world.

Sarah, a copy-editor, says: 'I'm a second eye, someone who can look afresh at a manuscript and see what the author and commissioning editor no longer see after multiple readings. So in fiction, I'm checking that the plot works, and works as well as it can do; and in non-fiction, whether the layperson can follow the thread or narrative pull of the argument.

'In fiction, chronology inconsistencies can be a pitfall, but I have learned to make scrupulous notes: the weather, what is flowering, historical events and songs and films signifying a particular year. A pet hate of mine is generic "historical settings": for example, "It was the sixties, all the girls were wearing miniskirts and the Beatles were high in the charts . . ."

'Sometimes, the changes can be bolder and more brutal: I once worked on a historical novel and was told it should be cut by a third. I did the work and sent the manuscript back to the author, who immediately rang me, pretty distraught. Their commissioning editor had not told them that they had asked me to cut it. The author then rang back a week later to say that, despite the cuts, nothing was missing, the characters were clearer, and the plot, narrative drive and energy were a lot tighter. And of course to do all this you need to give lots of tactful reassurance: the author must *always* feel that it is their book.'

Another copy-editor, Lesley, when I asked her about the kinds of structural issues that pop up in manuscripts, explained that 'depending on the sort of book – fiction or non-fiction, mass market or academic, etc. – I keep an eye out for plot errors, factual errors, internal consistencies, timeline impossibilities and suchlike. I am the invisible mender. I once worked on a novel in which one of the characters was in the midst of a difficult pregnancy and in the end, in a scene of great tension, gave birth prematurely. By this point, from detailed descriptions of the seasons passing, it was possible to work out that the mother had already been pregnant for eighteen months. This is the type of structural plot issue that you always need to be alert for.'

'THE WRITER IS YOUR NATURAL ENEMY': COPY-EDITING

Once words are born, how do we make them better? There are so many words out there, and the number increases with every moment that the Gutenberg Galaxy exists. Words emerge from a writer and are spotted, pursued and nurtured by agents and editors. With some help, those words are arranged into sentences – a basic unit of grammar – and then, hopefully, into paragraphs, chapters and, finally, a book. But it all starts with sentences. And to be a sentence – to make sense – it must contain a complete thought. If it doesn't make sense, it's not a sentence.

And once you get beyond sentence level, for words to make sense they also need to be correct, clear, coherent and consistent. These are known as the '4 Cs' of copy-editing – the cornerstones of making good words better, and what all writers and the people who work on their words alongside them strive for.

Correctness

'When I set out to write my first book, I wanted to write a book that examined the very nature of facts and how we turn them into stories. To do this, I knew, I would have to get every fact that was verifiable correct. The more you want to ask the big, shifty questions, the more your foundation must be rock solid.'

This is Emma Copley Eisenberg writing about the

process of fact-checking for her book *The Third Rainbow Girl: The Long Life of a Double Murder in Appalachia*. Why is fact-checking – correctness – important? Well, for a start, if something is incorrect then it doesn't – can't – make sense. So, who is responsible for making sure the basic facts are correct? Historically, it was a woman. Copley Eisenberg pointed me in the direction of what she called 'the definitive book on the subject': *The Fact Checker's Bible: A Guide to Getting it Right* by Sarah Harrison Smith. In her introduction, Harrison Smith discusses the long history of fact-checking in American magazines – beginning with *Time*, in 1923. She quotes a memo from Edward Kennedy, *Time* editor:

> Checking is . . . sometimes regarded as a dull and tedious occupation, but such a conception of this position is extremely erroneous. Any bright girl who really applies herself to the handling of the checking problem can have a very pleasant time with it and fill the week with happy moments and memorable occasions. The most important point to remember in checking is that the writer is your natural enemy. He is trying to see how much he can get away with.

Reading this, I wondered idly if this *Time* editor was in fact Edward Kennedy, younger brother of John F. Kennedy. I didn't know, so I had a look online to fact-check it for myself. And actually, I couldn't confirm it either way: fact-checking isn't an easy business. In an article about fact-checking for the *London Review of Books*, Christian Lorentzen quoted the same letter, credited to an unspecific 'editor'; nowhere could I find absolute confirmation. However, whoever said it, in their world there was a clear division of labour when it came to words. Men created them, and women checked them. And as Lorentzen described, the fact-checker 'was born to be a cheerful scapegoat, keeping roguish writers in line and protecting editors from vigilante readers, anonymous and grateful for a week full of happy moments of correcting misspelled place names'.

Harrison Smith explains that a fact-checker should be doing the following to a manuscript: reading for accuracy; determining what to check; researching the facts; assessing sources; checking quotations; understanding legal liabilities; looking out for plagiarism – perhaps a more sophisticated and vital contribution to making words better than 'correcting misspelled place names' suggests.

Harrison Smith's list demonstrates a high level of responsibility for fact-checker, author and publisher, with, in some cases, potential legal issues if it goes wrong. But testing our words for factual accuracy is one crucial way in which they get better. If we can't trust that the words we are reading are factually correct, where does that leave us? Harrison Smith quotes Sara Lippincott, a former head of fact-checking at the *New Yorker*: 'A little skepticism . . . is much to be desired, but if it is fed over and over again with a diet of mis-information, it eventually becomes cynicism, which is a different thing entirely. Then we are turned off. Then we cease to listen to each other at all, and so the journalist is in danger of becoming extinct – or ignored.'

Correctness doesn't mean that a copy-editor will be able to look at every fact, figure or statement and know immediately if it is true. But it does mean that they will be aware of what they should check, and how. A good copy-editor either knows that something is right or wrong, or, if they don't, will check it to confirm. The skill, of course, is in knowing what you don't know – the 'known unknowns'.

So for copy-editors, correctness really means 'enhanced awareness'. It means noticing the big things that need checking against a source to confirm if they are right or wrong, but also noticing the small things – that an abbreviation style used once on p. 83 matches the same abbreviation style on p. 623, or noticing that JPMorgan becomes JP Morgan between chapters 5 and 12. Nearly all the copy-editors I have worked with are experts in trivia, and generally possess excellent general knowledge and memories, but no one can know *everything*.

No experience, exam, training, pub quiz, round of trivial pursuit, obsession, drunken (or sober) conversation goes to waste when you are a copy-editor. Eventually, those years of accumulated shards of knowledge piling up untidily one on top of the other will find a use. I don't think there is a word in the English language for the bubble of satisfaction you get when you're editing a book and are able to correct the spelling of the name of the cyclist who was the fourth British wearer of the yellow jersey in the Tour de France from 'David Miller' (INCORRECT) to 'David Millar' (CORRECT), but there should be one.

And sometimes, as one of my copy-editors explained to me, correctness can be more crucial than avoiding embarrassment or legal issues. 'A medical dictionary I worked on had the decimal point in the wrong place for the maximum dosage of Valium – it was ten times too high! An erratum slip had to be added . . .'

In an interview with the *Atlantic*, Craig Silverman describes how when he wrote a book on media accuracy called *Regret the Error*, 'I did an anecdotal survey asking people: "Between books, magazines, and newspapers, which do you think has the most fact-checking?" the majority of people responded with "books".' As Silverman explains: 'A lot of readers have the perception that when something arrives as a book, it's gone through a more rigorous fact-checking process than a magazine or a newspaper or a website, and that's simply not the case.' In the interview he attributes this to the physical properties of books: 'Its ink and weight imbue it with a sense of significance, unlike that of other mediums.'

So why aren't books properly fact-checked? It's partly because there is an assumption that an author is an expert on whatever they are writing about – that they know more than their editor or copy-editor about the topic – which is why they are writing a book on it. (Another reason is that magazines often hold the copyright on articles they publish, rather than the author, so the accuracy or otherwise is their responsibility.) Accordingly, there is a belief that turning to books for fact-checking is safer than, say, web-based sources, which people tend to be suspicious of. But that's not necessarily the case – fact-checking in non-fiction books is the exception, not the norm, which means you could still be consulting a source that hasn't had its facts verified – and inadvertently disseminating those errors even further.

The very best way of checking a fact is to go to the original source – but of course that takes time and money, and it's money that publishers are reluctant to spend. These constraints mean that, ultimately, the final responsibility for the veracity of words has to lie with their creator. As Harrison Smith says, 'The collaboration of fact checkers, authors and editors should be a kind of holy trinity, (with the author, like God), getting credit for the effort of all three.'

Shifting sands

'Each time a writer begins a book they make a contract with the reader. If the book is a work of fiction the contract is pretty vague, essentially saying: "Commit your time and patience to me and I will tell you a story." There may be a sub-clause about entertaining the reader, or some such. In the contract for my novels I promise to try to show my readers a way of seeing the world in a way I hope they have not seen before. A contract for a work of nonfiction is a more precise affair. The writer says, I am telling you, and to the best of my ability, what I believe to be true. This is a contract that should not be broken lightly and why I have disagreed with writers of memoir (in particular) who happily alter facts to suit their narrative purposes. Break the contract and readers no longer know who to trust.'

This is the writer Aminatta Forna in an interview discussing the fine line between fiction and non-fiction writing. Increasingly, that line is now a disputed border, with incursions from both sides. When Truman Capote published *In Cold Blood* in 1966 it was after huge amounts of research, including eight thousand pages of notes. But as Philip K. Tompkins wrote in an *Esquire* article about the book: 'Capote has, in short, achieved a work of art. He has told exceedingly well a tale of high terror in his own way. But, despite the brilliance of his self-publicizing efforts, he has made both a tactical and a moral error that will hurt him in the short run. By insisting that "every word" of his book is true he has made himself vulnerable to those readers who are prepared to examine seriously such a sweeping claim.'

Shortly after publication there were claims that Capote had manufactured some of the dialogue and scenes in the book, but *In Cold Blood* was a bestseller on publication, and is now regarded as the original 'non-fiction novel', and a modern classic.

With other 'non-fiction novel' successes following, like Norman Mailer's *The Executioner's Song* (1979) and John Berendt's *Midnight in the Garden of Good and Evil* (1994), readers were set a new challenge: to decide if absolute veracity was more important than compelling storytelling. But actually, it turned out that what many readers wanted was *both*. 'The difference between fiction and non-fiction is quite reasonably assumed to depend on whether stuff is invented or factually reliable,' says author and critic Geoff Dyer – but increasingly, we want to read stories that are based on truth, while being written for us in a novelistic style.

As Dyer explains: 'In a realm where style was often functional, non-fiction books were – are – praised for being "well written", as though that were an inessential extra, like some optional finish on a reliable car. Whether the subject matter was alluring or off-putting, fiction was the arena where style was more obviously expected, sometimes conspicuously displayed and occasionally rewarded. And so, for a sizeable chunk of my reading life, novels provided pretty much all the nutrition and flavour I needed. They were fun, they taught me about psychology, behaviour and ethics. And then, gradually, increasing numbers of them failed to deliver – or delivered only decreasing amounts of what I went to them for. Non-fiction began taking up more of the slack and, as it did, so the drift away from fiction accelerated.'

Fiction addiction

In fiction, readers are used to the idea of the unreliable narrator – indeed, the suspect loyalties of these types of characters often add to our reading pleasure. But how do we feel about the words of the unreliable author – those who alter the facts to 'suit their narrative purposes', as Aminatta Forna says? The literary hoax has a long history, stretching from Onomacritos in ancient Greece, who was a collector and forger of oracles and poems, via the supposed 'Hitler Diaries' to James Frey, whose 2003 misery-lit* memoir *A*

---

*Misery lit seems to attract hoaxers. In 2008 *Love and Consequences*, a memoir by Margaret B. Jones that had received rave reviews, was revealed to be fake. The author wrote of being half white and half Native American, being fostered as a child and eventually being recruited as a drug

Million Little Pieces was exposed in 2006 as being substantially untrue. This 'fiction addiction', as one commentator described Frey's million-copy-selling work, was eventually unravelled by journalistic digging. *A Million Little Pieces* was rejected by seventeen publishers before it found a home: those seventeen rejections were of a book that was presented by the author as fiction. 'Initially I said, "I want it to be published as a novel so I don't have to get into all that. I don't wanna have to go through picking it apart, talking about what was changed and why." Things were changed for all sorts of reasons: effect, for respect, other people's anonymity, making the story function properly,' said Frey.

Did it matter if Frey's book was packaged and sold as fiction, memoir or non-fiction? Do readers enjoy his words any less because of uncertainty over how they are categorised? Are we attaching too much meaning to what is, after all, marks on a page that together represent the one thing we all want from a book: a story?

'To many, Frey and his novel were a big deal,' wrote Laura Barton, in a *Guardian* interview with him. 'Not just because he sold millions of books and was wept over by Oprah Winfrey, but because his was a tale of triumph over adversity, and it gave people hope.* Frey still insists that the bulk of his book is true . . . It is feasible too that Frey's booze-soaked, crack-addled brain did remember events differently from the

---

runner by the Bloods. Her true stable middle-class upbringing was revealed by her sister after publication, leading to the publisher recalling all copies of the book.

*You could make the same argument about cyclist and cancer survivor Lance Armstrong's 2000 autobiography *It's Not About the Bike*. Armstrong's 2013 confession relating to his extensive doping while riding as a professional makes parts of *It's Not About the Bike* more fictional than not. Did the words he chose taint the hope that he offered to people living with cancer, or not?

way they occurred; after all, a large section of his life exists like a half-remembered drunken night out. Take apart a lot of memoirs, he says, and you will find truth lying down with fiction. "Some people think memoirs should be held to a perfect journalistic standard," he says. "Some people don't. Obviously I don't. My goal was never to create or to write a perfect journalistic standard of my life. It was always to be as literature. I thought in doing that it was OK to take certain licences." All storytellers, he argues, are embellishers. "To tell a story effectively you manipulate information . . . I think that if stories were told always exactly as they really happened most of them would be really boring."'

Clarity

Once an author and their in-house editor have been through several rounds of structural edits, they will probably be too close to the text to be able to see where it is clumsy, repetitive, awkwardly phrased, or just plain unclear. If your copy-editor – your earliest impartial reader and reviewer – can't make sense of what you are trying to say, then how will your audience? This is why your copy-editor is there – to fine-tune the text until it sings on the page. Clarity means getting rid of any redundant words and phrases, or ambiguity caused by the wrong word order, or indeed the wrong word.

Here's what Sarah had to say about copy-editing for clarity: 'I work on books that are intended for a general rather than an academic readership, and I figure that my job is to be a lay reader, and if I don't understand something, another reader will struggle too, so if there is something that has been clumsily or ambiguously explained, or something that is simply missing, then it needs to be addressed. I think you have to have the confidence to say you don't understand something, and not assume that the author will think you are stupid or not up to the task – and generally, they can see my point.'

The idea of clarity cuts to the very heart of making words good. As George Orwell said, 'Good prose is like a window pane.' Good words are clear words: they express an idea thought up by one person in a way that another person can then understand – with a copy-editor there to check the scaffolding of the sentence that holds the entire thing up. Editing for clarity, like most aspects of copy-editing, involves a degree of tact and sensitivity when it comes to addressing it with authors. As Lesley explained to me: 'There are ways of making suggestions more palatable: "should this be" rather than "surely this should be"; "I think that" rather than "everyone knows that", etc. It's only polite to explain why you want to change something rather than just barging ahead. If an author's grip on grammar is shaky, if their sentence simply doesn't make sense, they are more likely to agree to a change if you explain why it's necessary. Every author will be slightly different and some are never going to warm to you (and vice versa), but it can't hurt to send an email at the start to say how much you're looking forward to working with them. In some ways it's a shame that everything is done via email now – it used to be fun meeting authors and going through the manuscript together, and it's so much easier to avoid misunderstandings face to face – now it's all scary-looking tracked changes and comment boxes.

'Sometimes you need to be firm, sometimes you need to be flexible, but you are always more likely to succeed if you work as a team. Oh, and a sense of humour helps – as in most areas of life. You can always laugh with friends afterwards – at authors if they've been unpleasant and at yourself if you've misjudged something badly . . . No one's perfect.'

Coherency

Coherence means the reader can understand the connection between one word and the next, and it helps them connect the words, ideas and arguments on the page in the way that the author wants. Simply, it means 'clarity of expression', making sure that there are no gaps in the text that will leave the reader floundering. Here are examples of a non-coherent and coherent piece of text: *

> **Non-coherent**: Dogs are canines that people domesticated a long time ago. Wolves are predecessors of dogs and they help people in a variety of ways. There are various reasons for owning a dog, and the most important is companionship.
>
> **Coherent**: Dogs are canines that people domesticated a long time ago, primarily for practical reasons. Even though dogs descended from wolves, they are tame and can be kept in households. Since they are tame, people have various reasons for owning a dog, such as companionship.

Ideas discussed in a paragraph need to flow from the topic, and they need to be arranged logically. But all the while you're copy-editing, as Sarah told me, 'Most important is empathy with the author's style: the ability to cut, rephrase, rewrite in a way that they would recognise as something they would have written. Each manuscript is like a crossword puzzle, and you have to work out the setter's style before you can crack it. Another analogy would be that a manuscript is a highly pixelated picture, and by looking at the small individual elements that go into building up the big picture, you

---

*www.enago.com/academy/coherence-academic-writing-tips-strategies/

can understand what the author is doing and work with these building blocks to clarify the whole.'

Consistency

Copy-editing is much further-reaching than just reading the text and spotting the odd typo. Copy-editors need to be able to make a series of decisions to stick to as they go through the text and impose them consistently. Most copy-editors will now work on a Word document, which can make things a little simpler. Many will turn off track changes initially while they work behind the scenes. Then they can let the author know what they have done without bombarding them with track changes. But of course, not all such consistency is as easily dealt with. You might want to change an American author's spelling of 'harbor' to 'harbour' throughout the text, but you certainly wouldn't want to change 'Pearl Harbor' to 'Pearl Harbour' – it's a proper name, so shouldn't be touched. A copy-editor needs to be mindful, even when imposing what appears to be straightforward changes, for *exceptions*.

Many copy-editors will draw up a style sheet as they edit – either just a straightforward list of the style they are using, or an A–Z grid – where they write down each word they encounter that needs a style decision to be made. As well as being a reference for them (and remember that copy-editing can take place over weeks, or months, and a copy-editor may be working on more than one book at a time, often for different clients, each with their own house style, so they will need to remind themselves of decisions they made weeks earlier, in some cases), a style sheet can be sent to the author for discussion or approval, and then on to the proofreaders at proof stage* so that they can catch anything that has slipped through. A style sheet is a way of ensuring consistency in a particular piece of work – no copy-editor can be expected to keep in their head every decision they have made about every word they encounter.

Here's the style sheet for this book:

A	B	C	D
AbeBooks	barcode	cash flow	data point
acknowledgement	baulk	catch-22	devil
A level	BC	cliffhanger	diple
all right	beat	Communism	dreamt
ancient (Greece	bestseller	Communist	dust jacket
etc.)	Bible	cooperate	
anglicise	bookmaking	copy-editor	
avant-garde	burnt	cyberattack	

E	F	G	H
ebook	FaceTime	ghostwriter	half-century
elite	face to face	Google (n)	halfway
email	fact-check	google (v)	head-on
encyclopedia	free-for-all	Gothic	home town
end matter	front matter	groundbreaking	
e-reader			
extraterrestrial			

I	J	K	L
internet	judgement	Koran	lay person
iPhone			leaned
			learned
			le Carré

---

*Words follow this path to publication. They are typed by an author in a Word doc (or similar, other programs are available) – usually referred to as a manuscript, even though no one writes by hand any more. After editing and copy-editing, the words are then laid out in a typesetting program that makes them look as they would appear in a printed book. These are called page proofs.

M	N	O	P
mea culpa	news-stand	off limits	PDF
metadata	Nielsen BookScan	OK	per cent
misspelt	nonetheless	Old English	pigeonhole
modernism	non-fiction	out of print	pixelate
movable	non-stop	overproduction	plotline
	no one	oversupply	POD/print-on-demand
			(computer) program
			proofread
Q	R	S	T
	re-check	*sans*	tagline
	reopen	sans serif	timespan
	reuse	serif	telltale
	rewritten	shortcut	transatlantic
	road trip	shorthand	tweet
		Skype	24/7
		storytelling	Twitter
		subsection	typeface
			typefounder
U	V	W	XYZ
usable		waterline	YouTube
		well-being	Zen
		well off	Zoom
		while	
		WHSmith	
		wish list	

Some of the decisions on this style sheet are ones of preference (per cent as opposed to percent, front matter instead of front-matter), while others (iPhone, le Carré) are proper names with no choice as to the correct presentation (but it's still important to have a reminder that it's not IPhone or LeCarré).

There are plenty of style books and fevered online debates about the 'correct' way to spell words, but as long as my copy-editors pick a style and stick with it, then I'm content. Making a decision and sticking with it is what I'm employing them to do, and the very best copy-editors are keen to make those decisions and then tell me what they've done.

The manuscript dating agency

When I was a child my favourite place to visit was the library (obvious, I know), but my best friend J and I didn't want to take any books out to read. Rather, we wanted to sit for as long as we could in front of the librarian and watch mesmerised as she fingered her way through the supple rows of library cards for each member. Nothing else could return me to the state of contented daydreaming that can sometimes come over you when you are five years old than a librarian's wooden box of tickets. Incredibly, 'library sounds' are some of the most searched-for ASMR* 'intoxicating sleep sounds' available online. Without stopping to consider why anyone would want their sleep sounds to be 'intoxicating', I read some online descriptions of 'library sounds'. 'Page-turning, whispering, writing' promises one; another 'features just the lovely sounds of a library front desk, with lots of dust jacket crinkling, some typing here and there, and a little bit of occasional inaudible whispering'.

Our department has an ancient blue card-index box with the names and contact details of freelance proofreaders, copy-editors and indexers. Made completely obsolete by databases and spreadsheets, we still keep it for posterity and reassurance. I briefly consider recording the sound of my leafing through this blue box, while inaudibly whispering the words contained within, and monetising my performance on YouTube. In fact, 'page-turning, whispering, writing' is a summary of what my ASMR mind hoped for when I embarked on a career in publishing.

I imagine our copy-editors would be horrified that such an old-fashioned relic as the blue box still exists, but who could resist the historical insights into the pre-digital

---

*Autonomous sensory meridian response. Not that I knew this when I was five.

freelance–editorial manager relationship contained within? The first card I pull out cautions, inexplicably, 'CAREFUL: BOLD WORDS AND EN RULE SPACING' (they use too many of them? they don't notice them? they don't know what they mean?), followed by 'likes classics'. Well, who doesn't? That's why they're classics. The next reads 'will rush and do anything' (*anything?*). Presumably as long as you can get whatever the 'anything' is to Surrey, which is where this particular freelancer lived. The 'will rush' on this freelancer's card is actually a positive in this context; in publishing, the clock is permanently set at 5 p.m. on a Friday afternoon, and you're always being asked to achieve the impossible: find a copy-editor who has working knowledge of Polish and doesn't mind converting 50 footnotes per chapter into coherent endnotes, can start work on the manuscript immediately because there are only ten days available for the job – and, by the way, the author is abroad and not accessing emails for four of them.

Next up is a freelancer who 'speaks Portuguese and Spanish and French', and who will tackle 'biography, crime, travel, politics' (all the good stuff, then). '<u>Not too much poetry</u>' the card ends. How much poetry is too much? I wonder. Enough that the note merits an underline. Finally, I pull out a card for an indexer that declares: 'Latin, ancient/ modern Greek, German, French, linguistics, archaeology, history, travel, biography, defence/intelligence studies, cookery, needlework'. Intelligence, cookery AND needlework? To be honest, this sort of wide-ranging list is excellent from my point of view – I could presumably persuade her to take on any old indexing job lying around by making it fit into one of those categories somehow, I think. If I can't make it sound like a travel book when I pitch it to her, I'll have to find a tenuous link to needlework.

All this is to say that trying to find the *right* copy-editor to work on a book requires patience, cunning and luck. I might, if I am the lucky one, receive a manuscript from a commissioning editor with a brief about what type of edit is needed. So, I then need to try to match up that brief with the copy-editors I have available. If I've had some warning that the manuscript is about to appear that helps, but it's not always the case. The copy-editor I want to use might be on holiday, booked up, or simply not interested in the manuscript I have. That's right, freelance copy-editors will sometimes turn down work, if they don't feel they have the time or interest to do a good job on it. Some superstar copy-editors can pick and choose who they work with and will turn down an author, or subject, owing to some past searing experience that has marked itself indelibly on their psyche.

Matching a manuscript to a copy-editor can sometimes feel like an impossible task. All the good copy-editors are busy, or about to depart for the south of France, or just don't fancy working on thousands of words on the Thirty Years War or even a brief illustrated pamphlet on healing stones. Or perhaps it's a nervous first-time author, and you know that they need a sympathetic copy-editor who won't alarm them with stern comments, or make them lose all confidence in their writing. Theoretically, any good copy-editor should be able to work on any type of text: they might not enjoy it, but that's not the point. Although most would like to spend their days being paid by the hour to copy-edit the next Booker winner, or a volume by a famous historian, sometimes you just have to agree to edit the book on statistics on a short schedule with a difficult author.

Combining the right copy-editor with an author, then, is more of an instinctive skill than anything else. It's a bit like matchmaking, but with the relationship generally being a long-distance one. The key is never to disturb a winning team once established, but of course establishing it in the first place is where much of the hard work lies. When you begin doing this type of work, you rely heavily on your colleagues to help you understand the strengths and weaknesses of the freelancers at your disposal, and deploying those resources across the number of books you work on at any one time can sometimes make you feel like you need one of those 3D maps that air chief marshals use in black-and-white war films. But the vital work that a copy-editor does on a text, and the closeness of the relationship between author and copy-editor, mean that choosing the right one is still the single most important decision I make when working on a book.

The Hemingway test

The application of 'sense' to our words is one of the most vital ways they get good. But, in these digital times, sense as applied by a human to words is in increasingly short supply. In some places, there is a belief that we just don't need human eyes to work on the 4 Cs any more. It's faster and cheaper to outsource 'sense' to a spellchecker or other computer programs. But precisely because so much text published online is now not edited at all, the sheer volume of content available means that, to stand out, well-copy-edited text is vital. And for that, you really do need a human: even if it can flag up words that don't make sense automatically, your computer still lacks the nuance that a real live copy-editor can bring to words.

Recently, BuzzFeed had an article on their website snappily titled 'This Quiz Will Tell You How Well You Can Copyedit For BuzzFeed News' – a challenge I couldn't pass up, especially as BuzzFeed have a policy of publishing what they call 'lower priority' posts without *any* copy-edits. I got 6/8 correct – make of that what you will. Apparently, many online publications have responded to the speed that content now needs to be produced at by publishing articles first and editing them only if the content is reported to need edits, or based on volume of traffic to the piece, in a process known as 'back-editing'. So the words must prove their worth before they are granted the attention that might be needed to make them better.

There are those who believe that in twenty years' time, copy-editors won't exist at all. Already there are programs like one I found online that promises to give you 'step-by-step recommendations for improving your manuscript based on what real readers want to see. Produce cleaner dialogue, eliminate needless filler, keep readers interested by perfecting your pacing, and even fine-tune the emotional tone of your writing with the click of a button. Feel unshakeable confidence in your book and leave worries in the dust.' If only it were that simple.

There is an app called 'Hemingway Editor' that claims to make your writing 'bold and clear'. You paste in your text, and it highlights sentences that it believes are too lengthy and complex, words that it feels are too long, adverbs and 'weakening phrases', and the passive voice that it thinks should be strengthened. It then grades your text for 'Readability'. Naturally, I put one of my paragraphs into the program and tested it against this one from Hemingway himself:

'All good books are alike in that they are truer than if they had really happened and after you are finished reading one you will feel that all that happened to you and afterwards it all belongs to you: the good and the bad, the ecstasy, the remorse and sorrow, the people and the places and how the weather was. If you can get so that you can give that to people, then you are a writer.'

How did we do? Well, Ernest's paragraph was graded '12' for readability. Apparently, that's only 'OK', and he should have aimed to score 9. My paragraph scored 6. According to the Hemingway app, I'm a more 'readable' writer than Hemingway. Which just goes to show . . . that in all the important ways, words really can't be improved by machines. They might be able to tell us if a full stop is needed or if a sentence is missing a verb, or if a word is repeated three times in a sentence, but words are how we communicate our most complex and profound thoughts – the 'ecstasy, the remorse and sorrow' – and for them to be 'good' for our readers, we need to sieve them through a human mind to ensure they make sense and to get the very best out of them.

A computer can learn the rules of words, but it can't recognise when those rules are being broken for effect – something that writers have been doing since the dawn of storytelling. Words can be used for the simple transfer of information, but they can do so much more than that. As Steven Pinker, in an article about his book *The Sense of Style*, reminds us, good editing is an art, not a science: 'Though bad writing has always been with us, the rules of correct usage are the smallest part of the problem. Any competent copy editor can turn a passage that is turgid, opaque, and filled with grammatical errors into a passage that is turgid, opaque, and free of grammatical errors. Rules of usage are well worth mastering, but they pale in importance behind principles of clarity, style, coherence, and consideration for the reader.'

SPECKS IN YOUR TEXT: GRAMMAR AND PUNCTUATION

'If I broke all the rules of punctuation, had words mean whatever I wanted them to mean, and strung them together higgledy-piggledy, I would simply not be understood . . . Readers want our pages to look very much like pages they have seen before. Why? This is because they themselves have a tough job to do, and they need all the help they can get from us.'

This is Kurt Vonnegut again, writing in 1980 in an article called 'How to Write with Style'. The rules of grammar and punctuation might sometimes seem a fiddly inconvenience, but they are a way for a writer to help a reader understand their words. It's important to acknowledge that when a reader agrees to read our words, we should do everything we can to help them enjoy the experience.

This part of *How Words Get Good* is about two related things that make the experience of reading better: the tiny and unobtrusive marks on a page (unobtrusive, that is, when all is going well and they are used in the right place and the right way) that we call punctuation and how we use grammar to order our words into sentences to create meaning. While the big-picture stuff – structure, sense – is one way that words get good, in the world of words the little details really matter. In fact, relative to their size, these specks in our text and the way we structure our sentences have an awful lot to say to us. Words can communicate emotion, feeling and meaning – but only if you put them together in a way that makes *sense* for the reader and that is familiar to them, 'very much like pages they have seen before', as Vonnegut reminds us.

Without grammar, words mean nothing – and they need the subtle assistance of punctuation to lend even more nuance. Punctuation reveals the relationship between words, the emotions we want a sentence to convey, and gives us breathing space – pauses – between ideas we encounter as we read. Ultimately, all words rely on the scaffolding of punctuation and grammar to take them from good to better.

'Like electricity or the soul, grammar is invisible. But when it is present among a group of words it comes to life – and minds can express themselves to other minds' is how Thoby Riddle describes grammar in *The Greatest Gatsby: A Visual Book of Grammar*. What could be more important than that? It's one of the beautiful mysteries of words that a completely invisible force – grammar – is what makes them far more than the sum of their parts. As soon as you put together one noun and one verb, you create meaning. 'Jesus wept' is famously the shortest verse in the Bible – and also a concise example of grammar doing its magic. Joining the verb 'wept' to the noun 'Jesus' signifies that Jesus was a real live person, who shed real bodily tears. A noun plus a verb is the building block of creating meaning – the very spark of life for words.

The rhythm section

The Greek word for grammar translates as the 'art of letters' – and that's how we should think of it: as an art form without which our words and letters can't reach their full potential.

I am an instinctive grammarian. Half the time I don't know why something is right or wrong, I just know that it is, or isn't. And actually, that's perfectly normal. Grammar is an instinctive and internalised skill – we learn the grammatical rules of our native language by hearing people around us speak it when we are very young. And that internalised skill is reinforced by reading. When you read, you absorb the natural rhythm and pace of a sentence and the grammar and punctuation it uses. A well-constructed line of words hums along; grammar and punctuation provide the rhythm.

But when grammar and punctuation go wrong, your reader is unceremoniously jolted out of their seat – it jars, sometimes in ways that are more effective or memorable than grammatical correctness. Think about Neil Armstrong's famous phrase, uttered when he first set foot on the moon in 1969. Armstrong said: 'That's one small step for man, one giant leap for mankind' – a grammatically incorrect sentence, since 'man' and 'mankind' mean the same thing – they both abstractly indicate all humanity, rather than one specific man. Armstrong always maintained that he said 'a man' (even if the crucial 'a' couldn't be heard in recordings), which was all that was needed for the sentence to, well, make sense. No doubt he had things on his mind other than semantics.

So why is grammar such a slog? If it's something innate, that we learn without having to study, why, when we write, can it feel so difficult? Why do people often feel ashamed or embarrassed about not knowing the rules of grammar? As Steven Pinker explains: 'The real problem is that writing, unlike speaking, is an unnatural act. In the absence of a conversational partner who shares the writer's background and who can furrow her brows or break in and ask for clarification when he stops making sense, good writing depends on an ability to imagine a generic reader and empathise about what she already knows and how she interprets the flow of words in real time. Writing, above all, is a topic in cognitive psychology.'

That's why the practice of reading and writing – lifelong exposure to both – helps us to understand how grammar should work. The more we practise, the easier it is to visualise and write for our generic reader. 'The flow of words in real time' and Thoby Riddle's 'minds can express themselves to other minds' are ephemeral feelings that we are hoping to capture. That's a lot to ask – and no wonder it can feel overwhelming. There's a tension at the heart of grammar: it is infinitely flexible yet hard-wired into our brains, it is part of what makes us human, yet over hundreds of years we have attempted to reduce it to a set of confining rules. Pinker again: 'Linguists and lexicographers have long known that many of the alleged rules of usage are actually superstitions. They originated for oddball reasons, violate the grammatical logic of English, degrade clarity and style, and have been flouted by the best writers for centuries . . . rules of usage should be interpreted judiciously, with a sensitivity to their historical provenance, consistency with English grammar, degree of formality, and effects on clarity and grace.' It's presumably no accident that his book was called *The Sense of Style* – for something that feels like it has a rigid set of hierarchical rules, when it comes down to the flow of words in real time, it's all about sense and sensitivity.

Hyphen wars

The word 'hyphen' comes from the ancient Greek word for a tie-like sign (‿) marked beneath two letters to show – in cases of ambiguity – that they belonged to the same word, before the space was in regular use, and also to separate syllables of a word. You can use them to link words in a compound adjective, to show that it is a single adjective (four-seater aircraft, eighteenth-century chair, etc.). Hyphens are often used incorrectly: the confusion comes about because a hyphen can be easily confused with a dash – which is a very different thing.

Here's a story from a copy-editor about the pitfalls of misunderstanding how hyphens should be used. 'I once worked on a wonderful history book written by a Cambridge academic. It was both informative and gripping, and in the covering email I sent when returning the copy-edited manuscript for his attention I said how much I had enjoyed it. His reply, which he copied to the commissioning editor and the publishing director, said that I had "ruined" his book by taking out his hyphens. He then backtracked slightly to tell me I could remove the hyphen after "especially" but not "specially", or maybe it was the other way round – he saw a difference, even if I didn't. Because my job is ultimately to keep the author happy, those hyphens went in and out as requested.'

This story doesn't really make much sense unless you know that there is no need to use a hyphen with adjectives that are an adverb / adjective compound: for instance, though you might hyphenate 'short-story writer', to make it clear that it's the stories that are short (not the writer), you would not hyphenate 'mildly unhinged author' as there is no such thing as a 'mildly author'.

All this is to say: hyphens may be small, but they are mighty. They can change the meaning of a sentence – indeed, they can add or take away sense itself. On 22 July 1962 NASA managed to waste $80 million when *Mariner 1*, a rocket whose mission was to conduct a fly-by survey of Venus, exploded less than five minutes into its flight.* A programmer at NASA

---

*In the language of NASA, the rocket actually suffered a 'destructive abort' by a 'range safety officer', after it lost all steering, which prompted concerns it might crash in an inhabited area or in a shipping lane. Did you know that NASA has its own online style guide? This is what it says about writing: 'The English language is one of the glories of Western civilization. It provides ample resources for elegant prose, whether of the simplest or most sophisticated kind. Good writers are readers of other good

had managed to miss out the hyphen in a complex code that the rocket relied on, which led to incorrect information being fed to it, ultimately causing it to crash. In sentences as in space exploration, hyphens can make or break your mission.

The overthrow of Czechoslovakia's Communist regime in December 1989 was so peaceful that it quickly became known as the Velvet Revolution. So how was it that, only weeks later, the majority of Czechs were 'at war' with the minority Slovaks? The *casus belli** lay in the debate about their country's new name. During the Communist years it had been known as the Czechoslovak Socialist Republic, and at the end of March 1990 the newly elected president, the playwright Václav Havel, proposed that the word 'Socialist' should be dropped from the name. So far so straightforward. The next problem, however, was how to make sure that both parts of the population – the Czechs and the Slovaks – were happy with the new designation. It turned out that the Slovaks weren't happy at all. They had never managed to enjoy independence, having spent too long being ruled by the Hungarians and, they felt, being looked down on throughout history by the Czechs. Now was their opportunity to demand equal billing, erasing their sense of inferiority by means of

---

writers. When difficulties are encountered in writing, the problem usually is with the thinking . . . Writers of history are writing not only for today, but also for tomorrow. They should avoid trendy language that will date their work among future readers.'

*I always feel that using Latin phrases is asking a bit much of the reader, but it's difficult to give them up completely as they are so *efficient*. 'The reason for the war' just doesn't have the same ring to it. On the subject of Latin and words, my favourite Latin phrase at the moment is *vox nihili*, which can mean an ambiguous phrase or sentiment, or a word that is born through a typographical error. Like the word 'covfefe' in Donald Trump's now-infamous tweet.

the simple introduction in their own territory of a hyphen. So if you went to Bratislava, the name of the new federation would be rendered as 'Czecho-Slovakia'. But if you were in Prague, the fledgling country would be referred to as 'Czechoslovakia'.

On 29 March 1990 the parliament agreed the hyphen solution. To complicate matters further, both sides referred to this high-stakes piece of punctuation as a dash (*pomlčka*), even though the Slovaks were actually demanding a hyphen (*spojovník*). Far from solving the problem, the use or non-use of the hyphen (or dash) only added to the ethnic tension. So three weeks later, in April 1990, the parliament had another go. This time they escaped the hyphen altogether by changing the name to the Czech and Slovak Federative Republic, passing a law which listed the long-form names in each language and pronounced them equal. But they still didn't *feel* equal, and eventually the two sides decided to part altogether. On New Year's Day 1993, the so-called Velvet Divorce was finalised, and what had been one country was now two: the Czech Republic and the Slovak Republic.

The so-called Hyphen War was not, of course, an actual war.* But it did throw a spotlight on the fundamental differences between the two countries, many of which dated back as far as the Austro-Hungarian Empire. As the Czechs and the Slovaks discovered, and the Austro-Hungarians already knew, in geographical and world-peace terms, hyphens are generally not good news.

---

*In fact, Czechoslovakia is the only former Soviet-dominated state to have had an entirely peaceful break-up, unlike those of say Yugoslavia or the Soviet Union.

Mutton and nuts

Punctuation is a way of fulfilling the contract between reader and writer. It can be used as an invitation – a way of encouraging the reader into the story to fill in the imaginative leaps that we want to inspire with words. It's easy to think of punctuation as a barrier, but some marks, for example the dot-dot-dot of the ellipsis and the white space of the dash, are important in creating space and emphasis for readers.

There are two types of dash: the en and the em. The en is so called because it was traditionally the width of a capital 'N', and known in printers' slang as a 'nut'. Quite fitting, as it can be used to bolt together two ends of a range of numbers (e.g. pp. 45–8; 1978–82), or to demonstrate a relationship between two things (mother–daughter alliance; Chinese–Soviet aggression).* It is also used instead of brackets or pairs of commas to mark off a 'nested' clause or phrase. It's easy for writers to mistakenly use a hyphen when an en rule – such as these ones – should be used; a copy-editor's bread-and-butter is to fix this kind of common error.

The em dash looks like this: —. And yes, it is traditionally based on the width of the letter 'M', and it is apparently historically known as a 'mutton'. So far, I haven't been able to find out conclusively why the en and the em are called the 'nut' and the 'mutton'. Perhaps it's just because 'nut' begins with 'n' and 'mutton' with 'm', and the word 'mutton' is twice as long as the word 'nut'.

One of the heavyweight clashes between American and British punctuation is that in the UK most publishers and

---

The Elements of Style by William Strunk Jr and E. B. White used this example to show why using a hyphen when you should be using a rule is a bad idea: after the *Chattanooga News* and the *Chattanooga Free Press* merged in 1942 the new publication was ineptly named the *Chattanooga News-Free Press*, which has a very different meaning to *Chattanooga News–Free Press*.

publications use 'spaced' en rules (i.e. there is space both before and after the dash – like that), whereas in the US 'closed-up' em rules are used. A closed-up em rule nestles up against the end of one word and the start of another, with no white space allowed. Many UK readers find unspaced em dashes awkward on the page when they first encounter them – I do, because it always looks to me as if the closed-up em is forcing two words to join together as a strange compound. Not only that, I have a feeling of panic when I look at them. Where is the space for me to breathe? Manuals of house style will often specify whether the publisher or newspaper use en or em dashes, and whether they should be spaced or unspaced.

The en and em are also used to signify when speech is interrupted. As my copy-editor interrupted me to explain, 'My own personal style is en dashes for speech interruption and em for word interruption – "Whatever –", "Whatev—" (and ellipses for speech fade-out "Whatever . . .").' See how the punctuation choice changes the tone of each 'Whatever'? Whatever.

Em and 2em dashes are used to cover up information that might need to be redacted. You might have encountered this in Jane Austen* or Charles Dickens, or more recently if you read the court filings of Paul Manafort's defence lawyer.[†] Using a 2em rule to redact something meant that authors were more likely to get away with criticising important or well-known figures – simply by not naming them, and instead coyly hinting at them from behind a dash.

---

*In *Pride and Prejudice* the Bennet sisters are enthralled by the men of the '———shire' Regiment.

[†]Manafort's lawyers failed sufficiently to redact the text that they wanted concealed: the 'redacted' sections were hidden by black bars in the documents, but if you highlighted the bars and copied and pasted the text into a new document you could see what had been obscured. They should have stuck with the Jane Austen method.

'To lead you to an overwhelming question . . .'

I am very fond of the origin story of the word ellipsis. It comes from a Greek word meaning 'omission', or 'falling short'. Haven't we all 'fallen short' at one time or another in our lives? How useful to be able to sum up our failings in three tiny dots. Even more evocatively, the ellipsis can be known as a 'suspension point', and according to Wikipedia it 'can also inspire a feeling of melancholy or longing . . .'.*

When an ellipsis indicates that someone, or something, has trailed off into silence, it is known as *aposiopesis*. Thus, you can use either a set of ellipses or an em rule (the earliest examples of ellipses were actually broken em rules) to indicate that you have been overcome with 'passion, fear, anger, excitement or modesty'.† In a 2015 *Slate* article, Katy Waldman writes that 'The three dots extend from the end of the phrase like a ledge into the surrounding silence. They co-mingle the thrill of possibility with the fear of irresolution. Who can say what varmints lurk, what vistas shimmer, to the right of those humble stepping stones? Who can say if there's anything there at all?'

The ellipsis invites the reader to draw their own conclusion based on what they think the author is trying to say, and in this way they become drawn into the narrative – part of the pact between writer and reader. It is a mysterious and atypical piece of punctuation that lets us share our own ideas about what we are reading – unlike other punctuation marks, which tell us exactly what to think. A full stop allows for no ambiguity. But an ellipsis encourages us to fill the silence with our own thoughts . . .

---

*Actually, the ellipsis at the end of that phrase wasn't in the Wikipedia entry. I added it myself to see if it did indeed lead to a feeling of melancholy. I think it did. How did you feel?
†Wikipedia again.

Anne Toner, author of *Ellipsis in English Literature: Signs of Omission*, points out that the ellipsis emerged when plays began to be printed, since drama 'is connected in the most concentrated way with speech as it is spoken'. It really found its home, however, says Toner, in the novel, where writers attempted to 'capture the sort of indefiniteness that is characteristic of all English conversations . . . that are almost always conducted entirely by means of allusions and unfinished sentences'.

Could the ellipsis be the most English piece of punctuation ever?

The ellipsis and dash are often tasked with conveying the most complicated and nuanced emotions. An ellipsis also changes the pace of what we are reading – it *demands* that we . . . pause. 'To lead you to an overwhelming question . . .' wrote T. S. Eliot in 'The Love Song of J. Alfred Prufrock' – and the trailing ellipsis here helps give us a sense of the magnitude of that question, while forcing us to slow down to give us time think about what it might be.

'Opinions differ as to how to render ellipses in printed material,' says the Wikipedia entry. This is an understatement: I have lost count of the number of heated discussions I have had with colleagues on this topic. At heart, the question is this: do you set your ellipses with a non-breaking* space between each dot, thus '. . .', or do you omit the spaces and cram the dots together, like this '...'? As with many ferocious disputes this one is important precisely because the stakes are so low. Does it really matter? Well, on balance, no. But

---

*A non-breaking space can also be known as a 'hard space'. It means that in digital typesetting and word processing you can prevent an automatic line break from happening. In this example it's because you don't ever want the dots of your ellipses to be separated from each other over a line. The three dots of the ellipsis must always travel together.

to me, it does. I feel extremely uncomfortable if my ellipses don't have a nice even space between each dot. The alternative just feels too … *squashed*. Claustrophobic. Spacing them out spaces out the suspense of the suspension point. To give a feeling of a thought trailing off into the distance I think you need your ellipses to trail off over the page, too. If you must use the unspaced version, then make sure you use it consistently. The absolute worst is to have a mixture of spaced and unspaced ellipses in the same document. Makes my head hurt.

Italics and **Boldfaces**

'Of all the conventions of print that make no objective sense, the use of italics is the one that puzzles most,' says Lynne Truss in *Eats, Shoots and Leaves*. Italics and other ways of **emphasising** text are not just an aesthetic – they are a way of using type that affects meaning. That's why I've included them in this section of the book. The thing about these ways of emphasising words is that they are contextual – they require the writer to use them in a way that the reader can usefully interpret, otherwise they are, as Truss says, just a puzzle. And you need to be careful they don't become an excuse for poor writing: a short-handed way of flagging something to the reader, but making them do all the work, rather than using better and more precise words to help them out.

So, why do we use *italics* (and other conventions: **boldface**, SMALL CAPS, colour* and s p a c i n g)? It's because the human eye loves brightness in a text body. Anything that changes the 'blackness' of a block of text is something that the eye is drawn to – known as 'inconspicuous stressing'.

---

*This is a mono (black-and-white) book, so we can't have colour here. You'll need to use your imagination.

Italics were first used in Italy (hence the name) in about 1500, and their original purpose was to help save space in small, portable editions of books. They are based on calligraphic handwriting, which is why they slant to the right. They should be used for:

- Emphasis (including, in novels, to indicate a character's internal thoughts: she daydreamed, *I am a bestselling author . . .*).
- The *titles* of works (books, newspapers, journals, paintings, plays, films) that stand alone. Works that appear *within* larger works (short stories, poems, songs) should be set in roman and in quote marks. If for some reason a sentence is in italic, then you simply reverse these rules and anything that would usually be set in italics should be in roman.
- The names of vessels. And don't forget satellites, like *Sputnik 1*.*
- Foreign words and phrases, unless they have been fully adopted into English, like fiancée and restaurateur.
- Algebraic symbols.

The Italian poet and founder of the Futurist movement, Filippo Tommaso Marinetti, published a manifesto in 1913 with the English title *Destruction of Syntax – Radio Imagination – Words-in-Freedom.*† In a section headed 'Typographical Revolution', he wrote:

The book must be the Futurist expression of Futurist thought. Not only that. My revolution is directed against

---

*Such a great word. It means 'on the same path' as someone. So *Sputnik 1* was a fellow-traveller with us through the solar system.
†*Words-in-Freedom* – this is how words get good.

the so-called typographical harmony of the page, which is contrary to the flux and reflux, the leaps and bursts of style that run through the page itself. For that reason we will use, in the very same page, three or four different colors of ink, and as many as twenty different typographical fonts if necessary. For examples: *italics* for a series of swift or similar sensations, **boldface** for violent onomatopoeias, etc. The typographical revolution and the multicolored variety in the letters will mean that I can double the expressive force of words.

I love the idea of 'doubling the expressive force of words' by simply slanting them or making them bolder on the page. Words set in italics do look *swift* and *urgent*, don't they? Literally dashing off the edge of the page to crowd into your mind and say what's needed. Italic words always look like they are rushing to catch the last train home.

Marinetti continued: 'I have no wish to suggest an idea of sensation by means of *passéist** graces and affectations: I want to seize them brutally and fling them in the reader's face.'

Bold weight text certainly flings itself into the face, which is why it is often used to highlight key words – the eye can scan down the page and identify important words immediately. Small capitals, drop caps (as seen at the beginning of this paragraph) or switching from a serif typeface to a sans serif one can be used to similar effect. Of course, you can also resort to ALL CAPS, but as we know from email etiquette, that's even ruder than seizing a word and brutally flinging it at someone.

Puzzling it may be, but I am a fan of italics and what puzzles *me* is that so many publications *don't* use them to

---

*Meaning an excessive regard for the past.

make the names of books, films, works of art and ships*
stand out. This is what the *Guardian* says in its style guide on
the subject:

> Use roman for titles of books, films, etc; the only excep-
> tions are the Review and the Observer, which by special
> dispensation are allowed to ignore the generally sound
> advice of George Bernard Shaw:
>
> > '1. I was reading The Merchant of Venice. 2. I
> > was reading "The Merchant of Venice". 3. I was
> > reading *The Merchant of Venice*. The man who cannot
> > see that No 1 is the best-looking, as well as the suffi-
> > cient and sensible form, should print or write nothing
> > but advertisements for lost dogs or ironmongers'
> > catalogues: literature is not for him to meddle with.'
>
> Use italics for foreign words and phrases (with roman
> translation in brackets); poetry and scientific names.

I just cannot understand a style guide that recommends
using italics for foreign words or phrases, but not for letting
the reader know the *proper* name of things, and that under-
mines its own rule by allowing two parts of its publications
to follow different rules. Truss is right when she says that
'Some British newspapers, notably the *Guardian*, have
dropped the use of italics for titles, which as far as I can see
makes life a lot more difficult for the reader without any
compensating benefits.' I could not agree more. Give me

---

*Bear in mind that although I firmly believe the names of vessels (includ-
ing spacecraft) should be in italics, any prefix (HMS, USS) should be in
roman. The only exception I can think of to this is if you are reviewing a
production of *HMS Pinafore*, where the *HMS* is part of the operetta's title.
If you really want to wow people with your ship-italicising skills, you can
take it a step further by making sure that you use italics for the *class* of a
ship as well (*Lion*-class battlecruiser; *Nimitz*-class aircraft carrier).

back my inconspicuous stressing. Italics are there to *help* the reader – to signal what the writer wants to emphasise in an immediate and intuitive way.*

The pling point

In 1956, Bobby Fischer and Donald Byrne played a game of chess in the Rosenwald Memorial Tournament in New York. Thirteen-year-old prodigy Fischer won the match, which later became known as 'The Game of the Century' – in part because of Fischer's youth, in part because of the audacity of his play. Fischer's gambit of sacrificing his queen in a strategic attack was rewarded by the annotators of the game with a !!, which in chess notation means 'brilliant move'. Other chess annotation symbols include ?? for a blunder, ? for a mere mistake, ?! for a dubious move, and !? for an interesting move. I love how reversing two tiny strokes can recategorise your move from 'dubious' to 'interesting'. So subtle, and yet so effective!

Chess annotators try to restrict their use of the ! and ?; and although a !!! has occasionally been awarded for an exceptionally brilliant move, generally it's agreed that !!! and ??? are unnecessary, with !! and ?? giving them sufficient room for manoeuvre. Perhaps we should all try to ration our points of exclamation. After all, how much more impactful than !! or ?? can !!! and ??? possibly be?!

The hybrid question/exclamation marks used in chess are called interrobangs – a form of punctuation that both asks a question and expresses the manner (excitement, disbelief) it is expressed in. The interrobang was dreamt up in 1962 by the wonderfully named advertising executive Martin

---

*There is no hope for me; I even use _italics_ and **bold** where I think it necessary in WhatsApp messages.

K. Speckter; he believed adverts would look better if copy-writers had one symbol to mark rhetorical questions. By the late 1960s, some typewriters included an interrobang key, although most modern fonts do not support it. The inter-robang key superimposes the marks over each other, like this: ‽ Pleasingly, to me this looks as if a small punctuation explosion has taken place.

So what is the story behind the marks that make up the interrobang – the ! and ? We all know what they look like, and, hopefully,* we all know that we should use the ! sparingly. In this, follow F. Scott Fitzgerald, who said: 'Cut out all these exclamation points . . . An exclamation point is like laughing at your own joke.' Someone has crunched the numbers on Fitzgerald's use of '!' for us. He used 356 per 100,000 words over the course of four novels. The most parsimonious user of the '!' studied was Elmore Leonard – a mere 49 per 100,000 words in the course of forty-five novels. Just below him is Ernest Hemingway at 59 per 100,000 (over ten novels). Down at the other end James Joyce couldn't get enough of exclaiming (as we'll see later, it was one of the few punctuation marks he seemed able to tolerate), manag-ing to use 1,105 per 100,000 words in just three novels. All this analysis was done by Ben Blatt in *Nabokov's Favourite Word*

---

*'Hopefully' is one of those words that people get irate about the usage of. Traditionally it meant 'in a hopeful manner' – e.g. 'hopefully they travelled on through the forest'. Now it is often used to mean 'it is to be hoped that' (as I have used it above). The online *OED* notes that 'hope-fully is a rather odd sentence adverb: while many others, such as sadly, regrettably, and clearly, may be paraphrased as "it is sad/regrettable/clear that . . .", this is not possible with hopefully. Nevertheless, it is clear that use of hopefully has become a shibboleth of "correctness" in the language – even if the arguments on which this is based are not particu-larly strong – and it is wise to be aware of this in formal contexts.' So hopefully you will forgive me.

is Mauve: The Literary Quirks and Oddities of Our Most-Loved Authors, a treasure trove of literary number-crunching.

The origin story of the exclamation mark is charming: it is derived from the Latin exclamation of 'joy' – *io*. As time passed, the 'i' moved over the 'o', and the 'o' became smaller and smaller, eventually shrinking down to just a point. From the fifteenth century onwards the exclamation mark was known as the 'mark of admiration', referring to its Latin origins in a word that meant a sense of wonderment. But it's been a sad decline over the centuries from a mark with a sense of wonder to one now with the slang names 'screamer', 'gasper', 'slammer', 'startler', 'bang', 'shriek' or 'pling'.*

The exclamation mark is now regarded with suspicion: easily overused in textspeak and online, it is no longer deployed to indicate admiration, although it is still used for emphasis. Writing in the *Atlantic*, Julie Beck explains that, whereas in the past one exclamation mark would suffice (after all, the exclamation point itself denotes exclamation – so why would you need more than one?), 'on the internet, it often doesn't. Not anymore. Digital communication is undergoing exclamation-point inflation. When single exclamation points adorn every sentence in a business email, it takes two to convey true enthusiasm. Or three. Or four. Or more.'

Until the 1970s, the exclamation mark didn't even have its own key on a keyboard. To produce one, you had to type a period, backspace and then finally an apostrophe. I bet that before having a dedicated key on the QWERTY keyboard, they were used far less liberally, what with the hassle of having to use three keystrokes to produce a single !.

---

*This last is used in 'Commonwealth Hackish' – this is apparently hacker jargon used by English-speaking hackers outside the US – presumably by hackers with RP accents.

Beck says that at journalism school she was taught that in the course of your entire career you only get *one* exclamation mark to use, so you should use it wisely. Think of how Arthur Conan Doyle ended the second chapter of *The Hound of the Baskervilles*: 'Mr Holmes, they were the footprints of a gigantic hound!' – one of the most compelling cliffhangers in literature. Nowadays, he'd have to put !!!!!* at the end of the line, just to get our attention.

In *This is Me, Full Stop.*, Philip Cowell and Caz Hildebrand call the exclamation mark 'the selfie of grammar', which might explain its twenty-first-century over-popularity. Gretchen McCulloch, who studies online communication, says that the exclamation mark is now no longer used for intensity, but rather to prove our sincerity in an online world where body language, tone and facial expressions are not available to help us judge each other. 'Five exclamation marks, the sure sign of an insane mind,' said Terry Pratchett, and looking at its overuse in our emails, texts and online today might well make you question our collective sanity.†

---

*When the playwright Joe Orton moved into his lover Keith Halliwell's flat in 1951 the first three entries in his diary read: 'Well!'; 'Well!!'; 'Well!!!' Here, the cumulative effect of all those exclamation marks works rather . . . well.

†Spare a thought for the residents of Westward Ho! in Devon (the only place name in the British Isles with an intentional exclamation mark – given in honour of Charles Kingsley's novel of the same name, which was set nearby) and even more thoughts for residents of Saint-Louis-du-Ha! Ha! in Quebec. The councillors of Hamilton, Ohio, attempted to increase publicity for their city by renaming it Hamilton! in 1986. Sadly, the exclamation mark was ignored by the United States Board on Geographic Names, and Hamilton! has now reverted back to plain old Hamilton, Ohio.

The love point

In 1966, the French writer Hervé Bazin wrote a book called *Plumons l'Oiseau* ('Let's pluck the bird' – no, I don't know why it's called that) in which he proposed six new punctuation marks (or points d'intonation):

> the 'irony point' (or *point d'ironie*: ⸮)
> the 'love point' (*point d'amour*: ♡)
> the 'conviction point' (*point de conviction*: †)
> the 'authority point' (*point d'autorité*: ⸮)
> the 'acclamation point' (*point d'acclamation*: ⸮)
> the 'doubt point' (*point de doute*: ⸮)

The best way to display irony or sarcasm, the first of Bazin's punctuation marks, has been under discussion by writers and readers since the 1580s – and probably since the dawn of time, when man first discovered irony and sarcasm. You can imagine that newly literate man very quickly realised that words and pictures on their own weren't enough – how do you indicate irony in a cave painting?

In the 1580s, Henry Denham, a printer, kicked things off by proposing a 'percontation point', which was a reversed question mark (⸮) used to denote a rhetorical question. Although use of this mark died out in the seventeenth century, in 1668 John Wilkins, an Anglican clergyman and author, suggested that irony in a text should be marked with an inverted exclamation mark.* In 1841 Marcellin Jobard, a

---

*You can see the inverted question and exclamation mark in the wild in Spanish. Its job is to sit at the start of the sentence and prepare the reader for the EXCLAMATION or question that is to come. Spanish syntax means that statements and questions have the same wording, so without the helpful inverted punctuation you'd have no way of knowing if you were being *asked* '¿You like learning about punctuation?', or *told*, 'You like learning about punctuation.'

Belgian newspaper publisher, proposed an irony mark in the shape of an oversized arrow head, with a small stem. Jobard thought that the mark could be used on its side, or upside down, to mark 'a point of irritation, an indignation point, a point of hesitation'. These days many online users deploy the closing tag </sarcasm> or </s> to denote a sarcastic or ironic comment; I am also fond of Tom Driberg's idea that ironic statements should be printed in italic type that leans the other way from conventional italics – to the left.*

Punctus interrogativus

Lynne Truss describes the eighth-century *punctus interrogativus* as 'a lightning flash, striking from left to right'. I love this description – while we might think of punctuation as being staid and fixed in position, Truss's description gives it energy, and purpose. It lives – it *strikes*. The *punctus interrogativus* eventually morphed into the question mark. In *This is Me, Full Stop.*, the authors reference the unproven but delightful theory that the question mark was first thought up by a monk who copied the shape of his cat's (presumably questioning) tail. It was probably originally used at the end of a sentence to let the reader know that what they were reading was a question, and that they should change the tone of their voice accordingly, so that it was clear to their audience.† As

---

*Driberg was a pretty opposite-leaning character himself, what with being a homosexual, journalist, politician, High Anglican churchman and possible MI5 informant and Soviet spy. Reading about his contradictions makes me feel that biographies of him should be printed entirely in backwards-leaning italics.

†'The question mark is alright when it is all alone when it is used as a brand on cattle . . . but connected with writing it is completely entirely completely uninteresting . . . anybody who can read at all knows when a question is a question as it is written in writing. Therefore I ask you

Truss points out, the mark was not known by the infinitely duller and more ponderous name of 'question mark' until the nineteenth century. Its alternative names of 'interrogation point', 'query' or 'eroteme' are much more beguiling.

Fly specks on the page

'I gave up quotation marks long ago. I found I didn't need them, they were fly-specks on the page,' wrote E. L. Doctorow. Another believer in a minimalist quote-mark style is Vladimir Putin. As two Brookings Institute scholars noted when they analysed Putin's dissertation for his advanced degree (awarded by the St Petersburg Mining Institute), there were sixteen plagiarised pages, no footnotes and no quotation marks. In 218 pages of text.

The final chapter of James Joyce's *Ulysses* is more than 24,000 words long (roughly forty printed pages), yet contains just one comma and two full stops. In many ways this is the pinnacle of Joyce's aversion to punctuation: he never used quotation marks in any of his books (he referred to them as 'perverted commas') – instead, he used em rules to denote when a person was speaking.

What is the story of these little marks that have been so shunned by some writers? In the chapter 'Foot-and-note disease' we will meet Aristarchus, the librarian in Alexandria, and see how he created the asterisk, but he also pioneered the use of the diple: >, which he used to highlight noteworthy text. The diple on its own wasn't enough, however; Aristarchus needed another symbol, because while a line or phrase might be noteworthy, he might also disagree with it. What to do? He came up with something called the *diple*

---

therefore wherefore should one use the question mark' was Gertrude Stein's view of things. Who brands their cattle with a question mark?

periestigmene: ⪢, to indicate where he found something notable, but didn't necessarily agree with it. As Keith Houston explains in *Shady Characters: The Secret Life of Punctuation, Symbols and Other Typographical Marks,* 'Authors praised, commented upon, and attacked each other's work, supporting their arguments with liberal quotations from the Bible – and what symbol could be more appropriate to the marking of this most noteworthy of texts than the familiar diple?'

By the fifth century, St Jerome was being berated by his one-time friend Rufinus of Aquileia for his inconsistency in his beliefs, and the diple and double diple were drafted into the fight. 'In order that the insertions I am now making in this work from elsewhere may cause no confusion to the reader, they have single marks at the beginnings of the lines if they are mine and double ones if they are my opponent's,' wrote Rufinus in his *Apology Against Jerome*.

The diple's big break into the mainstream came in the eighteenth century, with the rise of the novel. That led to writers needing a way to indicate direct and reported speech by their characters, and the diple's centuries spent morphing into the quotation mark meant it was a punctuation mark looking for a job – and in the novel it found one.

At this point the marginal diple mark became the quotation mark, used to open and close quoted speech. But how many marks? Do you single, ' / '? or double " / "?

Until the beginning of the nineteenth century it was a free-for-all: sometimes double and single marks would alternate as speakers did in the text, sometimes they were varied to distinguish direct speech from reported speech. Eventually, most printers settled on using the double quote mark, but sometime in the middle of the nineteenth century the contrary British began to use single quote marks exclusively – and that brings us to today, where the same transatlantic split still applies in books.

The waters have become even more muddied online and it's now common for online commentators to favour a hybrid use of speech marks instead of applying one style. This hybrid uses single quote marks for 'ironic' quotes and 'direct' quotations, and double for speech. Harvard English professor Marjorie Garber writes that quote marks these days can 'convey both absolute authenticity and veracity . . . and suspected inauthenticity, irony or doubt'. Trusted source? Use quote marks to indicate. Untrusted, suspect source? Also use quote marks to indicate. All this means that in a globalised world things are just a muddle. As journalist Andrew Heisel writes, 'When a word is in single quotes, is it being used as a word, ironically, or to quote someone else? Is that cliché in quotation marks for emphasis or because you think it's stupid? . . .'

Smart and dumb

Sometimes when I'm proofreading a cover, say, or some marketing material, I wonder what might be the most obscure correction I could make. The correction that only I would ever notice or think necessary, and that most readers wouldn't even be aware of. Spacing of ellipses is one, as is making sure that the possessive 's' in an italicised title is in roman (the *Guardian*'s, not the *Guardian's*, etc.); another is making sure that there is a hairline space at the end of an italicised word ending in, for example, an 'r', so that it doesn't crash into punctuation following it.

The tiniest, most obscure correction mark I probably make, though, is to change a ' into a ', or occasionally a " into a ". The difference is pretty subtle. The straight quote marks here are actually known as *dumb* quote marks; the curly ones are known as *smart* or typographer's quote marks. Smart quote marks look like classy little elevated 66s and 99s; straight quote marks do indeed look . . . dumb. We need to go back to 1893 to understand why smart and dumb quote marks exist. In a piece in *The Stenographer* that year, U. Sherman MacCormack wrote: 'For some time past the manufacturers of typewriters have adopted straight quotation marks, for the reason that the same character can be used at the beginning and end of the sentence, thus saving one key.'

So, the typewriter used only straight quotes to save a couple of keys, and some modern keyboards have followed suit. Straight quotes are the default online as they are safe (coding issues across platforms mean that they can survive in a copy-and-paste world better than their more glamorous curled cousins). Writing in the *Atlantic*, Glenn Fleishmann described how 'these humble symbols are a dagger in my eye when a straight, or typewriter-style, pair appears in the midst of what is often otherwise typographic beauty'.

Serial killer commas

Where do commas come from? The word comma means 'a piece cut off' in Greek, and Aristophanes of Byzantium, the librarian at Alexandria who keeps popping up in the history of punctuation, was credited with this bit, too. Like so much punctuation, it comes from a time when reading out loud was commonplace. For maximum dramatic effect, actors reading a text needed to know when and how to breathe when they were performing – how much breath was needed for a line, and how much for a longer piece of text? Aristophanes' system used a single point placed at different heights on the line to let them know.

American and British English disagree about almost every aspect of punctuation. In *Experience*, his 2000 autobiography, Martin Amis writes about receiving the US proofs of his 1995 novel *The Information*: 'Can't believe the US proofs of *The Info*. A termitary* of imported commas, each one like a papercut to my soul.' After seeing her views on the question mark, you won't be surprised by what Gertrude Stein has to say about the comma: 'Commas are servile they have no life of their own they are dependent upon use and convenience and they are put there for practical purposes . . . A comma by helping you along holding your coat for you and putting on your shoes keeps you from living your life as actively as you should lead it . . . the use of them was positively degrading.' It's difficult to read Stein's sentences without mentally adding in commas, and even more so when you read her thoughts on semicolons: 'They [semicolons] are more powerful more imposing more pretentious than a comma but they are a comma all the same. They really have within them deeply within them fundamentally within them the comma nature.'

It's true that US English can sometimes look like a termite mound of commas on a page – made worse by the fact that they are all in the *wrong place*. In *Dreyer's English*, Benjamin Dreyer deftly explains that US English makes use of a style of comma that separates the last two items in a list and that comes before 'and' or 'or' – for example: 'this type of comma can be called a Series, Serial, Oxford, or Harvard comma'.

In what is an otherwise delightfully mannered, informative, even-tempered and entertaining book, the series comma moment is the only place in all 278 pages of *Dreyer's English* where the author becomes . . . *firm*: 'Whatever you want to call it: Use it. I don't want to belabour the point; neither am I willing to negotiate it. Only godless savages eschew the series comma.'

So, in American English, the serial comma is A Thing. A Big Thing. Dreyer opines that 'everyone I've ever encountered

---

*I had to look this up. It's an anthill occupied by termites.

in US book publishing uses it' – which may be so, but then everyone I've ever encountered in British book publishing is a godless savage. The problem with the serial comma from a British point of view is that it is not *natural* to us to use it, and therefore it sticks out from a mile away. The other problem is that it can both resolve ambiguity in a sentence as well as create it – which means that it is a difficult beast to master. Like all the best illustrations of deep grammatical issues the best example is a sort-of apocryphal one, from a book dedication, which allegedly read: 'To my parents, Ayn Rand and God.'* Now, I agree that without a comma before the 'and' it does appear that the author was parented by Ayn Rand and God, and in this case we should allow the serial comma its moment. But in British English we should *only* use a serial comma to clear up ambiguity – not for any other reason, including if we just happen to feel like it.

Hanged on a comma

In August 1916, Roger Casement was hanged after a highly publicised trial for treason. Casement's defence was founded upon a comma: specifically, one that was missing. The Treason Act of 1351 seemed to apply only to activities carried out on British soil, and Casement's activities, while undoubtedly treasonous, had been carried out in Germany. The court decided, however, that although the original text of the 1351 Act was unpunctuated, a third comma should be read in the phrase 'If a man do levy war against our Lord the King in his

---

*The probable origin of this is a dedication from a book called *Electromagnetic Slow Wave Systems* by R. M. Bevensee, which contains the dedication: 'This Book Is Dedicated to my parents, Ayn Rand, and the glory of GOD.' Which isn't even an example of a serial comma, let alone an ambiguous one.

realm, or be adherent to the King's enemies in his realm, giving them aid and comfort in the realm, or elsewhere . . .".

This minor yet major tweak in interpretation meant that the phrase now applied to wherever the acts took place, not just to where the 'King's enemies' were. The verdict prompted Casement to write: 'God deliver from such antiquaries as these, to hang a man's life upon a comma and throttle him with a semi-colon.'

More recently but less dramatically, a class-action lawsuit in 2017 about overtime for truck drivers in Maine came down to a comma. As the *New York Times* explained:

> The debate over commas is often a pretty inconsequential one, but it was anything but for the truck drivers. Note the lack of Oxford comma – also known as the serial comma – in the following state law, which says overtime rules do not apply to:
>
> The canning, processing, preserving, freezing, drying, marketing, storing, packing for shipment or distribution of:
>
> (1) Agricultural produce;
>
> (2) Meat and fish products; and
>
> (3) Perishable foods.
>
> Does the law intend to exempt the distribution of the three categories that follow, or does it mean to exempt packing for the shipping or distribution of them?
>
> Delivery drivers distribute perishable foods, but they don't pack the boxes themselves. Whether the drivers were subject to a law that had denied them thousands of dollars a year depended entirely on how the sentence was read.

A lower court ruled against the truck drivers, but the decision was reversed by an appeal court, who reasoned that the absence of the Oxford comma in the law created enough uncertainty to overturn the original judgment. On this occasion, the Oxford comma and the Maine truckers won the day.

After all these legal cases, controversy and transatlantic tussling, the very best piece of advice I found on dealing with the serial comma comes from Lynne Truss in *Eats, Shoots & Leaves*:* 'There are people who embrace the Oxford comma,[†] and people who don't, and I'll just say this: *never* get between these people when drink has been taken.' It's just as well that most of the time we're separated by an ocean.

---

*Perhaps confusingly this is one example Benjamin Dreyer gives where he allows that the Serial Comma *can* be dropped – he believes that *Eats, Shoots, & Leaves* would look unsightly because of the ampersand–comma interface, so on this occasion he allows that we can have *Eats, Shoots & Leaves*. No wonder we're all in such a tangle.

[†]Although you might think that some of these people would include the band Vampire Weekend, whose 2008 single was called 'Oxford Comma', you'd be wrong. The songwriter Ezra Koenig explained that the song is 'more about not giving a fuck than about Oxford commas', a position I found myself increasingly taking as I wrote this chapter.

FIGHT LETTERS FROM CHARLOTTE BRONTË: SPELLING

A priest, a rabbit and a minister walk into a
bar. The rabbit says: 'I might be a typo.'

One of the more tedious jobs for a proofreader is checking
the end matter of a book. Notes, sources, bibliographies – it's
all a bit of a slog trying to stay awake in the face of page after
page of unoriginal content that rarely contains any surprises,
but that requires a high degree of concentration to check. So
when I saw that a proofreader had made a marginal comment in the notes section of a book she was looking at that
included the joyous pencil stroke of an exclamation mark
(see p. 120 for more on the story behind the !), I knew that her
numbed mind and eyes had stumbled across something that
justified deploying this excited shriek of punctuation.

'*Fight Letters from Charlotte Brontë to George Henry Lewes*'
was the line that had led to her comment. The *Fight Letters of
Charlotte Brontë*! Imagine. Charlotte writes to George Henry
Lewes (live-in partner of Mary Ann Evans, better known as
George Eliot) to challenge him to a bare-knuckle fight in a
backyard over his claim that Jane Austen and Henry Fielding
were the greatest novelists in the English language. Brontë
disagrees, you see, declaring that as a writer Austen was not
profound, only 'shrewd and observant'. *Pride and Prejudice*,

Brontë continues in her *Fight Letters*, was like a photograph of 'a carefully-fenced, highly cultivated garden with neat borders and delicate flowers – but no glance of a bright vivid physiognomy'. This is the kind of fighting-talk criticism that requires the gloves to come off and the brawling to commence.

This foray of my imagination into writing wild Brontë fan-fight-fiction was triggered by a typo – a simple mistake made by the typesetter (in this case, mis-keying an 'F' for an 'E') – that hints at a rich alternative world. The correct title of the book is of course *Eight Letters from Charlotte Brontë to George Henry Lewes*,* which, as my proofreader noted with some understatement in the margin, was 'less interesting!' A typo is different from a misspelling, which is defined as an 'error of ignorance' – i.e. one caused by whoever is writing the word not knowing how it is spelt, rather than the error being introduced as a book is produced. But how do these manglings happen to our words, and does it matter?

According to Mark Twain, 'The English alphabet is pure insanity. It can hardly spell any word in the language with any degree of certainty.'

As a reader, one of the first and unspoken things we expect from a book is that the words inside it are spelt correctly. Before something is printed and purchased for our reading pleasure, we assume that it will have been carefully checked and that any incorrect spellings will have been weeded out. We might initially feel gleeful at having noticed a typo, but if we keep finding errors in a text, we could start to lose faith. If the writer and their publisher can't be bothered to do something as basic as spell words correctly, then why should

---

*Lewes has been described as a 'witty, French, flippant sort of man', so he might well have enjoyed this whole excursion into a fantasy world where he receives menacing letters from a female novelist.

we trust that what they are saying deserves the investment of our time and attention? For a reader, spelling is a touchstone: if that's right, you can forgive a lot of other things. If it's not, the author hasn't fulfilled their side of the deal, and that betrayal is difficult to overcome. We should be able to lose ourselves in a book without being abruptly returned to real life by an intrusive mistake that takes us away from a story while we try to work out what the problem is.

But who decides what the correct spelling of something is? To notice that something has been spelt incorrectly, we need to have an agreed standard of correct spelling for it to deviate from. And like most things to do with words and language, that's not as straightforward as it sounds. Look at Shakespeare's grave in Stratford-upon-Avon:

> Good frend for Jesus sake forbeare,
> To digg the dust encloased heare.
> Blest be the man that spares thes stones,
> And curst be he that moves my bones.

As well as promising that you'll be cursed if you disturb the dust over his bones, to the modern reading eye it also appears to include a typo. And then look at Jane Austen's juvenile writings, titled *Love and Freindship*. I've worked on an edition of this, and I can tell you that not being able to correct what looks like a horrible typo on the front cover of a book is a sort of editing-induced OCD nightmare. I had to sit on my hands in order not to take a pen to it. But of course, to Shakespeare's gravestone-chiseller and to the fifteen-year-old Austen, these variant spellings of 'friend' were perfectly acceptable.

Briefly, here's how spelling in English became such a mine-field. First off, we had three centuries of Norman French rule. As that came to an end, English gradually became the dominant language. Early writers in English, like Geoffrey

Chaucer, were pretty good at standardising the spelling of their writing, but these efforts were consistently undermined by the Chancery clerks, who carried on spelling words based on French etymology. You'd have thought that when William Caxton brought the first printing press to London in 1476 that would have helped further the cause of a standard for spelling, but by the time he arrived, Caxton had spent thirty years living in mainland Europe. His grasp of English was shaky, and not helped by his assistants being a group of Belgian monks, who had even less command of English than he did. Even more deviation was added by individual printers developing their own house styles and then by typesetters who were fond of making words longer than they needed to be. They were paid by the line, so why not help things along a little, with a flexible approach to spelling?

If you picked up a copy of William Tyndale's translation of the New Testament you might expect the words inside to have set out on their journey to spelling standardisation. Henry VIII had made printing the Bible in English legal, and the whole *point* of a printing press was that you could produce standard editions of a work in great number. But even then, early print compositors faced numerous challenges in 'keying' texts correctly – there may have been printing presses, but there was still no agreement on spellings or punctuation, and text had to be constructed from reading handwritten manuscripts, with all the room for deviation and error that might suggest. The actual printing was done outside England, in Europe, and often followed Dutch orthography – which is why words with spellings like *ghost*, *ghospel* and *ghossip* sometimes appeared inside your holy book. We've retained the silent Dutch 'h' in ghost, gherkin and aghast, but lost it from ghospel and ghossip. Shame.

From the sixteenth century things became even more tangled as scholars attempted to link words to their Greek or Latin roots. Unhelpfully, this meant that spelling drifted further from the way words sounded, and that made them increasingly difficult to spell correctly: for example, sissors became scissors and ake ache – by this point, spelling was a complete headake.

The WORDS are deduced from their ORIGINALS

What was needed to get words better was some sort of agreed way of spelling them, written down and available for consultation by anyone who was interested. Enter the dictionary. The first modern dictionary in England was Samuel Johnson's *A Dictionary of the English Language*, published in 1755 – and 'The WORDS are deduced from their ORIGINALS' is printed on the title page. In the Preface to his dictionary, Johnson noted that the English language was 'copious without order, and energetick without rules . . . wherever I turned my view . . . there was perplexity to be disentangled, and confusion to be regulated'.

Before Johnson, dictionaries were in French, Spanish or Latin with English definitions. 'We must have recourse to the old Roman expedient in times of confusion, and choose a dictator. Upon this principle, I give my vote for Mr Johnson to fill that great and arduous post,' wrote Philip Stanhope of Johnson, and although Johnson never saw himself as a dictator, such was the reach and influence of his dictionary when it came to words and how to spell them that he might as well have been. But as Stanhope had surmised, lexicographical confusion and variant spellings meant that a firm hand was needed to take a decision and deduce the WORDS from their ORIGINALS so that all could know what order the letters should come in. Even Johnson was not infallible when it came to the tricky matter of *how* to spell – uphill but downhil, instill but distil, among others, meant the dictionary was not consistent, but at least it had an opinion, and one that other wordsmiths could lean on through the authority of print. Johnson had plenty of critics, but the *Dictionary* was generously reviewed and its scope, structure and style were emulated by all the dictionaries that followed.

Tung-tied

Johnson's equivalent in the United States was Noah Webster, who had a lasting influence on the way words were spelt there with his three-volume *A Grammatical Institute of the English Language*, which was made up of a speller, a grammar and a reader. By the end of the nineteenth century, the speller had sold 90 million copies, and became known as the 'blue-backed' speller, owing to the colour of its covers. Webster's aim was to rescue 'our native tongue' from the 'clamour and pedantry of English grammar and pronunciation'. He believed that the English language had been corrupted by the British aristocracy, and rejected the idea that knowledge of Latin and Greek was needed in order to study English grammar: he was adamant that the people must control the language.

Webster was (among other things) a teacher, and he believed that phonetic spellings were easier for children to learn. Gradually, he began to change the spellings in his blue-backed book – centre became center, colour morphed to color. Not every word that Webster tried to change the spelling of caught on. He attempted unsuccessfully to morph tongue to tung, soup to soop, sponge to spunge and ache back to the original ake. Although he didn't invent these new ways of spelling (the variant spellings were in some cases already in circulation – even Shakespeare used color and center as the dominant versions of those words in his First Folio), the popularity and reach of his dictionaries did much to make his choice of spelling take precedence over others.

Webster's dictionaries promoted a 'federal language' that would popularise an 'American' way of spelling. One of the outcomes of the work of lexicographers like Webster was the rise in popularity in the United States of the spelling bee. American children were encouraged to learn standardised ways to spell through informal classroom competition, and in 1925 the first United States National Spelling Bee took place, and still takes place annually.* Webster's dictionary continues to be the most popular and influential 'speller' in the US even today.

'All books are subject to these misfortunes'

The publishers of James Shirley's 1633 play *The Bird in a Cage* included a disclaimer: 'many other Errors, (though not for the most part literall,) thou shalt meete, which thou canst not with safetie of thy owne, interpret a defect in the Authors Iudgment, since all books are subject to these misfortunes.'

It's certainly true that all books – all words – have the potential to be subject to the misfortune of the error. It doesn't matter how successful or acclaimed a writer you are – it can happen at any time, and to pretty much any word. We all know words that we just can't spell, and that's why to make them better you need a team of eyes to scrutinise them. There are plenty of words that are just *difficult* – they aren't spelt as they are pronounced, they don't follow the rules.

According to the Oxford English Corpus, an electronic collection of more than 2 billion words, these are some of the repeat offenders when it comes to misspellings: assassination, bizarre, embarrass, fluorescent, idiosyncrasy,

---

*The winner of the first official spelling bee was an eleven-year-old called Frank Neuhauser, who won by successfully spelling 'gladiolus'.

millennium, occasion, tongue and weird. And that's just some of the common words that people have issues with – it doesn't even scratch the surface of words borrowed from other languages, or scientific, technical and medical terms. Actinobacillus. Dexamethasone. Pasteurellaceae.

What can we do to stop words being struck by the misspelling misfortune? We can use eyes. As many pairs of eyes as possible. The more people that look at a word, the more likely it is that at least one will generate that spark of electricity that shouts 'STOP! Something is WRONG here!'

In *Ex Libris: Confessions of a Common Reader*, Anne Fadiman describes what she calls the 'proofreading temperament' as being 'part of a larger syndrome with several interrelated symptoms, one of which is the spotting mania'. In other words, if you are afflicted with the temperament you won't be able *not* to spot errors that appear in front of you, wherever and whenever they occur. As Fadiman says, those who work with words 'tend to be good at distinguishing the anomalous figure – the rare butterfly, the precious seashell – from the ordinary ground'. It takes practice to override the assumption that a common word is spelt correctly – but the more you pay close attention when you read, the easier it becomes to spot the unusual butterfly.

So that's where the copy-editor and proofreader step in. Checking and correcting spelling is a fundamental part of their job. They need to be confident spellers, and to know when they need to check something, rather than assume it is correct. Copy-editors should be able to spot most misspellings or typos in a manuscript. But they probably won't spot all of them: as we've seen, our eyes can be lazy. And as well as that, humans are not machines. They get tired. They get distracted. They miss things. It's normal. It's why the burden of making words better is shared with the editor, the author, the proofreader. And on the subject of machines: hopefully

this book has shown that to get words good, there is no substitute for a person and a pen. Well, a person and some track
changes.

Keeping the words in line

Nearly all frontlist books these days will have been set from
a nice clean, edited Word file, which the typesetter will simply flow into the requested layout style. This means that
there are far fewer keying errors – typos – to spot than there
used to be. The transition from the traditional keying of text
to digital reflow means that errors introduced by the typesetter simply aren't there any more. But older titles that are
being reissued from backlists may well be keyed still, as no
digital file will be available. Recently I proofread such a title
– it was first published in an English translation in 1924, and
we had reset the existing text for a new edition. Although
when you're working on a book everyone involved wants to
see as few mistakes as possible, as a proofreader you can't
help but hope for a few juicy errors to pounce on as you go
through it, and to keep you on your toes. What's the point of
being afflicted with the spotting mania otherwise? How can
you demonstrate you are earning your money if there's
nothing for you to correct? There's a sense of something
dangerous lurking just below the waterline: there must be
errors, somewhere, but *where*?

The book I was proofreading contained a satisfying array
of keyed errors: bad breaks, entire sentences missed out and
typos. It also contained some OCR errors. Typesetters will
generally set from an old text setting that has been scanned
into an optical character recognition system, and this throws
up errors of a particular type: 'bum' for 'burn'; 'hot' for
'not'. Lower-case 'n' and 'm' are commonly mangled via
OCR, which makes sense when you think about how the

characters could get confused by a computer scanner, which unlike a human has no context for it to rely on. It's the context humans supply that means a living eye is always better than an electronic one.

Incidentally, in Shakespeare's *Cymbeline*, the princess Imogen's name may have been a misspelling of 'Innogen'. Shakespeare had already used the name Innogen for a character in early versions of *Much Ado About Nothing*, and although Innogen was probably a common Celtic name meaning 'young girl', the name 'Imogen' didn't exist until Shakespeare wrote *Cymbeline*. Perhaps his text was suffering from an early OCR error and he liked the result.

The typo hunters

Getting words better is a belt-and-braces business. Once the copy-editor has done their work, it's on to the proofreaders. Proofreading is as old as printing, and the original job of the proofreader was a simple one: to check the work of the type-setter (or compositor, as they were originally known). Unlike a copy-editor, who works closely with an author to improve and refine every aspect of the text before it goes to be made into proofs, the proofreader is traditionally only there to point out where the typesetter may have introduced further errors. They are the typo hunters.

When I started working in publishing, typesetters still keyed text into a digital typesetting system by hand. That meant we would send them a 'hard copy' (a physical print-out on paper) of a copy-edited manuscript, and they would literally read it line by line and key the text in. As you can imagine, it would be easy for a typesetter to introduce further errors into an edited text as they did so.* Errors are what the

---

*How about this one, supplied to me by a freelance proofreader: 'Get

proofreader is looking out for. This is why historically proof-readers marked corrections on proofs in red or blue pen. A red correction meant that the typesetter had introduced the error as part of the setting process, and a blue correction meant that the suggested correction was one that perhaps should have been picked up at an earlier stage (i.e. by the copy-editor and author) and was therefore not the responsibility of the typesetter. The distinction was important as red corrections could be charged back to the typesetter, whereas blue ones could not.* In *Copy-editing: A Practical Guide*, Karen Judd says: 'The proofreader is looking only for typographical errors or actual mistakes, not ordinary niceties.' The 'niceties' should have been fixed at copy-editing, partly because it is more expensive to fix a problem at proof than on manuscript. I like this description of the differences between copy-editors and proofreaders: 'If copyeditors are the gatekeepers charged with protecting copy against bad writing, proofreaders stamp the admission tickets.'† Of course, like nearly everything in the literary life some writers take exception to proofreaders – especially Mark Twain. 'Yesterday [my publisher] wrote that the printer's proof-reader was improving my punctuation for me, & I telegraphed orders to have him shot without giving him time to pray.'

'In the first place God made idiots. This was for practice. Then he made proof-readers.'

Mark Twain again. One of the first things I had to learn to do when I started working in publishing was to commission freelance proofreaders. I had only the vaguest idea of

---

thee behind me, Stan.' This is the sort of typo that, when you spot it, actually makes words, and life, better.

*Printers had a colour for their own corrections, too: green.

†This is from *Copyediting and Proofreading for Dummies*, by Suzanne Gilad.

what a proofreader did. It sounded self-explanatory, but what exactly was it? The first thing to know about proofreaders is that they fall into two categories: against copy, and blind. Yes, that's right – blind. In our index-card box of potential freelancers that we met earlier, some had the inexplicable notation 'blind' next to their name. Or even 'prefers blind'. *Prefers* blind? Proofreaders? Was there some secret society of blind proofreaders that I didn't know about? Actually, there is, but they aren't blind in the physical sense. Rather, these proofreaders look at proofs 'blind' – that is, without anything to read them against. Their opposite number, the 'against copy' proofreader, proofreads 'against' the original setting copy. Interestingly, although these proofreaders are doing the same job, the ways they proofread mean they often spot different types of errors. The against-copy reader is checking to make sure that the typesetter hasn't fallen asleep halfway through typesetting and missed out a word, or a line, or a paragraph, or even, as occasionally happens, an entire page or two. They read each sentence on the proofs against the setting copy's version of that sentence, and mark up any discrepancy between the two. The blind proofreader behaves more like you or I might do when we read a book: they might spot an error, which they would query, but they have no way of knowing if it has been introduced by the typesetter, or overlooked in the copy-editing, or if in fact it isn't an error at all, but the author's intention. But still: it doesn't matter – all they have to do is flag it up. Increasingly, publishers rely only on one proofreader because it is of course cheaper, but that does mean the error rate in a finished book will creep up, in part due to every pair of eyes on a text helping to keep errors down, and also because of the different ways in which the blind and against-copy readers operate.

The Mark Twain quote that opened this section is, I imagine, partly tongue-in-cheek. Here's how an author described seeing the work of a proofreader on his book: 'In nearly thirty years of writing I've never known anything like it. I'll be honest, in one or two instances I actually found it a bit spooky that he could have drilled down to a specific point of detail in the most obscure of primary sources. There is no doubt at all that he checked absolutely everything. It's also humbling to realise how careless I am even when I think I'm being meticulous.' So there you go. Not every author thinks proofreaders are idiots.

Proust's paperoles

'The unfurling manuscripts that comprised his interminable life's work' is one description of how Marcel Proust wrote. Working on *In Search of Lost Time*, Proust used cheap exercise books, bought in bulk. On the edges of the paper he would stick what he called 'paperoles' – loose scraps of paper that could be stuck, unstuck and moved around the manuscript as he wanted. Additions, digressions, unfinished thoughts – the paperoles even made it onto his proofs. 'Unfurling manuscripts' is a lovely thought, bringing to mind quiet publishing offices full of contemplative copy-editors surrounded by paper peacefully reading and absorbing – and of course, occasionally pouncing with a satisfyingly judicious edit.

'As the harbour is welcome to the sailor, so is the last line to the scribe,' wrote one medieval monk during a slow day at the transcribing and proofreading office. Proust's paperoles, no matter how romantic, were a pretty unwieldy mess that made sense only to him, and if you'd been involved in transcribing them you'd certainly have been looking for the safe harbour of the last line from the minute you started work on the first page.

Proofreaders needed a way of communicating suggested

Proust's paperoles

changes to proofs without resorting to bits of paper stuck to the manuscript. That's why we have proofreading marks that provide a universal standard for everyone involved in correcting text to work to. Since medieval times the margins of a page have been a useful and collaborative space to indicate where insertions, deletions and substitutions should go in a text. Generally, any errors that a proofreader finds are marked twice: once in the main body of the text, and once in the margin, directly in line with it. If the error is in the first half of a text line then the mark sits in the left margin; if it's in the second half then it goes in the right margin. This is so that a typesetter can work their eye down the margin, quickly spot a mark, then adventure into the thickets of the text to dig out exactly where the correction is. The standard proofreading marks should be 'clearly recognisable, memorable, and quick and easy to reproduce'. The first agreed 'standard' for proofreading marks was established in 1976, and then updated in 2005. You can easily find the standard proofreading marks online; you'll see that they are a mixture of abbreviations ('ital' for italics; 'sp' for spelling') and symbols.

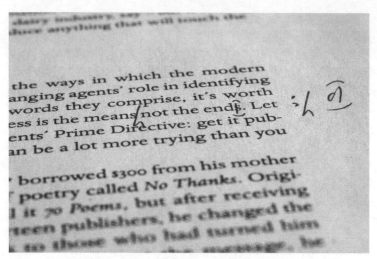

Proof correction marks. Shown are symbols for insertion
and deletion – there are many more to explore.

Photographing with your mind

There are lots of views about what a proofreader is responsible for. We can probably all agree that they should be
checking for spelling, punctuation and grammar, and making sure that the style sheet of the copy-editor has been
followed and the house style adhered to. They should also
cross-check any references in the text to illustrations, artwork, notes, etc. They should make sure that the formatting
of the proofs has been done consistently. Proofreaders are
not responsible for querying facts or rewriting text – that
should all have been dealt with during the editing stage. Of
course, that doesn't mean a proofreader would ignore something they thought might be wrong, or not try to improve a
clumsy sentence. Although it's not their job to spot these
things, most of them will. That's how the spotting mania
works, and they can't resist.

What happens after proofreading? All the sets of proofs
– author's, proofreader's, any other interested parties – are

likely to go back to the copy-editor (or, if not to them, to the editorial manager or equivalent – someone very much like me) for collation. That's where somebody looks at the proofreader's set of proofs (which are the 'master' set) and the author's proofs and the editor's proofs and translator's proofs and the proofs of all other interested parties (and it is surprising just how many interested, or uninterested-but-still-have-something-to-say parties there can be) and distils all the comments, suggestions, corrections and rewrites into one 'marked set' of proofs. When I began working in editorial a 'collation' to me was a light meal in lieu of dinner, but for a copy-editor, a 'collation' is the moment when you have to confront, in writing, all the decisions you made, or failed to make, or worse, made, but failed to execute consistently, when you worked on the manuscript. Like a badly assembled buffet, for a copy-editor, being faced with your mistakes can be pretty indigestible.

Alarmingly, this stage of editorial work is actually one of the most dangerous in terms of mistakes being made and typos slipping through. There are a couple of reasons for this: at this point, everything is generally being done under time pressure.* That pressure applies to the author, the in-house

---

*Sometimes proofs will be marked up with a 'global change' – an instruction to the typesetters that asks them to apply a change 'globally' – i.e. throughout the proofs. It's actually a very handy instruction – if you realise that something has gone awry in copy-editing, or a late decision has been made about using a particular form of a word, instead of having to go through and mark up every individual occurrence, you can simply issue one command, and let the typesetters automatically search for and replace it. Very occasionally this can go quite wrong, as my colleague B explained to me. She had been working on a set of proofs where it had been decided to change the word 'pants' to 'trousers' throughout (presumably the original version was using US vocabulary). The typesetters dutifully followed this instruction, leading to the word 'participants' appearing throughout the text as 'particitrousers'.

editorial team and of course the typesetters. The second reason is that at this stage, instead of having nice, clean electronic text to use, the typesetters are now having to decipher handwritten corrections marked up by the proofreader and added by the copy-editor, or whoever does the collation. No matter how careful and precise everyone involved tries to be, when it comes down to it the typesetters have to do a heroic job and try to untangle what remains on the proofs. Sometimes, despite everyone's best efforts, what the typesetter is looking at is a mess. Eventually, the typesetters will deliver a set of corrected revised proofs, so that once again their work can be checked, and then approved by the author (remember them?).

Most big publishers now use typesetters not based in the UK (they are often in India), so there is also a language barrier. That doesn't matter too much given that proofreading symbols should be universal, but when it comes to deciphering handwriting it can be a problem. My handwriting is really not good, and although I try to be as clear as I can, sometimes when you are manually marking up hundreds of corrections over an 800-page book, you start to scrawl. The typesetter then has to make sense of your scrawl, which is how you often end up with a much higher error rate at this stage of text preparation. To make matters worse, as you go through each stage fewer and fewer people are looking at the text. At the beginning you have the copy-editor and author working together; then you have the author again and the proofreaders, along with the copy-editor or editorial manager. But in the final stages you might have only one person (OK, usually me) looking at the sixth round of corrections while the clock ticks. That's how errors sometimes end up in what gets printed: a mistake at this stage won't necessarily be picked up by anyone else. Next time you spot what looks like an obvious mistake in a book, this might explain how it got there.

The lovely thing about page proofs and revises is that they are the ultimate physical record of how words get better. It's very satisfying to see the progression of a book from unedited manuscript to clean, edited text for setting, then on to page proofs, revises and so on. It's like taking the author's original words and putting them through a sieve – at each stage, the words are refined further and further, getting better and better, until all that should be left at the end are the good words – spelt correctly, full of meaning – that help the author say what they intend to the reader.

The other side of paradise

Described as a book that 'unfurled like a banner over an entire age' by A. Scott Berg, and also as 'one of the most illiterate books of any merit ever published' by literary critic Edmund Wilson, the first printing of *This Side of Paradise* was riddled with errors, beginning with the dedication page.* F. Scott Fitzgerald was known to be a terrible speller.

> Much has been said about F. Scott Fitzgerald's illiteracy, and *This Side of Paradise* has been singled out for notice as the worst offender. Fitzgerald's inattentive years at Princeton and his vagarious† reading produced an only partially educated young writer. Though he came to perfect his ear for English, throughout his career he remained a wretched speller.‡

---

*The dedication in the first printing read 'To Sigorney Fay', later corrected to 'Sigourney Fay'.

†I had to look this word up. According to the *Collins* online dictionary it's a 'rare' word. It means irregular, or erratic, or wandering.

‡This description is from Matthew J. Bruccoli, 'A Collation of F. Scott Fitzgerald's *This Side of Paradise*', *Studies in Bibliography*, vol. 9 (1957).

By the summer of 1920 the *New York Tribune* columnist Franklin P. Adams had invented a parlour game based on spotting mistakes in *Paradise*. 'The first printing was an inexcusably sloppy job, and . . . the blame must be distributed between author and publisher.'

The Great Gatsby, published five years after *This Side of Paradise* in 1925, was similarly, but perhaps unfairly, also noted for its misspellings and typos, beginning with the jacket. The first edition of Francis Cugat's famous jacket (see also p. 242) has a lower-case 'j' for Jay Gatsby, which had to be amended by hand before the copies were sent out. This error in the first printing of the first edition means that this jacket is 'the most expensive single piece of paper in twentieth-century book collecting' – apparently lifting the value of a first edition from four to six figures. That's the thing about mistakes – they might not make for good words, but in some circumstances, they can certainly add value. Depending on how you measure what makes something 'better', a typo can sometimes end up being a *good* thing.

On page 205 of the first edition of *The Great Gatsby*, Meyer Wolfsheim's secretary tells Nick Carraway that she is 'sick in tired' of young men trying to force their way into the office. This sort of typo is tricky to spot. In total, there were only five actual errors in the text – not a huge amount spread out over 50,000 words. Could it be that the reputation as a poor speller that Fitzgerald had inadvertently established for himself early on in his writing career meant that even a small number of errors in later books would be pounced on and pored over? Fitzgerald's commercial and literary success was ultimately undamaged by his inability to spell. His 'ear for English' and his storytelling abilities made up for any deficiencies in his spelling. Errors always do find a way of slipping through, but perhaps it doesn't matter so much if as readers we acknowledge the strengths in what we are reading, rather than the weaknesses. And, as Mary Norris quotes in the dedication to *Between You & Me: Confessions of a Comma Queen*: 'Of course, when you correct the errors of others, do so with kindness, in the hope that later writers will be as kind when they correct yours.'*

The yolk of oppression

Ask any freelance copy-editor or proofreader for the 'best' typo they have encountered in their careers and you will inevitably turn up some gems. In a way, it's a tragedy (although perhaps not for authors) that these get spotted and dealt with at edit or proof stage, and corrected before they can head out into the world for readers to encounter. There's a fine line between misfortune befalling a misspelt word and humour, and it often depends on your relationship to the word: whether you are the producer of it, or the recipient. Some selected highlights passed on to me while writing this book include an explorer who stumbles across a yawning abyss that somehow became a 'yawning abbess', and the phrase 'under the yolk of Mussolini'. These types of words are not-quite-homophones (homophones are words like flower and flour, which have the same meaning, just with different spellings). Further down this road, words with the same spelling but different pronunciation (row and row for example, or lead and lead) are known as homographs. A homonym can cover both.

For a time when I was younger I confused homonyms, homophones and Houyhnhnms, the fictional race of hyper-intelligent horses in Jonathan Swift's *Gulliver's Travels*. That book must have been a proofreading nightmare,

---

*Norris's dedication is from *The Art of the Footnote*, by Francis A. Burkle-Young and Saundra Rose Maley.

containing (among other spelling horrors) the words Lug-gnagg, Glubbdubdrib, Struldbruggs and Balnibarbi. I once had to copy-edit an article about the Roman emperor Elagabalus (described by Edward Gibbon as someone who 'abandoned himself to the grossest pleasures with ungoverned fury'; Elagabalus was said to have married a man named Zoticus at a public ceremony – unusual at the time, to put it mildly – and was eventually assassinated in a plot devised by his own grandmother) – I don't think I have ever struggled as much over a spelling.

However far you want to go with these words, I challenge you to read 'under the yolk of Mussolini' without imagining what a Mussolini-style egg yolk would look like.* Or indeed what it must be like to encounter a sleepy abbess on a remote glacier high up in the Transantarctic Mountains.

Hilterlands

Most of my career has been spent working on long, serious non-fiction titles. Inevitably, one name crops up again and again: Adolf Hitler.† I've worked on books solely about him and – European history being what it is – he often makes a

---

*See also this line in Karen Harper's *The Queen's Governess* (2010): 'In the weak light of dawn, I tugged on the gown and sleeves I'd discarded like a wonton last night to fall into John's arms.' Delicious dumplings.

†Even Hitler was concerned with getting his words better. The original title of *Mein Kampf* was 'Four and a Half Years (of Struggle) Against Lies, Stupidity and Cowardice'. If you'd like to guess at some more well-known titles from their authors' original efforts, try these: 'Tom-All-Alone's Factory That Got into Chancery and Never Got Out', 'All's Well That Ends Well', 'The Un-Dead', 'From a Sense of Duty', 'The Mute', 'Blanche's Chair in the Moon', 'The Last Man in Europe', 'Llareggub', 'What's That Noshin' on My Leg?', 'Forks'. Answers at the end of the chapter.

joyless cameo in other volumes navigating the twentieth century. And here's the thing: a pattern began to emerge. Once you had sent a book off to print, you would wait for the advance copies to land on your desk before spending the next six weeks Hiltering in the Hilterlands.

The commissioning editor responsible for most of the Hitler books I have encountered would often ask me if I thought it was possible for us ever to publish a book about Hitler without a rogue 'Hilter' slipping through. If you're publishing an 800-page book about Hitler, this tiny fat-finger transposition typo is very easy to make. 'Fat-finger' is the official name for it – and anyone who has used a QWERTY keyboard will recognise that feeling. I just tried typing out 'Hitler' and 'Hilter', and both feel very natural when you move your fingers over the keyboard. When I type 'Hilter', my brain* doesn't (as it sometimes does when I am typing other words) even register that there is something wrong with how I have spelt it. After all, it's the same number of letters, and something about where they are placed on the keyboard makes a Hilter almost indistinguishable from a Hitler. I suspect that the reason the odd Hilter slips through is that this type of error is so easy to make, and so tricky for even the best pair of editing eyes to pick up. The 'itl' and 'ilt' look almost indistinguishable from each other.

Admittedly, of all the criticisms you can level at Hitler, the ease with which he can blot the page with a typo resides in the lower ranks. Nowadays I try to remember to search through an electronic PDF of the text to weed out any lurking Hilters,† but in much the same way that Persian

---

*As my colleague Ruth reminded me when she proofread this book, it's important to make sure when publishing books about the brain that a rogue 'brian' doesn't slip through . . . and yes, this has happened to me.
†I like to call this process 'setting your Hilter Filter'. I suppose the town

carpet weavers would supposedly include a deliberate mistake in their rugs,* coming across the occasional Hilter does no harm and reminds us all that we're human, and we can all create (and spot) typos.

Atomic typos

In historical terms, we know that after the Second World War we enter the atomic age. The same is true of typos: after Hilter comes the unclear age. Sorry, nuclear age. 'Unclear' versus 'Nuclear' is a transposition error (like Hitler and Hilter, two letters in the word have been transposed with each other into the wrong place in the word), but it is also an example of a class of errors known as 'atomic typos' – the 'atomic' in the name comes about because these typos are very small mistakes that lead to very big differences in meaning. 'Pubic' and 'public', 'dairy' and 'diary', 'fight' and 'eight'.

Not only do they cause havoc by changing the entire meaning of a sentence, the chances of you setting off this sort of uncomfortable uncontrollable typo chain reaction are increased by the fact that they won't be picked up by a spell-checker either – the 'wrong' word is a perfectly valid one, just not in the context in which it appears.

Atomic typo fallout

In 1962 the United States conducted a shallow underground nuclear test in Nevada. Storax Sedan, as the test was officially

---

of Hilter in Lower Saxony in Germany might have to do the opposite and Fitler out the Hitlers in their printed matter.

*Followers of Islam believe that only Allah makes things perfectly, hence to weave a perfect rug would be an offence to him. I have never tried using this argument to placate an author angry about an error, but one day I might.

known, is the largest human-made crater in America and its fallout was twofold: it contributed just under 7 per cent of the total amount of radiation that fell on the US population during the series of nuclear tests known as Operation Plowshare, and in 2005 it also contributed to a diplomatic incident with Sudan.

TYPING ERROR CAUSES NUCLEAR SCARE ran the headline of a BBC article on 11 March 2005. 'The Sudanese government had a nasty shock this week, when it read on a US Congress website that the Americans had conducted nuclear tests in the country,' the piece continued. More prosaically, what had actually happened was that Ellen Tauscher, a Democratic member of the House of Representatives from California, had used the Sedan explosion as an example of a nuclear test that led to excessive radiation fallout. The name 'Sedan' was incorrectly transcribed in the *Congressional Record* as 'Sudan'. The Sudanese Foreign Minister was so alarmed at the news of these hitherto unknown nuclear tests in his country that he raised it with US officials in Khartoum. Although the Foreign Minister pronounced himself 'very relieved' to learn that it was a simple typing error, he said that 'our investigations, which are already under way, will continue until we get to the bottom of this matter'. An atomic typo in every sense of the word.

'Don't make any mistakes'

The differences in spelling between American and British English are only the start of the problems in sharing words and language across two continents. There is divergence in grammar, spelling and vocabulary to contend with, and sometimes it can lead to unexpected and unintended results. In 2003, Nicole Mowbray, a foreign desk assistant at the *Observer*, was asked to type out a printout of an email. The only instruction given was 'Don't make any mistakes'. In a 2019 interview about what happened next Mowbray describes how 'Fastidiously typing in the memo, and not knowing what the document was or its origins, I'd changed all the American spelling "mistakes" to British English. "Recognize" became recognise, and "emphasize" emphasise. "Favorable" was amended to favourable. I thought I was being helpful. Instead, it was a disaster.'

What Mowbray had been asked to type was a copy of a leaked US memo which the *Observer* had headlined on 2 March 2003 as REVEALED: US DIRTY TRICKS TO WIN VOTE ON IRAQ WAR; with Mowbray's typed-up version of the memo below it on their front page. But because Mowbray had corrected the 'mistakes' in the memo from American spellings and usage to British ones,* its provenance was immediately called into doubt. How could it be a leaked US memo if all the spelling was in British English? As Mowbray says:

'The wobble caught on. Was it a fake? Some outlets due to report on the *Observer*'s story cancelled interviews over doubts about the memo's authenticity. It was decided the readers' editor should publish a special dispatch to counter the thousands of complaints from readers, many American, calling us "lying limey bastards", claiming that the story's authors had fallen victim to a hoax and that the email was part of a campaign of misinformation.'

Mowbray's story and what happened next are told in the 2019 film *Official Secrets*, and her error was only one in the context of what she had been asked to do.

The house style I am most familiar with and have spent most of my career imposing on the words on my desk is to use '-ize' spellings for words like organize and realize. I have lost count of the number of times that people have told me that '-ize' spellings are *wrong* because they are

---

*Not unreasonably, Mowbray was following *Observer* house style guidelines.

American.* In fact, using '-ize' in *British* spelling has been happening since the fifteenth century, which meant that the first settlers from England who made it to America in the seventeenth century had loaded up their boats with dogs, sheep, goats, poultry and -ize spellings – and they stuck to it and that's why people now think it is an American way of doing things).

The '-ize' ending for words like organize and realize comes directly from the Greek root '-izo', whereas '-ise' endings come from the French suffix ('-iser') – and that variant was not in use until almost a century later. The King James Bible and Shakespeare use '-ize' spellings throughout, and using '-ize' is part of what is known as Oxford spelling, since it is used by Oxford University Press, and the *Oxford English Dictionary*.† But it's no wonder that there is permanent confusion about which is and isn't correct – and really, it depends on where you are and who you are writing for. Oxford spelling is generally used by NATO, the WHO, UNESCO, the United Nations, the *Encyclopedia Britannica*, Cambridge University Press and *Nature*. But most British newspapers use '-ise' – perhaps because that is what their readers expect, given the widespread belief that '-ize' is an Americanism. *The Times* used '-ize' until 1992, when it changed to '-ise'. Naturally some of its readers wanted to know why – hence this

---

*When *The Defence of the Realm: The Authorized History of MI5* was published in 2009 there was much controversy over the use of the -ize spelling of 'Authorized'. If you look at MI5's own website, they insist on using the -ise spelling of 'Authorised' when mentioning the book. And in the US edition they changed the title to *Defend the Realm*. Perhaps to sidestep the potential trauma of trying to untangle spelling defence (the UK way) versus defense (the US way). What an Anglo-American mess.

†But Oxford (nor, indeed, anyone else) do not use -ize if the word is not traced to the Greek -izo suffix – which is why we have, for example, analyse, prise and chastise.

exchange in their letters page between a reader and Richard Dixon, the then Chief Revise* Editor:

> I recently picked up the London *Times* and noticed the unexpected spelling of certain verbs. The *Oxford English Dictionary* spells words such as 'colonize' and 'modernize' with a 'z', yet *The Times* spells those words 'colonise' and 'modernise'. When did *The Times* convert these spellings, and why?

> In the great -ize versus -ise debate, *The Times* has opted latterly for simplicity over a sort of erudition . . . The rule at the newspaper was that any verb said by the etymological experts to derive from Ancient Greek and with a zeta in the suffix got the -ize treatment in English. But in the *Style Guide* of 1992, the following entry appeared: '-ise, -isation: avoid the z construction in almost all cases. This is volcanic ground, with common usage straining the crust of classical etymology. This guidance is a revision of the Greek zeta root ending in the direction of a Latin ending and common usage: apologise, organise, emphasise, televise, circumcise. The only truly awkward result is capsize, which should be left in its Grecian peace.'

'Volcanic' is an excellent description of the -ise/-ize debate. Unstable shifting ground that is liable to explode underneath you at any moment.

---

*The etymology of 'revise' is Latin and French, which is why he was not known as the Chief Revize Editor.

Enter the king

In 1906 H. W. and F. G. Fowler wrote in their book *The King's English*: 'The English and the American language and literature are both good things; but they are better apart than mixed.' In 1997, Kingsley Amis wrote his own version of *The King's English*, the index of which has the following sub-entries under 'American English': accent; accentuation; 'alternate world'; '-athon'; 'bath'; 'billion'; 'convince'; dangling participles; 'elevator'; Germanisms; 'gorged-snake' construction*; 'kids'; letter-writing; 'penultimate'; pronunciation; 'shall' and 'will'; 'should' and 'would'; 'show me a good loser'; 'specialty'; spellings, and subjunctive; 'suckling pig'†; 'too'; vowels (long or short).

I hope the extent of this sub-entry demonstrates the breadth and depth of uncommon ground that it's possible to find between US and UK English – or at least the breadth and depth of uncommon ground it was possible for Amis to find.

This brings us to the anglicising of text, which many publishers did until fairly recently, by resetting American editions before they were published here. Before the world became much more interconnected, British publishers felt that their readers would need their texts anglicising, so that

---

*This brilliant description is of what Amis calls the 'American name for a journalistic trick' of coupling together disparate facts while writing a story. His made-up example begins: 'Briton Chris Mankiewitz, twenty-six, has been named to lead England's soccer squad against Ruritania next month. The Warsaw-born father-of-two said at his recently-rebuilt £150,000 Deptford home, "My attractive blonde wife, Samantha, twenty-four, and I are just over the moon with the news."'

†According to Amis the 'ordinary name for a piglet not yet weaned' is a sucking pig. He suggests that the alternative of suckling pig is an Americanism, 'perhaps an ancient one . . . The gain in tastefulness from sucking to suckling may seem small, but every little helps, as the old lady said when she made water into the sea.'

they wouldn't have to deal with potentially unfamiliar vocabulary. Would British readers be able to cope with drugstores, pacifiers, cookies, apartments and vacations? What about diapers, freeways, zip codes and railroads? Anglicising text is fraught with difficulties, however – is it really right to change Americanisms to Britishisms if the author is American, and has chosen those *exact* words? Can you really substitute one word for another without altering its meaning or impact? You can go too far with this sort of thing.

Anglicising text takes time and costs money, and while in the past many publishers would seek to anglicise everything they published by resetting the text for their own edition, it is very rare nowadays. All readers are much more exposed to variants of the words they are commonly used to – the internet and globalisation mean that we are increasingly less bemused by American (and other foreign) vocabulary.

Driller thriller

In 1947, George Orwell wrote *Nineteen Eighty-Four*.* According to University College London, which houses his manuscript notebooks, diaries, letters and photographs,

---

*My favourite Orwell novel is *Keep the Aspidistra Flying*. *Aspidistra* has one of the best-ever descriptions of a hangover in literature, in Gordon Comstock's awakening in a police cell after a night of debauchery: 'Gordon emerged from some long, sickly dream to the consciousness that the books in the lending library were the wrong way up . . . Apart from the minor pains that stabbed him every time he moved, there was a large, dull sort of pain which was not localised but which seemed to hover all over him.' The second-best is Kingsley Amis's description of Jim Dixon's hangover in *Lucky Jim*: 'His mouth has been used as a latrine by some small creature of the night, and then as its mausoleum. During the night, too, he'd somehow been on a cross-country run and then been expertly beaten up by secret police. He felt bad.' The economy of that 'He felt bad' at the end is a perfect example of how words get good.

Orwell kept 'very few personal papers and even fewer manuscripts' (in fact, the only manuscript of his that survives in any form at all is less than half of *Nineteen Eighty-Four*). When in 1984 Secker & Warburg published *Nineteen Eighty-Four: The Facsimile of the Extant Manuscript*, they were only able to reproduce just over 40 per cent of the manuscript of Orwell's final novel. I know this because I have been trying to track down a copy of it to see if I could trace the history of a particularly infamous typo that is spoken about in hushed tones by those in my line of work. As copies of the *Facsimile* currently sell for roughly £100 a time, that purchase will have to wait until this book becomes a bestseller.

The typo we are interested in comes very near the end of the book, as Winston Smith sits in the Chestnut Tree Café at 'the lonely hour of fifteen'.* The chapter progresses in Orwell's usual style – every word doubleplusgood, every word exactly as it should be, and where it should be. Until you come to the following passage: 'A shrill trumpet-call had pierced the air. It was the bulletin! Victory! It always meant victory when the trumpet call preceded the news. A sort of electric drill ran through the café. Even the waiters had started and pricked up their ears.'

There are four different editions of *Nineteen Eighty-Four* on my shelves but none of them retains this doubleplusungood typo. I know that every time I come across it I commit facecrime; of course, Winston Smith's job in *Nineteen Eighty-Four* was to spend his days rectifying and rewriting malprints and misquotes from *The Times*, to ensure that events always appeared to accord with Big Brother and the Party, but I am sad that this typo has been rewrite fullwise upsub antefiled by a diligent pair of editing eyes at some point over the years.

---

*Such good words – who hasn't known the lonely hour of fifteen?

Errata, corrigenda and addenda

'We can both pity and make fun of the person responsible for the error knowing full well how they will feel when they spot the mistake,' writes Martin Toseland in his introduction to *A Steroid Hit the Earth.** It's even worse than that in my experience, because when you work in publishing it's not usually *you* who spots the mistake (I mean, it's my job to spot it, but if I'd spotted it, I'd have done something about it, that's sort of the point of what I do), but invariably the commissioning editor, author, colleague, reviewer, kind-hearted friend, vocal internet blogger or outraged member of the public. As most people who work with me know, I have a superstitious inability to look at the advances of any book I have worked on when they are given to me. Instead, I leave them to marinate under a pile of paper on my desk for a week or so, and after that time if no one has approached to point something out, I might allow myself to look at them.

You can't work in publishing for as long as I have without coming across some errors-of-note, and some of them have been signed off by me.

So, what do you do if the worst happens and, despite deploying copy-editors and typo hunters, mistakes have slipped through? One of the earliest examples of corrected errata – an attempt to make a bad word good – is found in what is known as the 'Judas Bible', from 1613. In Matthew 26:36 a tiny slip of paper saying 'Jesus' has been pasted into a line. Underneath, you can see the edge of another 'J', which the paper was intended to cover up. The original printing had Judas, not Jesus, saying, 'Sit ye here, while I go and pray yonder.'

Some mistakes in the King James Bible are so infamous

---

*Other gems in his collection include 'He leaned his head against her hair. A wasp strayed across his face. He kissed it' (from Alison Bold, *Moments to Cherish*).

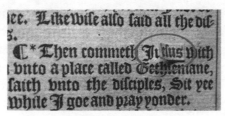

The Judas Bible

that copies are now known by the name of their errors. A well-known one is the 'Wicked Bible', where an omission of a 'not' from the Ten Commandments means that readers are instructed to commit adultery. Other variations include the 'Vinegar Bible', which features 'The parable of the vinegar' (instead of 'The parable of the vineyard'), and my personal favourite, the 'Printers' Bible', which states that 'Printers have persecuted me without a cause . . .', rather than the correct 'Princes' doing the persecuting.

An errata slip (they are also known as corrigenda; there is nothing like dressing up your failings in fancy Latin terms to make you feel just a tiny bit better) traditionally listed the errors and their corrections on a piece of paper for insertion into the book. According to *The Chicago Manual of Style*:

> An errata sheet is definitely not a usual part of a book. It should never be supplied to correct simple typographical errors (which may be rectified in a later printing) or to insert additions to, or revisions of, the printed text (which should wait for the next edition of the book). It is a device to be used only in extreme cases where errors severe enough to cause misunderstanding are detected too late to correct in the normal way but before the finished book is distributed.

The 1922 edition of James Joyce's *Ulysses* had an eight-page errata slip. Nicholas Blincoe in the *Telegraph* quotes a book dealer who claimed that the first edition was 'compiled by seven typists, all in various states of drunkenness and decrepitude, working alongside a blind author'.* As if things were not tangled enough, some of Joyce's 'errors' were deliberate, and were wrongly 'corrected' by printers or editors. Leopold Bloom (the novel's protagonist) sees his name misprinted in a newspaper as 'L. Boom'; the French edition (un)helpfully amended this. A copy of *Ulysses* with the errata slip is worth five times more than one without.

It's not often that you find errata slips in books nowadays. Publishers' first print runs are generally smaller than in the past, so it may be just as economical to pulp the entire print run and reprint the corrected book as to issue an errata slip. But these pieces of paper from the past are an echo of the 'connection' that Adam Smyth, an academic who specialises in the instability of modern texts, talks about – a connection with the production of a book and the thought processes of its author. See this passive-aggressive example of an errata slip highlighted by the book historian Dennis Duncan on Twitter, from a 1904 book by Mary Petherbridge called *The Technique of Indexing*. The text that the errata slip applies to reads: 'This research work necessitates the possession of one or two good reference books and possibly a visit to the British Museum, where every author's name will be found entered correctly in the catalogue.' The errata slip reads: 'ERRATUM: Page 25, line 3, "Where every author's name", *should read* "Where nearly every author's name". Ouch.

---

*James Joyce wore an eyepatch because of vision issues that meant he did much of his writing on large sheets of paper, in red crayon. Recently one of my proofreaders spotted in a book we were working on that we had the eyepatch over his right eye when it was generally worn over his left. The same proofreader also pointed out we described a character in a book as 'soap-eating' rather than the more usual 'soup-eating'.

'All history was a palimpsest'

In *Nineteen Eighty-Four* Winston Smith describes how in the one-party state of Big Brother 'All history was a palimpsest, scraped clean and reinscribed exactly as often as was necessary . . . Books, also, were recalled and rewritten again and again, and were invariably reissued without any admissions that any alteration had been made.'

The internet age has led to two competing views about errors. The first is that the ability to correct and edit in real time on the internet and in ebooks means that typos and other errors can be easily erased from history, 'scraped clean' as often as needed until only the correct version remains. The contrary view is that erroneous information and errors posted online are impossible to erase – unlike print editions of books, which can ultimately be destroyed. Craig Silverman, author of *Regret the Error: How Media Mistakes Pollute the Press and Imperil Free Speech*, argues that 'Corrections only work if they are easily accessible and written in a way that clearly communicates both the error and the correct information. In the online world, a correction must also exist within the context of the offending article.' This context is of course what was missing from Winston Smith's job at the Ministry, where errors are erased from history with no acknowledgement of what went before.

To error is human

In 1644 John Milton published *Areopagitica*, in which he opposed licensing and censorship. Milton argued that it was the right of every person to read through a book themselves to determine its quality, rather than have another person decide it for him. This even applied to books that were banned or considered heretical, since we can learn from books we disagree with. Each person is born with their own

free will and conscience, Milton believed, and should therefore decide for themselves what words have value – not be
dictated to by a licensing authority. In the early days of printing, mistakes were not just tolerated, they were expected,
and provided a means of discourse and conversation between
texts and their readers. As Adrienne LaFrance remarks in
'A Corrected History of the Typo':

> print's long history is riddled with errors and strike-
> throughs and rewrites – a fact worth celebrating and in
> some ways emulating, actually. In the earliest days of the
> book, writers and readers gathered around mistakes as a
> means of discourse about the work. When books were
> new, people saw them as fluid, changeable. Mistakes
> weren't as much lamented as they were expected, and
> people scrawled corrections over the text itself, in the
> margins, and on errata lists slipped between pages.

I love the idea that the arbiter of the quality of the text is
ultimately the reader, and that mistakes were a way to generate conversation, air differences of opinion and communicate
strongly held views. Nowadays, we generally assume that if
something is in print it is *correct*. The process of printing
itself lends an authority to each word, fact or argument on
the page. If it has made it into print, we feel, it must be right.
In her article, LaFrance discusses errors in early modern
texts with Adam Smyth. Smyth points out that in the early
days printing of texts led to the 'dissemination of blunders',
and that errors were 'not hidden away', as they often are
now. He argues that errors remind us of the 'connection
between the book going wrong, momentarily, and a sense of
the process of production being briefly revealed, or implied'.
This, I think, is why people like to hear about these mistakes
– they give us a very brief glimpse of the hard work behind

the scenes involved in publishing anything, and they allow us occasionally to see the very human fallibility of all involved. Not to mention giving us a laugh, and who doesn't enjoy that?

As Adam Smyth says: 'We might think of error not as a bug to be killed off, but as an inevitable presence; and not, perhaps, even as something always regrettable, but as an aspect of writing, printing, and of life, that is always there.'

So, if there are errors in this book (there will be), then sit back and enjoy them. Vent your ire in the margins. Laugh. Smugly whip out a blue pen to mark them up. Send me a strongly worded email. Revel in my fallibility. It's what Milton would have wanted.

Answers to quiz on p. 152

'Tom-All-Alone's Factory That Got into Chancery and Never Got Out' (*Bleak House*)

'All's Well That Ends Well' (*War and Peace*)

'The Un-Dead' (*Dracula*)

'From a Sense of Duty' (*Where Angels Fear to Tread*)

'The Mute' (*The Heart is a Lonely Hunter*)

'Blanche's Chair in the Moon' (*A Streetcar Named Desire*)

'The Last Man in Europe' (*Nineteen Eighty-Four*)

'Llareggub' (*Under Milk Wood*)

'What's That Noshin' on My Leg?' (*Jaws* – apparently this was a tongue-in-cheek suggestion from the author's father; other contenders were 'A Silence in the Water' and 'Leviathan Rising'.)

'Forks' (*Twilight* – congratulations if you knew this one: Forks, Washington, is the setting for *Twilight* and is the rainiest town in the USA.)

FOOT-AND-NOTE DISEASE:* FOOTNOTES

'Having to read footnotes resembles having to go downstairs to answer the door while in the midst of making love,' observed Noël Coward,[†] but come *on*. It's worth a trip down the stairs. I *love* footnotes. Answering the door to find a footnote on the doorstep would be a joy and I would invite it to come right in and entertain me. Funny, arch, passive-aggressive, enlightening, diverting, interest-piquing, footnotes are among the most playful and exuberant things you can find in a text. More than that, if used imaginatively, a footnote can be as moving or as touching as anything else in a book.

Fussnotenwissenschaft[‡]

The invention of the footnote is usually credited to Richard Jugge, who became the Royal Printer for Elizabeth I.[§] At a

---

*'Foot-and-note disease' was a phrase conjured up by John Betjeman, who used it to disparage writers of legal and academic texts who, in his view, made use of extensive footnotes to get round word-count limits. I don't see the problem.

†When asked why there was a diaeresis (those little dots over the 'e' in his name), Coward remarked, 'I didn't put the dots over the "e" in Noël. The language did. Otherwise it's not Noël but Nool!' Where else in a text can you include this sort of fun aside, if not in a footnote, Noël?

‡This handy German word literally means 'footnote science'. Which makes me in this chapter a footnote scientist.

§Sadly, Jugge was not a very satisfactory royal printer and proved to be intolerably slow in producing versions of the Bible for the Church and government. After a 'long hearing and debating of grievances' he was

time when the margins of Bible printings were littered with notes pointing readers to obscure doctrines or having a dig at the pope or indicating misrepresentations by other analysts of religion, Jugge had the foresight to use the bottom of the page to array these annotations in neat lines as the first footnotes. By 1729, when Alexander Pope published *The Dunciad Variorum*, footnotes were no longer being used only to give the reader straightforward, helpful additional information, but had become a way for a writer to mock an entire profession.* Despite that mockery, half a century later Edward Gibbon's six-volume *History of the Decline and Fall of the Roman Empire* featured an estimated 8,000 footnotes in 1.5 million words of text.† While reading about *Decline and Fall* I kept coming across this phrase: 'Gibbon has often been said to have lived his sex life in his footnotes.'‡ Most footnote scientists (there are more than you would think) agree that the longest footnote in history was by the Reverend John Hodgson in his *History of Northumberland*, written in 1840. It runs to 264 pages, which does make you wonder if it wasn't

---

apparently ordered to limit himself to the quarto Bible and the New Testament in sextodecimo. A quarto page was roughly the same size as our A4, and a sextodecimo was a quarter of that.

*There isn't the space here to go into *The Dunciad*'s footnotes in detail (and neither is there the will on my part; it's probably the most off-putting thing I've ever tried to read). Pope starts as he means to go on by giving the title a footnote. John Mullan writes in the *Guardian* that 'the verse is encrusted with Pope's own prefaces and notes and appendices – an apparatus of mock-learning that mimics the pretensions of would-be scholars and critics'.

†'Due to its large file size, this book **may** take longer to download,' says the Amazon information for the ebook version.

‡I have read none of *Decline and Fall*, footnotes or otherwise, but it's interesting that this quote (usually attributed to the historian Philip Guedalla) and the Noël Coward one both associate footnotes with sex. Who knew they could arouse such passion?

actually meant to be a footnote. Perhaps the Victorian type-setters had enjoyed a long liquid lunch and accidentally set it as such.

Even when footnotes go on a bit I find them a delight. The back-cover blurb for Paul Auster's *Hand to Mouth* describes the book as ending with 'three of the longest footnotes in literary history: a card game, a thriller about baseball, and three short plays. *Hand to Mouth* is essential reading for anyone interested in Paul Auster, in the figure of the strug-gling artist, in the nature of poverty, or in baseball.' This is clearly next-level footnoting ('give a footnote an inch and it'll take a foot'[*]) and I admire the chutzpah of an author who decides to Trojan-horse a thriller about baseball into their own autobiography by way of a footnote.

Footnotes can be used in a variety of ways – to insert a digres-sion or qualification which may be too distracting to the reader if included in the main text; to provide citations or attributions to support claims in books (often academic ones) that feel the need for them; or as an aside[†] or additional sign-post to the reader, which allows the author to break the fourth wall. In non-fiction the use of footnotes is routine (actually, as I hope you'll learn from reading this chapter, in academic works it tends to be *endnotes* that are used), but

---

[*]Frank Sullivan, apparently.

[†]How about this for a footnoted aside? 'This is the only reference in the canon to Holmes's eyebrows' (Leslie S. Klinger, ed., *The New Annotated Sherlock Holmes*). Incidentally, Klinger's book on the Sherlockian universe is almost 2,000 pages long and weighs 10lb; it also reports on the work of fellow Sherlock obsessive Roger T. Clapp, whose study of Victorian rail timetables leads him to conclude that in the entire corpus of Sherlock writings only one train connection was correct. You see, as this isn't a book about Sherlock Holmes I wouldn't be able to bring this to your attention without a footnote.

footnotes can also be employed inventively in fiction. Talking about his novel *An Abundance of Katherines*, author John Green comments on the footnotes he deploys in the text: 'They can allow you to create a secret second narrative, which is important if, say, you're writing a book about what a story is and whether stories are significant.'

And this is, I think, what I relish about footnotes in fiction – that they can add a second, hidden-but-seen story to the text. Terry Pratchett's *Discworld* novels are beloved for many reasons, and one is their parallel universe of footnotes (there are entire Reddit threads devoted to the question of people's favourite Pratchett footnotes). While writing *Good Omens*, Pratchett and Neil Gaiman often footnoted each other's sections, allowing them to have a backwards-and-forwards discourse about their writing, and then to share it with the reader. J. G. Ballard's story 'Notes Towards a Mental Breakdown' consists of a single sentence,* with each word having an elaborate footnote that tells the story. 'Each plot-thickening annotation blurs the author–subject divide, so that the structural breakdown reflects the mental one.'†

When footnotes . . . aren't footnotes

I've had so many conversations with authors about footnotes, when what they actually mean are *endnotes*. It's puzzling that this leads to so much confusion – the clue is in the name – but it happens often. Footnotes go at the foot of the page, and endnotes . . . well, they go at the end of the book, or sometimes at the end of each chapter. This

---

*The sentence: 'A discharged Broadmoor patient compiles "Notes Towards a Mental Breakdown", recalling his wife's murder, his trial and exoneration.'

†Ed Park, 'On his Distinctive Returns', *Los Angeles Times*, 11 October 2009.

confusion is not confined to the authors I have worked with. Vladimir Nabokov's *Pale Fire* and David Foster Wallace's *Infinite Jest** are often cited as examples of heavily footnoted texts, but in fact both make extensive use of endnotes. In his blog 'On the Fine Art of the Footnote' Jonathan Russell Clark explains that *Pale Fire* 'consists of a Forward† written by the fictional Charles Kinbote, a 999-line poem called "Pale Fire" written by the fictional John Shade and then a section called Commentary also written by Kinbote, who we soon come to realize is a lunatic who believes himself to be the King of a country called Zembla.'

Nabokov's use of endnotes forces the reader to move back and forth between Shade's poetry and Kinbote's commentary, giving the reader of this fictional work the experience of a referenced academic read. It transpired, however, that in *Pale Fire* Nabokov was just warming up in the matter of notes and annotations. Two years later, in 1964, he published a translation of Alexander Pushkin's poem *Eugene Onegin* – 'Apparently unhampered by his publishers in the matter of space,' the *New York Times* commented tartly in their review. Nabokov certainly was unhampered – his version of *Eugene Onegin* was printed over four volumes and 2,000 pages – but only 228 of those pages featured the actual poem. The rest were taken up with annotation, commentary, notes, variant versions of

---

*In *Infinite Jest*, David Foster Wallace deploys more than four hundred *endnotes*. Not only that, he pretty much forces the reader to engage with them by making one of them (note 324) an entire chapter of the book. It runs for seven pages of tiny, set-down footnote text. 'Set-down' means that the text would be roughly the same size as this text. For seven pages. Urgh. As well as nudging the reader to engage with the endnotes, this technique also means that readers of *Infinite Jest* have to use two bookmarks.

†This should of course be a 'Foreword'; the error is Clark's, not Nabokov's. Thank God for footnotes – where else could I point this out?

the poem and two appendices. 'In art as in science,' observes Nabokov in his commentary, 'there is no delight without the detail, and it is on detail that I have tried to fix the reader's attention.' At the outset of his translation he wrote to his collaborator and friend Edmund Wilson that the work 'could be quite smoothly combined with other pleasures'. After a year of working on it he wrote again to Wilson: 'I was . . . on the verge of a breakdown, and not fit for company.'*

In 1970 *The Annotated Lolita*† was published with a commentary by Alfred Appel Jr. Described in a *New York Times* article on footnotes as a 'worshipful Nabokovian', Appel, the *NYT* continued, 'plods through the text, explaining what, in most cases, needs no explanation. Unwittingly he does an uncanny impression of Charles Kinbote, the mad annotator whose scholarly notes take over the narrative poem in Nabokov's *Pale Fire*, like a parasite consuming its host.' You feel that Nabokov would have approved.

The death dagger approaches

There are various ways of signalling a footnote to a reader. Straightforward sequential superscript‡ numbering can be

---

*Although Nabokov's *Onegin* was published in 1964, he continued revising it until well into the 1970s, partly in response to a damning review by Wilson in the *New York Review of Books*.

†*Lolita* was originally published in 1955 in an edition 'swarming with typographical errors', according to Brian Boyd in *Vladimir Nabokov: The American Years*. It was the book that made Nabokov's name, although as he subsequently noted, it was also perhaps the reason that the name 'Lolita' fell out of fashion: 'I am probably responsible for the odd fact that people don't seem to name their daughters Lolita any more. I have heard of young female poodles being given that name since 1956, but of no human beings,' he said.

‡When you use a note indicator in your text it should be placed in the 'superscript' position in the line. That means that the number or symbol

used, sometimes within a bracket. But who would want to use 'straightforward superscript sequential numbering' when instead you could use these beauties?

$$* \dagger \ddagger \S \| \P$$

In my opinion these are some of the most charming and graceful ornaments you'll find on a page. Don't they make you want to add footnotes whenever and wherever possible? Let's find out more about them.

* The little star

The paleoarchaeologist Genevieve von Petzinger spent five years compiling a database of geometric signs at 370 rock sites across Europe. What she discovered was that over 30,000 years and the whole of Europe, just thirty-two signs appeared again and again. Pretty incredible when you consider how isolated by distance and time the people sharing this diction-ary of symbols would have been from each other. One of those thirty-two was the asterisk, the 'little star'.

We know that Aristarchus of Samothrace* was the librar-ian at the Library of Alexandria two thousand years ago. As well as spending his days looking after the 400,000 papyrus scrolls stored there, he also found time to edit the work of Homer, and in doing so resorted to a symbol called the *asteriskos* (⁂) which he used to mark lines that had been dupli-cated. Aristarchus was clearly a freelance copy-editor and proofreader who took his craft seriously, as he also invented

---

will appear above the baseline (the invisible line that each letter sits on) in your line of text.

*According to Wikipedia, Aristarchus 'had a remarkable memory and was completely indifferent to his own appearance'.

symbols to show where lines were in the wrong place (the 'dotted lunate sigma': Ꞇ), and various other notations based on the lunar symbol to show where something had gone wrong in a manuscript. That the word 'aristarch' is now used to signify that someone is a judgemental critic suggests that he may perhaps have wielded his symbols a little too liberally.

† The dagger

While Aristarchus of Samothrace was a deployer of what became the first footnote symbol, his predecessor at the Library of Alexandria, confusingly, is associated with the second footnote symbol, the dagger. The dagger is a variation of a symbol called the obelisk,* and was invented by Zenodotus. Zenodotus is noted for overseeing the original use of metadata – which in 280 BC meant that the scrolls in his library had tags attached to the bottom edge listing author, title and subject, so that readers wouldn't have to unroll the whole thing to find out what it was. As we'll see a bit later in this chapter, footnotes and endnotes are the ancestors of modern-day hypertext links, which probably wouldn't surprise Zenodotus at all.

The obelisk symbol represented (among other things) a roasting spit, or the end of a javelin – a literal drawing of something used to 'dig out' or 'cut out' unwanted text. St Jerome neatly summed up the differences between an asterisk and a dagger: 'an asterisk makes a light shine, the obelisk cuts and pierces'. I love this way of thinking about these symbols: the asterisk illuminating what needs to be highlighted, while the obelisk literally digs out errors in our words. I hope my copy-editor refrains from using an obelisk to cut and pierce too much of my text. It could be even worse, though. The

---

*The obelisk symbol began as a -, then evolved into ÷, before settling on its current dagger-shaped form of † or ‡.

dagger is sometimes referred to as the 'death dagger', as it was often used before or after a person's dates, to indicate that they were . . . well, dead.

‡ The double dagger

As if a single dagger by your name wasn't alarming enough, you could find yourself even more dead, denoted by a double dagger next to your name. The third footnote symbol obviously has much in common with the straightforward dagger, although it's worth noting that it can also be used in chess notation to indicate checkmate. Wherever it appears (unless being used as a footnote symbol) the dagger, and especially the double dagger, are generally bad news.

§|¶ The section sign, the pipe and the pilcrow

The Pipe and Pilcrow might make a good name for a pub frequented by typographers and typesetters, but I've grouped these three symbols together, because after the asterisk, dagger and double dagger there is much less consensus about the order in which the footnote symbols should be used, or indeed about what the symbols should be. Naturally, the further down the list a symbol is the less likely you are to see it – so the section sign,* pipe† and pilcrow‡ are much rarer beasts than the asterisk and daggers. This unfairness is made even worse by organisations like the UN, whose editorial

---

*The section sign is made up of two 'S' glyphs, probably from the Latin *signum sectionis* – 'section cut-off'. In *The Good Soldier Švejk* by Jaroslav Hašek it is used to mean bureaucracy.

†The pipe is a type of *caesurus*, which means 'cutting', and was originally used to signify a pause or break in the text.

‡Pilcrow comes from the Greek word *paragraphos*. It morphed through *paragraphe, pelagraphe, pylcrafte* and then pilcrow.

team state in their 'Editorial Manual Online' that the order of indicators used in their official documents is: *, **, ***, ****, †, ‡, §. They are obviously *big* fans of the asterisk, even if its overuse might at first glance make it look as if they are busy blanking out swear words in their texts.

'Amusement, charm, a chance to rest'*

The footnote began life as a way for people with different religious viewpoints to fight out their opinions on the same page – a way for the feisty words to pick up their daggers and duel it out with each other. Perhaps that's why the precise, sharp dagger shape works so well to highlight these types of disagreements. Footnotes pierced right to the very heart of a matter; scoring a direct hit on your opponent supported by your argumentative little dagger would have been extremely satisfying. But gradually, the footnote grew up, stopped picking quite so many fights, and over time became a respected symbol of academic thoroughness.

In his book *The Footnote*, Anthony Grafton says that 'the text persuades, the note proves'. As he explains, the job of the footnote is to 'convince the reader that the historian has done an acceptable amount of work'.† As well as Grafton, the other

---

*Chuck Zerby, *The Devil's Details*, p. 5. I put this footnote in to demonstrate a footnote that really should, in my view, be an endnote. I'm sorry to disappoint the reader with this useful, but not exactly interesting, source note. I'm hoping that all the other footnotes in this chapter will be amusing or charming or a chance for the reader to rest.

†Grafton certainly displays his own industrious work rate to the reader: in his 244-page book, there are 423 footnotes. That's 1.73 footnotes per page. Nearly all his footnotes are used to indicate sources – which, to my mind, means that they should actually be endnotes, and gathered neatly in one section in the end matter of the book, not lying about all over the place for the reader to trip over.

professor of *Fussnotenwissenschaft* I consulted was Chuck Zerby, who wrote *The Devil's Details: A History of Footnotes*. Like *The Footnote*, *The Devil's Details* has many, many footnotes. However, Zerby has gone one better than Grafton and really mixed things up – he employs two types of footnote system simultaneously on the page. He uses the *symbols* to indicate notes that consist of an aside, or a development or elaboration of the main text. But he also uses *numbers* to indicate his sources. So nearly every page is speckled with a proliferation of tiny symbols and numbers. It would look far more welcoming for the reader if the numbered 'source' footnotes had been tidied away neatly in the end matter, allowing his (very funny and informative) 'aside' footnotes to shine on the page. As Zerby says, 'the main job of the footnote is to interrupt. Simply interrupt' – which does make me question why he has chosen to treat his source notes as footnotes as well. I don't mind being interrupted on the page (or indeed in real life) by some amusement and charm, but I do mind being stopped in my tracks while I'm skipping across the page by something as pedestrian as a source. Much better to turn to the back of the book for those at a time of my own convenience. Or never.

Zerby describes how the footnote 'lets us hear the missteps of biases,* and hear pathos, subtle decisions, scandals and anger' – which is why these small textual asides carry so much heft. Footnotes add much to our understanding of what a writer is trying to do – they require tact, skill and timing, but when it pays off, it really pays off.

---

*Speaking of bias, the following footnote makes mine and many others' top ten footnote lists: 'It becomes wearisome to add "except the Italians" to every generalisation. Henceforth it may be assumed.' A. J. P. Taylor, *The Struggle for Mastery in Europe, 1848–1918*. The line in the main text to which this footnote was originally attached read: 'All diplomatists were honest, according to their moral code.'

In 2000 Martin Amis published *Experience*, a memoir of his life.* He explains early on how he uses footnotes in the book: 'to preserve the collateral thought', a way of showing 'the novelist's addiction to seeing parallels and making connections'. The footnotes are some of the most entertaining,[†] interesting and moving elements of *Experience*.

In *Experience* Amis writes about the moving and difficult story of his cousin Lucy Partington, who disappeared in 1973 and whose remains were only discovered in 1994 during the excavation of Fred and Rose West's house in Gloucester.[‡] Zerby notes that while Amis writes about Lucy in the main text of *Experience* (and briefly notes that she was killed by Fred West) he then relegates West to the footnotes. West is only allowed back into the main text once more in a chapter that begins with his suicide in January 1995 – '(And in death, as it were, he drifts up from the footnotes and into the text.)' – and in this way, Amis manages elegantly to separate his cousin from her killer, allowing her to be freed at last from having her name always bracketed with his.

In praise of the endnote

I've been a bit unfair on the endnote, I know. Unlike its close friend the footnote it has no glamorous signs or symbols to charm the reader, and, as I hope I have made clear, endnotes

---

*Amis has published many other books, including *Dead Babies* (1975), a book title that was so challenging that for the paperback edition it was changed to *Dark Secrets*, although it seems to have reverted to the original title in recent printings.

†Take this example, from p. 49 of *Experience*: 'In my house, back in South Wales, you could have a cigarette on Christmas Day at the age of five.'

‡Fred West (1941–95) was a serial killer who committed at least twelve murders between 1967 and 1987. The majority of those murders were carried out in conjunction with his wife, Rosemary.

should be reserved for purely functional matters: sources and credits. If footnotes are sometimes irritatingly distracting and show-offy, the endnote is a trusty, solid workaday hero. If you can trust an endnote, then you can trust an author, and a book. The footnote shows an author's creativity, while an endnote reveals the sources used and confirms that the research has been properly done. 'The footnote's power comes from its disruptive nature,'* whereas an endnote's power comes from the way it backs up the veracity of a text, visible but discreet, like a Romanesque buttress.

Notes from the future

The joy of the footnote for me is that, when I see one indicated, I think 'Ooohh! Further elaboration right here, at the bottom of the page.' All I need do is glance down, and then (when they work at their best) be amused, charmed or moved. But increasingly we don't read words on a page – instead, we read them on an e-reader, or a tablet, or a screen. When you read text digitally, you can click into, or hover over, note indicators, and then be instantly taken to the note in question. But to me it abruptly divorces the note from its 'home' text – which is a shame, since footnotes in particular should be there to enhance the page they are on. Cut off from their place on the physical page, endnotes and footnotes are now free to roam round hyperspace – but do we still feel the same about them?

Increasingly, authors are encouraged to put their footnotes and endnotes not on the pages of their books, but

---

*This is from www.barnesandnoble.com/blog/consider-the-footnote-why-dont-more-authors-use-the-most-powerful-tool-in-fiction/. It should be an endnote, of course, but we're not having them in this book, so I'll leave it here for you.

online. In 2011 in an article in the *New York Times* about the future of footnotes in a digital age,* Alexandra Horowitz neatly summed up the problem: 'Footnotes really presage hyperlinks, the ultimate interrupter of a stream of thought. (But footnotes are far superior: while hyperlinks can be highly useful, one never finds oneself looking at an error message at the bottom of the page where a footnote used to be.)'[†]

Zerby's issue with notes in hyperspace is that moving notes from physical to digital space removes the 'dramatic possibility' of a well-judged footnote. He illustrates this point beautifully with an example written by the explorer Ernest Shackleton. Shackleton's account of his journey to the South Pole between 1907 and 1909 has, says Zerby 'almost no notes'. The page bottoms are 'almost as feature-less as ice fields to the unobservant'. As the text advances across the page and the explorers across the ice, Shackleton describes the men gathering up samples of rotifers,[‡] which were somehow able to survive the harsh climate, to take home and examine.

In transit to Australia, the rotifers were exposed to much warmer temperatures and all were found to be dead upon

---

*www.nytimes.com/2011/10/09/books/review/will-the-e-book-kill-the-footnote.html?_r=2&ref=books&pagewanted=all. Well, who knows if this hyperlink will still be around when you try to follow it?

†Adds Horowitz: 'Even the audio book has solved the problem of how to convey footnotes. Listen to David Foster Wallace reading his essay collection "Consider the Lobster," with its ubiquitous show-stealing asides: at a certain point, his voice is unnaturally distant, the result of a production trick intended to represent the small type of a footnote.' I love this.

‡Tiny animals nightmarishly described in 1696 by the Reverend John Harris as 'an animal like a large maggot which could contract itself into a spherical figure and then stretch itself out again; the end of its tail appeared with a forceps like that of an earwig'. Apparently they are microscopic (which makes things a little less alarming), although Harris's description omits to mention this.

arrival in Sydney. 'A sad business,' as Zerby says. He then describes how 'one of the text's rare asterisks is encountered; its [Shackleton's] note informs us: "Since this was written, examination of the rotifers in London . . . has shown that they are still living . . ."' As Zerby points out, the 'brief moment' the reader has between reading of the death of the rotifers and then, miraculously, the news that some have survived, 'allows us to experience the disappointment of Shackleton's crew and then their elation, an experience we would have missed had the text simply been corrected'.

Here the footnote's unique ability to disrupt is harnessed to create. Bringing to life a quantum of the contrasting emotions that Shackleton's scientists experienced by bridging the gap between dismay and delight. That's the power of the footnote.

INDEX, MISSOURI*: INDEXES

My colleague Richard loves indexes. I'm certain he would rather read an index than a book. What makes a good index? I once asked him. What elevates it above the norm? 'Any index,' he replied, 'that elevates "it" above the "norm" is at least in alphabetical order.'

Undeterred by this welcome outbreak of indexing humour, I asked him what his favourite index was. I assumed I'd misheard his answer; he *seemed* to have said 'snicker-snack fateful psychosis'. Further interrogation revealed that what he'd *actually* said was 'snicker-snack, fateful, of psychosis'.†

As most people would be if presented with a string of seemingly unrelated words, I was puzzled. It transpired Richard was referring to an entry in the index to Will Self's collection of essays *Feeding Frenzy*. When I tracked down

---

*There are seven places in the US called 'Index'. Index, Missouri, is a ghost town ('not to be confused with "Index of Missouri-related articles"', according to Wikipedia), and you can find the others in Arkansas, Kentucky, New York, Virginia, Washington and West Virginia.

†Not to be confused with Richard's favourite index *entry*. That is apparently 'Duguid, Richard, xxiii', from a book with an author who wanted to index every named person in the text ('fair enough', according to Richard), those in the acknowledgements ('unusual') and the bibliography ('bizarre'). Although, as Richard explains: 'His thinking is sound. In academic fields, the first thing that anyone does when a new book appears is look in the index for their names. He wanted to keep as many people as possible happy. Even me!'

the *Observer*'s review (it was published in 2001) I found the exact same phrase mentioned in it: 'snicker-snack, fateful, of psychosis'.

'Before reading *Feeding Frenzy*,' said the reviewer, 'it is advisable to consult the index.' According to Self (the review continued), it covers 'people, places and things', but also ideas, obsessions, and my own irritating stylistic tics'. The reviewer then mentioned some of these index entries: 'tongues, locking', 'matching socks and shoes', 'co-ordinated foot- and sock-wear', and finally, 'snicker-snack, fateful, of psychosis'. Well, I thought, I'll order a copy.

'The baby figure of the giant mass'*

WHY DOESN'T MICHELLE OBAMA'S MEMOIR HAVE AN INDEX? BLAME TRUMP ran a *Guardian* headline in November 2018. 'What were her publishers thinking?' wrote Ann Treneman in *The Times*. 'Why in the world wouldn't they want to provide what amounts to a road map for readers?' One reason, according to a quote in the article from Ruth Ellis, executive board member of the Society of Indexers, is the unrelenting speed at which books now have to be published. Indexes are constructed right at the end of the publishing process and increasingly there just isn't time in a squeezed schedule to let an indexer do their work.[†] A thorough index for a non-fiction

---

*This is from *Troilus and Cressida* (c.1602): 'And in such indexes, although small pricks / To their subsequent volumes, there is seen / The baby figure of the giant mass / Of things to come at large.' An even earlier mention can be found in Christopher Marlowe's *Hero and Leander* from 1593: 'Therefore, even as an index to a book / So to his mind was young Leander's look.'

[†]John Sutherland, a one-time president of the Society of Indexers, high-lighted in a 2012 article about Salman Rushdie's memoir *Joseph Anton* that sometimes *authors* may deliberately choose not to have an index.

book can often take four to six weeks to complete, and in many cases even longer.

The 'road map' analogy for an index is also used by Sam Leith (the honorary president of the Society of Indexers), in his charming article in praise of indexes, published on National Indexing Day. Leith quotes Harold Macmillan, who said that a good index is 'much more than a guide to the contents of a book. It can often give a far clearer glimpse of its spirit than the blurb-writers or critics are able to do.' Leith continues: 'The index is, in any non-fiction book, more useful than anything else in the apparatus. It is a map of the text; a cunningly devised series of magical shortcuts.' As Richard says: 'There are lots of good indexes and lots of bad ones, but a good index should give the lie of the land, as it were; and to that extent it is also a marketing tool in the bookshop: I assume a significant number of book-buyers do look at least briefly at an index to help them make a decision.'

Unrolling the Dead Sea Scrolls

Before the index, there was the concordance. A concordance lists every word found in a text (unlike an index, which is a limited *selection* of concepts and themes from the text), and they are so labour-intensive that they have only been done for works of magnitude – the Bible, or Shakespeare's plays, for example. You can see why when you consider that Hugh of Saint-Cher, who compiled the first biblical concordance in

---

'Indexing is as necessary to (non-fiction) books as oxygen is to lungs,' says Sutherland, but by not having an index in his 656-page book, Rushdie forced journalists and reviewers to read every page of *Joseph Anton* to find what they might be looking for, rather than skip straight to the index. Rushdie's approach is presumably to catch out people like Edwina Currie, who was reportedly hurt that she wasn't included in the index of John Major's memoirs.

1230, had to employ five hundred monks to help him produce it. The first concordance to the Hebrew Bible took ten years to assemble – beginning in 1946, after thousands of written fragments were discovered in caves on the shores of the Dead Sea by archaeologists assisted by Bedouin shepherds. The earliest fragment dated from the eighth century BC, and publication and control of the Dead Sea Scrolls, as they were named, quickly became mired in academic controversy, with many scholars arguing that access to them was being denied by a small group. In 1991, Martin Abegg, a Dead Sea Scrolls researcher, was able to use a computer to 'invert' a concordance that had made its way out into the wider academic community in the 1950s. Using this concordance, Abegg was then able to reconstruct (approximately, anyway) some of the documents, which eventually led to the release of the original text of the scrolls. This would be, I suppose, like taking the index of a book and trying to reverse-engineer the entire text from it.

Pointing the way

The word 'index' comes from Latin, and it means 'one who points out'. Sam Leith highlights the index of Douglas Hofstader's 1979 book *Gödel, Escher, Bach*,* which includes entries for 'index: challenges of; as revelatory of a book's nature; as

---

*Gödel, Escher, Bach was one of the first books I ever had to send to print when I started working in publishing. It was (and still is) one of the most baffling books I have come across. The tagline describes it as 'A Metaphorical Fugue on Minds and Machines in the Spirit of Lewis Carroll'; in his 2007 book *I Am a Strange Loop*, Hofstader writes: 'In the end, we are self-perceiving, self-inventing, locked-in mirages that are little miracles of self-reference.' This reminds me of those indexes that under the entry 'infinite loop' send you to the page you are already on, so that you really get the whole infinite loop experience, via an index.

work of art'. That 'work of art' is generally misunderstood – especially in a digital age. Many people believe that indexing a book now is just a case of taking an electronic form of the text, sticking a name or theme into a search function, and attaching the page numbers that get thrown up to the index entry. As the Society of Indexers explains on its website, 'the intellectual task of selecting appropriate terms of index entries, and deciding what is significant information in a text, can only be done by a human indexer'. The Society of Indexers highlights the problems with assuming readers can just use a 'search' function on an ebook, and why an 'index' can't be compiled simply by searching a PDF: indexes are about subjects, not just words. Indexers are able to anticipate how a reader might approach a topic; electronic searches often leave the reader with a huge number of unhelpful 'hits' – which forces the reader to attempt to do the work of sorting out what is really relevant. Or, more likely, they will close the covers, give up and go home.

I asked Richard to explain the key attributes of a good index. 'It's stating the obvious, but still has to be said: usability. That the entries are in alphabetical order and the page numbers are correct. The latter is often the victim of late changes in a book's production process; no excuse, though! An index should be of value to the reader (more than to the author's ego): it needs entries that take you to where the key points are made, that make links with each other, that do not send you somewhere that is not worth going (an entry for something which the author refers to only in passing, i.e. without saying anything about it), and so on.'

'A reduction of a life's experiences'

In *Indexers and Indexes in Fact and Fiction*, Hazel K. Bell*
writes that the indexer of 'soft texts' is 'often dealing with
personal relationships and emotions, with recurrent or continuous themes rather than isolated facts, and has to make
assessments as to the selection of items to index and the
terms in which to express them on the basis of subjective
value judgement. The indexer then becomes the interpreter,
not the reporter, of such texts.' By 'soft texts', Bell means
stories of human lives, rather than, say, academic texts.
'Human lives are generally not lived in accordance with strict
principles, and irregularities in lives that are being indexed
must be met by flexible indexing practice.'

In a 1997 article in the *Indexer* magazine, Bell wrote a
piece on Douglas Matthews, who Richard would always tell
me was the master indexer to whom all others were compared, and one of the few indexers often thanked by authors
in their acknowledgements (as they all surely should be). In
her article Bell quotes Matthews's opinion that 'indexers do
more than compile the index, functioning also as "longstop
copyeditors", or "test drivers", finding unnoticed errors and
inconsistencies in the text'.† As Matthews says of the art of
indexing, 'There can be no shortcutting that basic, dogged,
analytical reading of the whole work and then arranging it
to make the text easy for consultation, which is the essential
function of the indexer.' When Matthews died in 2020, one
of his authors recalled how he had an 'astonishing ability
to keep hundreds of thousands of names and places in his

---

*Bell is a prolific indexer who has worked on more than nine hundred
indexes, as well as being the editor of the *Indexer* magazine from 1978 to
1995.
†This is true; nearly every indexer I commission will politely submit
along with their index a list of typos or errors they have noticed while
combing through the text.

head all at once, like doing a Rubik's cube without the cube'.

In another article in the *Indexer* (this one from 2012), Bell quotes from a letter that Kurt Vonnegut sent to the Society of Indexers in 1978: 'I would have said that you were much like the poets of olden times, fitting thoughts and feelings and impressions and hard facts into orderly, severely limited, preconceived schemes.'

Chapter 55 of Vonnegut's 1963 novel *Cat's Cradle* is titled 'Never Index Your Own Book' (the question of who should compile an index is one we will return to). In the novel, Claire Minton, the wife of the new American ambassador to San Lorenzo is a professional indexer. 'She can read character from an index,' says her husband. 'It's a revealing thing, an author's index of his own work . . . It's a shameless exhibition – to the trained eye,' says Claire. 'Never index your own book.'

The heading of this section comes from a quote by Philip Hensher in a 2004 *Independent* article about indexes, where he summarises the function of an index: 'If a biography is a reduction of a life's experiences to the span of a single volume, then the index is a further reduction, indicating the general characteristics, or recurrent themes, of the bare truth which a book cloaks in prose.' On the importance of a real live indexer over a mechanical process, Hensher echoes the feelings of every reader who has encountered an index that supplements and expands the joy of a good book:

> Indexers, in general, are admirable, scrupulous people who undertake a task demanding great skill and intelligence. To provide an index to a long and perhaps complex work of non-fiction requires them to come to terms with the subject, to understand an unfamiliar argument which may not have been put forward at all competently by the author, and to master the significant points of the debate. It is inconceivable such a task could

be done by mechanical means, and this arduous and demanding work will continue to be done by modest and highly intelligent people for very little money and no public acclaim whatsoever.*

Books that don't have indexes are missing out. As Hensher says: 'Indexes are not just neutral summaries, but occasions for ruthless wit, surreal juxtapositions, and sheer, brutal, revenge. If the index goes beyond a mere list of names mentioned, it often becomes a weird, loaded narrative of its own, with vicious agendas and grotesque jokes.'

In his biography for the article Hensher is described as a 'novelist and index-addict'. In it he discusses his novel *The Fit* (2004), which features as its hero an indexer. Hensher's indexer dreams of writing an '"Index to a History of the World"; an index so beautiful and complete that there would be no reason whatever to write the book itself'. Hensher compiled his own index for *The Fit*, and comments that 'though it finds itself providing entries for bizarre moments in the narrative, such as "HRH Princess Margaret, irrational fear of being transformed into", it was an incredibly demanding thing to put together, even in a spirit of jokiness'.

Index, author

In 1977 J. G. Ballard wrote a short story called 'The Index'. The entire thing is typeset as an index, enabling us to trace the life of the mysterious protagonist (Henry Rhodes Hamilton, or 'HRH') over the course of the twentieth century: 'Hitler, Adolf, invites HRH to Berchtesgaden; divulges Russia invasion plans; impresses HRH; disappoints HRH', etc.

---

*I can confirm that three things are true of indexing and indexers: they are modest, highly intelligent and definitely underpaid for their work.

Eventually, the reader realises that the story unfolds in linear fashion, from A being the birthplace of HRH ('Avignon'), to the entries for U, V and W, where 'HRH's downfall is revealed to the reader: Westminster Abbey, arrest of HRH by Special Branch; Wight, Isle of, incarceration of HRH; Windsor, House of, HRH challenges legitimacy of'. The final 'entry', under Z, is revealed to be that of the indexer himself: 'Zielinski, Bronislaw, suggests autobiography to HRH; commissioned to prepare index; warns of suppression threats; disappears'.

So, who should compile an index? The author, or a professional indexer? I asked Richard what he thought.

> Some authors should, of course, i.e. if they are good at it (it'll save them money, if nothing else).* Most shouldn't, because it is a skill that, while fundamentally self-taught in most cases, usually requires some training or at least the application of considered judgement honed over time. There are also many indexing principles that are usefully applied and need to be understood (it is surprising how many authors, who presumably use indexes frequently, haven't really grasped how they are put together). Here's a list of pros and cons of an author doing their own index:

PROS	CONS
They know their subject	They know their subject too well

'If an index is to illuminate the text, is to expose its inner workings to make them more accessible to the reader, then

---

*Nowadays most publishers insist that an author pay for their own index, if they want to have one.

the person holding the torch should be reacting with wonder to what they find, making concise but revealing notes of interesting discoveries, arranging them in a way that most excites fellow explorers; an author can be to some degree inured to the potential fascination and novelty of their own subject, and will when indexing perhaps focus on things that are of value to the expert more than the general reader.

'A very big reason for authors not doing their own indexes is that some can't help but want the index to show how comprehensive the coverage of the book is, how widely they have trawled the seas for our benefit, and so they expect there to be far more entries than a professional would put in. The pro indexer is always thinking about the usefulness of a potential index entry: would anyone actually look up that heading (or at least would it mean anything if they were browsing the index), and does the author really say anything useful about it? ("But I mention Sappho!" "Yes, but only in passing; you say nothing of value about her at all," is a common enough, if hypothetical, exchange.) The number of page references for an entry can similarly surprise an author. ("But I mention Sappho far more times than that!" "Yes, but only on pages 75 and 77 do you say anything concrete about her.") So, you sometimes find an author-compiled index is excessively long and crowded with unuseful entries.

'Another reason is that a good index takes a lot of time to compile. The total hours cited on invoices for indexes I have seen range from 15 for a tiddler to a hundred or more for really huge things.* Of course, an author may not want to compile their own index but may still have perfectly

---

*The Society of Indexers recommends an indexing rate (as at 31 December 2019) of £25.90 an hour, £2.90 a page or £7.80 per thousand words. So you can see that if an indexer is spending 100 hours plus on the job, it's a relatively significant outlay on a book.

legitimate opinions about it, perhaps keen to see some particular concepts or phrases used as headings and so on; often, a good index will emerge from a collaboration between a professional indexer and an author. In all cases, the author is anyway given the chance to comment on or amend the indexer's work – an occasional source of conflict as well!'

Indexes, entries in

We're all used to the idea that the entries in an index will appear in alphabetical order. Generally, index entries shouldn't start with an article ('a'; 'the') or a preposition ('in'; 'on'). An indexer needs to consider what will be the most useful way to help a reader find what they are looking for in the text – 'feeding habits of elephants' might not be an especially useful way for a reader to find 'elephants, feeding habits', for example.

Subentries are incredibly important in non-fiction titles because they help the reader navigate complex topics and relationships between people and events. An index to a biography is useless unless it breaks down the subject's life into manageable topics and themes – if it doesn't, you end up with hundreds of entries for them, and that won't help the reader at all.* As well as entries and subentries, indexers will use cross references within an index to point the reader to further information ('see also'), or to another entry entirely ('see'). Then there are double entries (where something could appear in the index in two or more forms – 'cars'

---

*Subentries are also where indexers can have the most fun. As Paula Clarke Bain points out in her review of Francis Wheen's index of his own book *How Mumbo-Jumbo Conquered the World* (2004), he masterfully uses subentries to qualify people in his index, including 'Elizabeth II, Queen: accused of cocaine-smuggling' and 'Philip, Prince, enjoys *Flying Saucer Review*; praised by extra-terrestrials'.

or 'automobiles' for example) which allow more than one access point for the reader, but they may take up too much space in the index, so somebody needs to make a decision about how useful each double entry is.

Indexing is usually done at page proofs (you can't do it before then, because you need the text to be anchored to the correct page numbers, and you only know those once it has been typeset) – which is one of the reasons why allowing authors to rewrite at this stage is such a problem. Any edits that cause text reflow can mean that every carefully selected index entry is then incorrect – a nightmare situation. I have lost entire weeks of my working life to dealing with 'minor' text reflow changes to an index. I always start off by optimistically thinking that it will just be a small job that I can take on myself, but two entries in I realise it is going to take me hours to adjust each index entry, that I am going cross-eyed with the effort and that I should have hired a professional. You can't ask the typesetter to do it automatically, since generally insertions and deletions in the text don't cause reflow to be a neat one page over or one page under: it's far more likely that only five or six lines on each page will need their index entries adjusting, and until you check you don't know which ones. Even with a searchable PDF this is a long, laborious job that requires a lot of concentration.

Another potential nightmare occurs when an index betrays you. It's not uncommon for changes made to a text for, say, legal reasons not to be applied at the same time to the index (often because changes of this sort tend to arrive very late in the day, when an index may already have been delivered); this means that although your *text* might no longer be libellous, your index might point to the ghostly shadow of something that was once there. There is nothing more likely to arouse the suspicions of interested parties than an index entry that points the way – to a suspiciously dead end.

Index, a history of the

The first 'indexes' weren't indexes at all – they were slips of paper attached to scrolls of text, so that you could know what you would be looking at before you went to the bother of all that unrolling. Detailed 'Tables of Contents' were the closest thing to an index, and they began to appear about two thousand years ago. Indexes as we think of them had to wait for three things to happen before they could become useful: alphabetisation (probably invented by the Greeks, though we don't know for sure); page numbers (which began to be used from about 1470*); and the printing press (from the mid-sixteenth century, which meant that identical copies of a book could be manufactured).

The index as readers today would recognise it began life in the eighteenth century. The 'Prince of Index-makers' was Samuel Ayscough, who in 1787 compiled a catalogue of books in the British Museum and followed this up with the first concordance to Shakespeare, for which he was paid 200 guineas.

Samuel Richardson prepared some of the earliest 'indexes', including one for his edition of *Aesop's Fables*, published in 1739. Richardson was the author of *Pamela; or, Virtue Rewarded*, published in 1740 and regarded as a critical point in the development of the novel. While we usually associate indexes now with non-fiction work, Richardson was an inveterate reviser of his work,[†] and by the time the sixth

---

*Page numbers started out as a tool for printers to know that they were collating sheets in the right order; it wasn't until the early 1500s that writers started using them to refer their readers backwards and forwards to locations within books.

†Richardson was so devoted to the idea of revising *Pamela* that he set up a 'reading group' of middle- and upper-class ladies to advise him on how their fictional counterparts were represented in the novel; although *Pamela* was popular with this audience there was disquiet over how the women of these classes were represented in his pages.

edition of *Pamela* arrived in 1742 it had acquired 'An ample TABLE of CONTENTS; Being, an EPITOME of the Work', which summarised Pamela's letters and worked as a 'copious INDEX', which would 'direct the Reader where to find the most material Passages, as well as give an Idea of the entertaining and instructive Variety to be found in the Work'.

The length of Richardson's novels may have encouraged him to supply indexes for his readers to help them keep track of what was going on. *Clarissa: or, The History of a Young Lady*, published in 1748, is estimated to be 1,927,870 words long;* Richardson, at the urging of Samuel Johnson, supplied a 'Table of Contents' to the second edition and an index to the third and fourth editions, to 'facilitate its use', allowing 'the reader [who] recollects any incident . . . [to] easily find it'.

Indexes, jokes about

Henry B. Wheatley† is known as 'the father of indexing' (or 'indexing, father of', I suppose), and in 1902 he opined that 'One of the last things the genuine indexer thinks of is to make his work amusing.' Despite Wheatley's views, there is a fine tradition of humour being used in indexes. Although

---

*The Guinness World Record holder for the longest novel is *À la recherche du temps perdu* by Marcel Proust, which comes in at 1,267,069 words. That's nothing compared to the more than 11 million words in *Devta*, a serialised fantasy thriller novel written in Urdu and published every month in *Suspense Digest* between 1977 and 2010.

†Wheatley founded the Index Society in 1877, which failed through lack of funds; he was an inveterate setter-upper of societies, it seems – he also established the Library Association and the Samuel Pepys Club. There was even a Wheatley Medal, awarded by the Society of Indexers until 2012, to recognise and encourage excellence in indexing. 'I fear that the interest of the public in the production of indexes (which is considerable) does not go to the length of willingness to pay for these indexes,' Wheatley once said – a state of affairs which is sadly true.

they can often appear dry and too academic, indexes can be (appropriately) used for comic effect. Fortunately for those of us who appreciate humour in indexing, Paula Clarke Bain, a freelance indexer, highlights the best examples of playful and humorous indexes on her blog (if this chapter has ignited a burning fire in you about indexes, do take a look at her writing – it's both entertaining and educational). She picks the indexes in *I, Partridge: We Need to Talk About Alan* (published in 2011) and *Alan Partridge: Nomad* (2016)* as being particularly rich in humour. Partridge might be a fictional character, but he understands that to be taken seriously his memoirs must feature an index. Subentries for 'Norfolk' in *I, Partridge* include 'backward underachievers of', 'sex in' and 'starvation in'. Of course, the index subentries for Partridge himself ('Partridge, Alan Gordon') give the reader a sped-up synopsis of Alan's life and times, including 'as ineffective leader', 'waterproof trousers, discontinued', 'Toblerone addiction', 'as Norwich Don Juan'.

Indexes, playful

In 1928 the Hogarth Press published *Orlando: A Biography* by Virginia Woolf, acknowledged as a subversive satire of English literature, a feminist classic and an experiment in literature. *Orlando*'s subtitle sets up Woolf's playful approach to her writing; like all good biographies, *Orlando* includes an index, which Woolf compiled herself.† The index echoes the

---

*As well as the excellence of its parody index, *Nomad* also features 144 endnotes, to further bolster Alan's credibility as a non-fiction author. 'Not a euphemism', 'My description' and 'My publisher' appear often in Alan's notes, as do snippets of his ongoing bromance with Eamonn Holmes.

†*Orlando* was not the first index Woolf had created – in 1926 she produced one for *Castles in the Air*, a memoir by the actress Viola Tree, also published by the Hogarth Press.

restless shape-shifting qualities of Orlando; and Woolf uses 'and' to link subentries within it, which means that just by looking at the index the reader can sense the narrative arc of the story. The entry for the character of Orlando begins with the subentry 'appearance as a boy', runs through the events of the first half of his life ('buys elk-hounds'; 'his first trance'; 'retires into solitude') and then, halfway through the subentry, the casual index browser is brought up short by 'becomes a woman', then a few entries later there is 'declared a woman', and finally 'birth of her first son'. Woolf subverts the traditional scholarly notions of the index and uses it as a conspiratorial way of indicating to readers how *Orlando* should be approached; additionally the reader who browses through the index is given a taster of the shape-shifting Orlando's gender-fluid adventures.

Index, a universal

In Jorge Luis Borges's *The Library of Babel*, the narrator describes an infinite library, in which all possible permutations of the written word are stored: 'Like all the men of the Library, in my younger days I travelled; I have journeyed in quest of a book, perhaps the catalogue of catalogues.' And although Henry Wheatley's Index Society eventually had to close, it could never be said that it lacked a similar kind of quixotic ambition. It was established on the back of an idea to create the most ambitious index of all – a universal index of everything – a catalogue of catalogues of words. In 1877, at the International Conference of Librarians, a paper written by J. Ashton Cross called 'A Universal Index of Subjects' was presented.

Such was the enthusiasm among the librarians for producing a universal index of everything that the Index Society was formed. As Dennis Duncan, author of *Index, A History of the*, explains in a piece for the *Literary Review*:

First, the society would identify important or 'standard' works that lacked indexes and ask members to do the needful. Second, it would draw up a list of disciplines – anthropology, astronomy, botany, and so on. Indexes from canonical works in each field could then be consolidated into subject-specific general indexes. Finally, these subject indexes would be fed upwards into the all-knowing vastness of the universal index.

'The all-knowing vastness of the universal index'. Just imagine such a thing: an index where everything and anyone and anything that has ever existed could be found. Alphabetised, catalogued, ordered. Except we no longer need imagine it. Every time we sit down at our computers, we have access to the biggest searchable index in human history via our web browser of choice. Ashton Cross concluded his lecture with these words: 'the question . . . ought to be, not whether a Universal Index shall be made, but only in what way it can be made'. Now we know the answer.

HOW WORDS GET FREE

Movable type and the invention of the printing press liberated words from the constraints of being painstakingly transcribed by monks copy by copy. The mass printing of words truly freed them – and changed everything. That freedom to finally reach a readership can also happen through translation, which allows words to cross borders, continents and cultures, and through persuasion – the art of the blurb writer, which encourages the potential reader to complete the circle of how words get good, by picking up a book and committing to buying it. And words also achieve freedom through typography: the physical properties of the printed page are part of the contract between writer and reader that allows each side to understand what the other is trying to say.

INSPECTOR MAIGRET AND THE
POGO STICK: TRANSLATION

'Not word for word but sense for sense'

'They don't have to show us Catch-22,' the old woman answered. 'The law says they don't have to.'

'What law says they don't have to?'

'Catch-22.'

In 1962, Joseph Heller told a *Newsweek* interviewer that he'd received a letter from his Finnish translator. It read: 'I am translating your novel *Catch-22* into Finnish. Would you please explain me one thing: What means Catch-22? I didn't find it in any vocabulary. Even the assistant air attaché of the U.S.A. here in Helsinki could not explain exactly.' 'I think in Finland,' concluded Heller in the interview, 'the book will lose a great deal in translation.'

The problem for the Finnish translator was that looking up catch-22 wouldn't have enlightened him: the term was popularised by the novel, and then used retrospectively as a handy shorthand for any paradoxical situation, as demonstrated in the conversation above between Yossarian and an old woman at the end of the book. A catch-22 was exactly what the Finnish translator faced. He couldn't translate catch-22 because at the time there was literally no translation possible: catch-22 just meant . . . catch-22. Incidentally, Heller's original title was *Catch-18*; he was forced to change it by the publication in the same year of *Mila 18* by Leon Uris. 'I was heartbroken. I thought 18 was the only number,' he said. However, in Ian McEwan's 2019 novel *Machines Like Me*, which is set in an alternative post-war Britain, people are reading a book called *Catch-18*.

Humans have been discussing how to translate since antiquity, which perhaps indicates the value writers place on freeing their words to travel. The ancient Greeks distinguished between literal translation (metaphrase) and more explanatory clarifications of words – paraphrase. 'Not word for word but sense for sense' is how St Jerome described the process of translating the Bible from Greek into Latin in the fourth century BC: the first major attempt of its kind. The Roman playwright Terence's six plays were adapted from earlier Greek plays and his clear, entertaining conversational language meant that many scribes learned Latin through copying his texts. Like Jerome, Cicero* cautioned against word-for-word translations, believing that the translator was an artist: 'I did not think I ought to count them [the words] out to the reader like coins, but to pay them by weight, as it were.' The English poet John Dryden believed that good translation was a mixture of these two types of translation: 'When [words] appear . . . literally graceful, it were an injury to the author that they should be changed. But since . . . what is beautiful in one [language] is often barbarous, nay sometimes nonsense, in another, it would be unreasonable to limit a translator to the narrow compass of his author's words: 'tis enough if he choose out some expression which does not vitiate the sense.'

But freeing our words through translation also carries a risk – that we might lose the original meaning of those words. The thought of what words *lose* in translation might be one of the reasons that the process is often looked down

---

*'You will like Cicero, or you will be whipped,' read one graffito in Pompeii, in reference to the quality of his works and translations.

on. Translation is always approximate. As David Bellos says in *Is That a Fish in Your Ear: The Amazing Adventure of Translation*: 'any utterance of more than trivial length has no one translation. All utterances have innumerably many acceptable translations.' He then goes on to point out: 'The variability of translations is incontrovertible evidence of the limitless flexibility of human minds. There can hardly be a more interesting subject than that.'

So the translation of words from one language to another has been around for a long time – and is crucial in allowing words to find a global audience. Without translation, writers would only be known in their own countries, or at least only in those countries that shared their language. Translation is the ultimate liberation for words.

What do translators really do? Although I've had lots of translated texts pass across my desk, and even worked on David Bellos's book, I have no direct experience of it. I was lost in translation. Fortunately, editor, copy-editor and French-to-English translator David Watson was willing and able to help make sense of it all.

On a sticky wicket

'Of course, it's a truism of translation that you cannot translate word for word,' said David. 'Translation is not decoding, a one-for-one substitution, and there is no Enigma machine that can do the task mechanically (and, so far, no computer program has been able to achieve translation beyond a crude approximation, or by aggregating a lot of previous human translations). Give the same piece of text, even something ostensibly simple and prosaic, to a hundred different translators and you are highly likely to end up with close to, or exactly, a hundred different versions. All of them (ideally) will convey more or less the same sense, but the words will not be the same.

'So St Jerome's dictum that a translation should be "not word for word, but sense for sense" does tell us a little bit about the nature of translation. But sense is a many-headed hydra, it doesn't just lie in the dictionary definitions of the words, and if that complexity is not enough to deal with there are other things besides – style, voice, idiom, register, irony, dialect – that you have to try to convey through translation, and these bring in their own challenges and difficulties.

'Let's take a simple example of the type of problem a translator might encounter. Harold Pinter's Japanese translator apparently wrote to him in some perplexity over the phrase "a sticky wicket". Hardly surprising – cricket isn't big in Japan, and the translator was further hindered by the fact that "wicket" can mean three different things in cricket: the strip of pitch between the bowler and batter, the stumps and bails themselves, and what happens when the batsman's innings is terminated by the bowling team ("taking a wicket").* It's possible to use all three meanings in one sentence: "The batsman lost his wicket when the ball turned off the wicket and hit his wicket".† Well, in Pinter's use, it is a reference to the pitch itself, but that isn't the end of the translator's problem, far from it.

'Firstly, very few Japanese would recognise the cricket terminology, so perhaps the translator might consider coming up with an equivalent sporting analogy – a slippery sumo ring, perhaps. Well, that might be OK if it were a set phrase or cliché in Japanese, as sticky wicket is in English, but if it is a fresh coinage of the translator, then it wouldn't do at all. Besides, how would it read if characters in an English setting were using sumo wrestling analogies? OK, so maybe

---

*If ever a sport were untranslatable, it would be cricket.
†Imagine trying to explain this to someone who had never seen a game of cricket.

a sporting metaphor just can't be found, but perhaps there is a more general Japanese set expression that at least gets the meaning, albeit losing some of the colloquial colour – let's say for the sake of argument (and because I don't speak Japanese)* that "a slippery slope" is a Japanese analogy for a tricky situation. But what if Japanese is a language not much given to colourful metaphoric sayings at all, in which case talk of wickets, wrestlers or slopes would be puzzling, perhaps nonsensical, to the average Japanese playgoer? So, the translator was stumped (sorry)† and forced in the end to adopt a bland denotative phrase such as "a difficult situation". It was adequate in conveying the basic sense, but loses a lot of the flavour of Pinter's dialogue. Almost as much as his famous pauses, Pinter's mordant juxtaposition of anodyne, banal English colloquialism with dramatic situations of unspoken menace creates that sinister tension in his writing that is so characteristic it has its own adjective – "Pinteresque".‡ Recreating those layers of one language in another language context with its own linguistic conventions and baggage of received meanings and cultural references is part and parcel of the task facing the translator. A sticky wicket indeed.'

English as She Is Spoke

'Nobody can add to the absurdity of this book, nobody can imitate it successfully, nobody can hope to produce its fellow; it is perfect.' This was Mark Twain describing *O novo guia da conversação em portuguez e inglez, ou Escolha de dialogos familiares*, which translates as 'The new guide of the conversation

---

*No, I don't either.

†This was David's apology; I add my own.

‡Pinter's early plays were described as 'comedies of menace', a particularly evocative coupling of words.

in Portuguese and English, or School of familiar dialogues'
– usually known as *English as She Is Spoke*. Written by Pedro
Carolino and published in 1855, the book was intended to be
a guide to Portuguese–English conversation. Unfortunately,
Carolino could not actually speak English – so he used a
French–English dictionary to translate a Portuguese–French
phrase book, with some incredible results. Carolino was an
extremely literal translator: when faced with the Portuguese
term *chover a cântaros* he rendered it as 'raining in jars', apparently unaware of the idiomatic English phrase 'raining
buckets'. According to Carolino, 'The walls have hearsay'
(rather than ears), 'That not says a word, consent' ('Silence is
consent') and 'I have mind to vomit' ('I feel sick') were for
him all perfectly acceptable translations.

The 1883 edition of *English as She is Spoke* included an
introduction written by Twain, who opined that:

> In this world of uncertainties, there is, at any rate, one
> thing which may be pretty confidently set down as a
> certainty: and that is, that this celebrated little phrase-
> book will never die while the English language lasts . . .
> Its delicious unconscious ridiculousness, and its enchant-
> ing naiveté, are as supreme and unapproachable, in their
> way, as are Shakespeare's sublimities. Many persons
> have believed that this book's miraculous stupidities
> were studied and disingenuous; but no one can read
> the volume carefully through and keep that opinion. It
> was written in serious good faith and deep earnestness,
> by an honest and upright idiot who believed he knew
> something of the English language, and could impart his
> knowledge to others . . . a man who believes he has done
> a high and worthy work for his nation and his gener-
> ation, and is well pleased with his performance.

Carolino's 'English' also entertained Abraham Lincoln and kept his mind diverted from fighting the American Civil War, and inspired both *Monty Python's Flying Circus's* 1970 'Dirty Hungarian Phrasebook' sketch, and *Britain as she is visit*, a 1976 spoof tourist guide. And even when translation is perhaps a little fast and loose, we can enjoy it. There is certainly space in my corner of the Gutenberg Galaxy for *A Man Without Scruples* (the Swedish translation of *The Great Gatsby*) and *The World is Not a Factory for Fulfilling Wishes* (the very pessimistic Macedonian translation of *The Fault in Our Stars*). When it comes to words, sometimes nonsense makes for entertainment.

In search of lost translations

In 1922 Joseph Conrad wrote to Charles Scott Moncrieff after reading the first volume of Marcel Proust's *À la recherche du temps perdu* in Scott Moncrieff's English translation – which he had called *Remembrance of Things Past*. 'I was more interested and fascinated by your rendering than by Proust's creation,' Conrad said. 'You have a supreme faculty akin to genius.' The difficulties of translating a work from one language to another are demonstrated in how Scott Moncrieff translated the title of *À la recherche du temps perdu*. He was aware that there was no English equivalent to the French title, so he decided to use a line from Shakespeare's Sonnet 30: 'When to the sessions of sweet silent thought / I summon up remembrance of things past.'

There have only been three English translations of *À la recherche* – Scott Moncrieff's original, which he worked on from 1921 until his death in 1930, one in 1981 by Terence Kilmartin,* and one published in 2002 by Penguin, where

---

*This version took Scott Moncrieff's original translation and weaved in 300,000 more words that Proust's brother, Robert, and his publishers,

seven translators took on Proust's seven volumes over seven years. The French edition Scott Moncrieff worked from was littered with typesetting errors. He had to somehow see through this unstable text, intuit what he thought Proust was saying and then find a way to express it in English. And unlike the translations that followed, he had no other English version of the text to help him. As Jean Findlay, Scott Moncrieff's great-great-niece and author of *Chasing Lost Time: The Life of C. K. Scott Moncrieff, Soldier, Spy and Translator*, describes, 'in 1921 Scott Moncrieff was working alone, like a man scaling Everest for the first time: he had no route marked out, no helpfully drilled footholds'.

Proust was still alive when Scott Moncrieff began his endeavour, and shortly before his death in November 1922 he began a correspondence with him. Although the first volume of the translation, *Swann's Way*, was well received, Proust wrote to Scott Moncrieff that the work was 'no substitute for the internal ambiguity of my *Temps perdu*'.

Scott Moncrieff died in 1930 when he was only forty years old. He was exhausted by a punishing work schedule – in part because he had to financially support nine of his nieces and nephews – but along with translations of Stendhal, Abelard and Héloïse, and Pirandello, he completed all Proust's volumes bar the final one.*

I asked David for his thoughts on how that 'internal ambiguity' is rendered in Proustian translations.

'Umberto Eco describes translation as a form of "negotiation". It is a dialogue, a haggle between yours and the

---

Gallimard, had added to the original. The extra words were based on the stuck-in notes called paperoles (see pp. 144–5) that Proust had left on his manuscripts – many of which had fallen off and had to be painstakingly reinserted. Kilmartin's work was revised in 1992 by D. J. Enright, who retranslated the title as *In Search of Lost Time*.
*It was completed after his death by Stephen Hudson.

author's texts: it involves trade-offs. And, as in all negotiations, compromise is inevitable: you win some and you lose some.

'The opening sentence of Proust's *À la recherche du temps perdu* – "*Longtemps, je me suis couché de bonne heure*" – has an echo of "happiness" (*bonheur*) in the phrase "*de bonne heure*" (early), which simply isn't possible to convey by means of sound in any direct English rendition. So maybe, as a translator in negotiation with this text, you have to let that subtlety of meaning go – you can't win 'em all.

'But another tactic might be to be to adopt a looser, less literal approach in order to translate the sense rather than just the words on the page. For example, you might hazard "I happily went to bed early". But that is fraught with risk, of course: you are interpolating something into the original; you are changing the flow and rhythm of the sentence; crucially, you are making an implied meaning into an explicit one, and so rendering the sentence less subtle. (And this is just the first sentence in a novel that is a million and a quarter words long. . .) So, what do you choose to do in the end? Well, there is no right or wrong answer to that.'

Roundheads and cavaliers

'It's a parlour game of mine,' David said, 'to divide translators into two camps: roundheads and cavaliers. Roundheads like to play it straight, and translate as literally as possible to match the forms of expression used in the original text; cavaliers set as their main aim the achievement of a translated text that sounds as if it were originally written in English, even if it means finding different idioms and forms of expression to the original text. Roundheads would assert that the text is foreign by definition – different cultures express themselves, linguistically and otherwise, in their own unique ways; why would you want to lose the flavour of Frenchness or Italiannness or Chineseness and impose an inappropriate English idiom on the text? Critics of this approach would claim that it can lead to an awkward "wooden" translation and perhaps smacks of a certain academic arrogance.

'Cavaliers would say that readers in English should not have to encounter a stiltedness that readers in the original language would not have endured; critics of their approach would say that they can sometimes interpolate too much of a style and voice that is nothing to do with the author's choice of expression, that they can play fast and loose with the text they are supposed to be serving ("cavalier" of course can suggest a sense of reckless abandon).

'But my English Civil War metaphor is something of a false dichotomy; at least insofar as translators range out along a spectrum rather than forming two distinct camps. No one is so literal that they will not veer away from the specific wording of the original; no one so cavalier that they simply make up their text with no regard to the limits imposed by the meaning of the text they are translating. Word-for-word literalness is anathema to any good translator. German, for example, tends to place verbs at the end of clauses, and no translator would this word order replicate, otherwise he like Yoda sounding end up would.

'Mark Twain once satirically translated an especially florid French translation of one of his works back into English using a word-for-word literalness and ended up with something rather different from his original: "It there was one time here an individual known under the name of Jim Smiley; it was in the winter of '49, possibly well at the spring of '50. I no me recollect not exactly . . ."*

---

*This is the original: 'There was a feller here once by the name of Jim

'As a self-confessed cavalier, I have often felt immensely pleased with myself by coming up with a snappy English phrase, only subsequently, and often reluctantly, to abandon it because it just wasn't a close enough match for the sense or style of the original. Another problem inherent in the "cavalier" approach is that, if your aim is to render the text in a natural-sounding English voice, which type of English voice do you use, and how do you decide whether it is an appropriate equivalent of the voice of the author or narrator of the original text?

'To return to Proust, as we have seen, the original translator, Scott Moncrieff, produced a magisterial piece of work. However, one criticism often levelled at him is that his English text has a tendency towards a somewhat flowery Edwardian style of prose, which may have been the height of British literary taste at the time but has not aged very well and in many ways is seen as not appropriate to Proust's style.

'So how should the modern translator approach texts? Obviously you always seek to avoid anachronism (you wouldn't have characters in Flaubert or Tolstoy greeting each other with "Hey, dude, how's it hanging?"), but you can't avoid the issue of whether you choose a style that sounds more natural to the modern ear or whether you try to render it in an English style that is contemporary with the author. In general, if a translator is commissioned to do a new translation of a classic text, they are probably expected to do a version that sounds more of their own time. But that of course raises the question of how much a translated text is a work in its own right and in its own voice.*

Smiley, in the winter of '49 or may be it was the spring of '50 I don't recollect exactly . . .' It's the opening line of Twain's 1865 short story 'The Celebrated Jumping Frog of Calaveras County'.

*An indication that translations are viewed as works in their own right is

'My own personal take on the subject is based on my own approach to translating a text. I will read a sentence, make a first stab at translating it, listen to how it sounds in my head, try to refine it into a more natural English-sounding version if possible. I don't apply a method, just an instinct – or rather not an instinct, but a response based on a lifetime of reading and using the English language (and it is often under-estimated how much good translation requires a command of one's own language as well as knowledge of a foreign language).* As translator you are not a creator of an original work in the way that an author is, of course, but the art or craft of translating is creative nonetheless. The translation is a new text, and every word in it is a choice you make. You should have the humility to self-efface, not show off, but your voice is inevitably there, ghosting the voice of the author. The neutral, transparent translation simply does not exist.'

James Joyce's *Finnegans Wake* includes ten words of one hundred letters, scattered throughout the text. The first of these appears on page 1, and reads like this: 'The fall (bababadalgharaghtakamminarronnkonnbronntonner-ronntuonnthunntrovarrhounawnskawntoohoohoordenen-thurnuk!) of a once wallstrait oldparr is retaled early in bed and later on life down through all christian minstrelsy.' Is it untranslatable? I asked David.

'Well, many works have been described as such, yet it is quite remarkable how many seemingly impossible texts have been rendered by hook or by crook into other languages. *Finnegans Wake* is a novel so linguistically challenging that the French version took thirty years to complete, while the

---

that generally in most territories around the world translators retain the copyright of their translations – even if that translation is unauthorised.
*Translators almost always translate from a foreign language into their mother tongue, and rarely the other way round.

Japanese version* required three separate translators after the first disappeared and the second went mad.

'Georges Perec's novel *La Disparition* includes no word containing the letter "e" – not a problem if every e-less word in French had an e-less English equivalent, which of course it doesn't.[†] So Gilbert Adair's translation, *A Void* (because a literal translation of the title – 'Disappearance' – would already break the rule), had to find a way to somehow tell the same story using an entirely different lexicon of e-less words in English. To say it is a loose translation is an understatement, and it is an interesting test case of how "loose" a translation can be while remaining recognisably consistent with the original work. It also shows how fluid the term "translation" can be. Perhaps a better question than "Is anything untranslatable?" would be "Is anything translatable?", to which I would say "Yes, but only if we have no way of defining exactly what a translation is", which approach you will have noticed I've adopted throughout this conversation.'

---

*It's called フィネガンズウェイク. Apparently, the subatomic particle known as a 'quark' is named after the phrase 'Three quarks for Muster Mark' from *Finnegans Wake*. The physicist Murray Gell-Mann, who named it (them?), had already thought of using the sound 'kwork'; Joyce merely provided the spelling.

†Naturally, after writing *La Disparition* in 1969, Perec then wrote a novella in 1972 called *Les revenentes*, where the only vowel used was the letter 'e'. *La Disparition* is a lipogram, which comes from ancient Greek and means 'leaving out a letter'. *Les revenentes*, on the other hand, is antilipogrammatic (what a word!) – which describes constrained writing that only uses a single vowel. These types of 'constrained' writings are known as Oulipo.

The philosopher versus the sorcerer

When we think of translation, we generally think of it as being between two different languages. But even when two countries share a language, like the US and the UK, there can be 'translation' from one edition of a book to another. *The Seven Deaths of Evelyn Hardcastle* by Stuart Turton was published in America as *The 7 ½ Deaths of Evelyn Hardcastle*. 'Our editorial team decided to Supersize it' was the publisher's initial response, although more prosaically it was due to a potential title clash with another novel: Taylor Jenkins Reid's *The Seven Husbands of Evelyn Hugo*. And Ted Hughes's *The Iron Man* had to be changed to *The Iron Giant* in the US. Why? Because Marvel had already trademarked the name Iron Man.

To the list of reasons for changing a book's title between one market and another we can add obscurity. That's why in 1998 when Scholastic published the first Harry Potter novel in the United States, the title was changed from *Harry Potter and the Philosopher's Stone* to *Harry Potter and the Sorcerer's Stone*.* In his 2015 biography of J. K. Rowling, Philip W. Errington described how Arthur Levine, the head of Scholastic, 'noted that he needed a title that said "magic" more overtly to American readers'. The American title might have had more magic to it, but as Philip Nel, an American scholar of children's literature, points out in his essay 'You Say "Jelly", I Say "Jell-O"?: Harry Potter and the Transfiguration of Language', changing the title to *Sorcerer's Stone* 'lacks the reference to alchemy implied by *Philosopher's Stone* in the title of the British edition'.

---

*In 1989 the James Bond film *Licence to Kill* also suffered a US-induced title change. It had originally been called *Licence Revoked* (which describes the film's plot – M revokes Bond's licence to kill, making him a rogue agent), but the name was changed during post-production. Apparently, American audiences thought it referred to Bond's driving licence. Sorry, license. In the US you can use the one word for both noun and verb.

After changing the title, Levine went on to 'translate' the text for an American readership. It was the first book in the Harry Potter series, and it suffered from the most intervention of all seven of them – perhaps because at the time of publication in the USA J. K. Rowling was an unknown author. As well as the title change, vocabulary changes in the book include 'Quidditch pitch', which becomes 'Quidditch field'; 'mum' becomes 'mom'; 'jelly' becomes 'Jell-O'; 'jumper' becomes 'sweater'. As Philip Nel explains, changing 'pitch' to 'field' does two things: it divorces Quidditch from cricket (played on a pitch, not a field) – which means that the many jokes about how long Quidditch matches can last (jokes that are clearly based on the potential length of a real-life cricket match) become meaningless (although perhaps that matters less, as most Americans are not familiar with cricket anyway); and it destroys the rhyme of the English phrase.

Although J. K. Rowling is careful to create a world that reflects the cultural diversity of England, for example by using dialect, and drawing characters like Parvati Patil and Cho Chang, the change from 'mum' to 'mom' – even when used by a character of Irish descent, like Seamus Finnegan, who in the British edition says 'mam', but in the US edition says 'mom' – demonstrates how cultural subtleties can be lost when these types of 'translation' changes are made. Where some words are translated there is also a loss of puns: 'Sellotape' in the UK becomes 'Scotch tape' in the US, but this means that American readers will miss out on the pun between 'Sellotape' and 'Spellotape.' At one point in the US version Dumbledore sits in a 'high chair', which is very different to the British edition, where we find him in a 'high-backed chair'. Of course, one of these chairs is usually used for restraining a toddler, while the other suggests prowess and gravitas.

But was this necessary, or was it in fact an act of cultural appropriation – since, as Nel writes, 'all acts of translation can be read as acts of appropriation'. Nel sets the translation of the Harry Potter series into the context of American children's publishing, where it is so common that it usually passes without any comment at all. He refers to Jane Whitehead's 1996 study of these types of changes, '"This is NOT what I wrote!": The Americanization of British Children's Books', where she says: 'The range of alterations made under the umbrella of Americanization is vast . . . these changes include titles, setting, character names, culturally specific allusions . . . in addition to spelling, punctuation, vocabulary, and idiom.'

As well as changing meaning and introducing distortion, translating texts between two markets that speak the same language in this way also deprives readers of the opportunity to learn about linguistic difference. Levine explains his approach to Harry Potter: 'I wasn't trying to . . . "Americanize" them. What I was trying to do was translate, which is something different. I wanted to make sure that an American kid reading the book would have the same literary experience that a British kid would have.' As Nel says in his essay: 'Were it possible to create "the same literary experience" for children from different countries, why would it be desirable?' English children are very used to American popular culture, to American spellings on their spellchecks – so they are generally able to understand any differences in the two languages without real difficulty. 'Britons receive plenty of American culture that has not been Anglicised, but the economic imperative of selling to the vast American market gives U.S. publishers the belief that they have license to Americanize British texts.'

Personally, I don't agree with the idea of 'translating' like this – from UK English to American English, or the other way round. One of the joys of reading as a child is that it exposes to you to words, phrases and concepts that you would otherwise never encounter. As one eleven-year-old wrote to the *New Yorker* in 1999 on publication of *Harry Potter and the Prisoner of Azkaban*, children 'have large imaginations, and can usually figure out . . . what words mean from their context'.

When I was a child I actively enjoyed spotting the 'differences' between British and American language. It was intriguing – and part of how I learned about the world. I hadn't been to America (I hadn't even left the country, let alone been on a plane), but I already considered myself an experienced traveller because even though I was only nine I knew through reading that our shared language was not always the same. Growing up in rural Essex in the mid-1980s I was the most unsophisticated child imaginable, except when it came to words. I knew that you could spell colour as 'color' if you were American, or walk on the sidewalk rather than the pavement, and this knowledge made me feel like I was cracking a secret code. These differences were part of the rich background of a story, and always enhanced my enjoyment, rather than diluting it.

Just one more translation story in this chapter from David:

'The only truly reprehensible crime on which I have no compunction in passing judgement is when a translator decides that the original text isn't quite good enough and needs editing or rewriting, or when a translator simply gets it completely wrong – mistranslates, in other words.

'As one of the translators for a recent new series of Georges Simenon's Maigret novels,* I encountered both

---

*There were seventy-five Maigret novels to be translated, and Penguin published one a month for six years, with eleven different translators working across the series. Georges Simenon wrote the novels between 1931 and 1972, although Maigret himself began and remained elderly for the duration.

types of barbarity in earlier translations. One hilarious mis-translation had Maigret borrowing a vehicle to travel along a river. The French word is *"youyou"*, a type of dinghy, but for reasons best known to himself the translator under-stood this to mean a "pogo stick". Perhaps dimly sensing the absurdity of the stocky Inspector Maigret pogoing up a towpath, and feeling a batsqueak* of doubt whether a pogo stick is really a mode of transport at all, the translator, rather than face the likelihood that he might have got something wrong, simply tacked on an explanation: ". . . he was given a pogo stick, *which was the latest craze. He had never been on one before* . . ."† and obviously felt that that cleared the matter up satisfactorily.'

---

*At the time of writing the rights to this book have been sold to South Korea, Japan, China and Turkey. I'm interested to see how my translators approach this phrase.

†Italics are David's. And mine.

BLAPS, BLOVERS AND BLURBS

What do we use to try to convince someone to buy our words – to commit to them? It's more of the same, of course. We use words to persuade people to pick up a book or click on a 'buy it now' button and begin the adventure of reading. Blurbs, or cover copy – the text that adorns the back cover, and more recently the Amazon page – are the launch pads for books as they make their way out into the world – and arguably, this means that they need to be the best of all words. How did this very particular form of persuasion come about, and why?

Are you a bromide?

Well, are you? This intriguing question was the headline to the first piece of text known to have used the word 'blurb'. In 1907, American Frank Gelett Burgess needed to present his book *Are You a Bromide?** to an annual trade association dinner. According to Burgess's publisher B. W. Huebsch, 'a damsel on the jacket of every novel' was the done thing at the time: 'the picture of a damsel – languishing, heroic, or coquettish'. Inspired by this, Burgess's jacket included an image of a fictitious young lady called 'Miss Belinda Blurb', pictured 'in the act of blurbing'.

---

*Burgess used the word 'bromide' to describe dull, boring people, saying dull, boring things. Try it next time you need a new way of insulting someone, or something.

YES, this is a "BLURB"!

All the Other Publishers commit them. Why Shouldn't We?

MISS   IN
BELINDA   THE ACT OF
BLURB   BLURBING

ARE YOU A BROMIDE?

BY

GELETT BURGESS

Say! Ain't this book a 90-H. P., six-cylinder Seller? If WE do say it as shouldn't, WE consider that this man Burgess has got Henry James locked into the coal-bin, telephoning for "Information"

WE expect to sell 350 copies of this great, grand book. It has gush and go to it, it has that Certain Something which makes you want to crawl through thirty miles of dense tropical jungle and bite somebody in the neck. No hero no heroine, nothing like that for OURS, but when you've *READ* this masterpiece, you'll know what a BOOK is, and you'll sic it onto your mother-in-law, your dentist and the pale youth who dips hot-air into Little Marjorie until 4 Q. M. in the front parlour. This book has 42-carat THRILLS in it. It fairly BURBLES. Ask the man at the counter what HE thinks of it! He's seen Janice Meredith faded to a mauve magenta. He's seen BLURBS before, and he's dead wise. He'll say:

This Book is the Proud Purple Penultimate!!

Miss Belinda Blurb

Far from being a boring old bromide, Belinda appears to be blurbing on speed. You'd definitely want to go for cocktails with her. 'WE consider that this man Burgess has got Henry James locked into the coal-bin, telephoning for "Information",' she begins. 'WE expect to sell 350 copies of this great, grand book. It has gush and go to it, it has that Certain Something which makes you want to crawl through thirty miles of dense tropical jungle and bite somebody in the neck.' In twenty years of editing book blurbs, I don't think I've ever come across such an array of unusual endorsements. Why is Henry James locked in a coal-bin, for a start? And have you *ever* read a book that makes you want to crawl through thirty miles of dense tropical jungle and bite someone in the neck? Maybe this book will be it.

'A sound like a publisher'

Having invented the word 'blurb', in 1914 in his *Burgess Unabridged* Burgess went on to define it further:

> Blurb 1. A flamboyant advertisement; an inspired testimonial. 2. Fulsome praise; a sound like a publisher . . . On the 'jacket' of the 'latest' fiction, we find the blurb; abounding in agile adjectives and adverbs, attesting that this book is the 'sensation of the year.'

In the unlikely event someone ever asks you what sound a publisher makes, then 'blurb', it turns out, is the answer.

Burgess's first definition of the word 'blurb' – 'A flamboyant advertisement; an inspired testimonial' – gradually morphed over time to describe all the copy on the back cover of a book.

Like so many words in publishing, 'blurb' can be used both very specifically and very generally. 'Blurbs' where I work describes the cover copy, the flap copy, as well as the endorsements on the cover and first couple of pages. A 'jacket' in publishing usually refers to a removable dust jacket on a hardback book, whereas a 'cover' generally applies to the boards that a paperback book is bound in. Most people use these words interchangeably, and so can we in this chapter, but it's worth noting that there is a difference. And although we lazily use the word 'blurb' to describe all this, writing cover copy is very different from hunting out blurbs from reviews and other authors.

In 1855, some half-century before Belinda and her bromide

appeared, Walt Whitman published *Leaves of Grass*, a book of poetry which inspired Ralph Waldo Emerson to write and congratulate him on its success. 'I greet you at the beginning of a great career,' said the letter (among other things, presumably), and the following year Whitman took these words and had them stamped (in gold leaf, no less) on the spine of the second edition of *Leaves of Grass*.* In so doing Whitman was perhaps giving a nod to the first line of his poem 'Song of Myself', which famously begins: 'I celebrate myself.' Emerson's endorsement of Whitman is one of the earliest examples of one writer 'blurbing' another, but how did all this begin?

The Blurb's Progress

In 1678 John Bunyan published a Christian allegory called *The Pilgrim's Progress*. As well as being recognised as the first novel written in English,[†] *The Pilgrim's Progress* and the novels that followed it were important steps on the road to the blurbs we see today. Take a look at the frontispiece of the first edition of *The Pilgrim's Progress* shown overleaf.

This is *way* more than a standard title page. The title and

---

*Whitman spent four decades revising *Leaves of Grass*. The first edition had twelve poems, and the last, four hundred. Mission creep.

†Well, this depends a bit on your definition of what a novel actually *is*. Some critics make a distinction between allegories and novels (which would exclude *The Pilgrim's Progress*); other criteria for a novel are that they are of a certain length, are wholly original, and that they don't fall under the category of romance (these types of stories were often fantastical in nature) or picaresque (which describes a connected series of episodes, rather than a unified narrative). Once you have used these criteria to screen the candidates, you are left with Daniel Defoe's *Robinson Crusoe*, written in 1719, as the first novel – but that's only if you're English. *Don Quixote* was written more than a century earlier in 1605 and is considered to be the first 'European' novel.

subtitle, 'The Pilgrim's Progress: From this world, to that which is to come', give the reader the basic narrative arc. Then it tells us that the story is 'Delivered under the Similitude of a DREAM' – so the reader knows *how* the story is going to be conveyed to us – and then it hints at the final outcome: 'And safe Arrival at the Desired Countrey.' When *The Pilgrim's Progress* was first published, there was no established mechanism (or agreed physical space) for communicating with the reader what a story was *about*. This didn't matter so much when the earliest reading material was generally based on the retelling of existing stories (your audience had heard it all before), but as soon as new, or 'novel',* tales were being told, printers and authors had to find a way of explaining what the story *was* to encourage readers to be drawn in. This

---

*The word 'novel' comes from the Italian word *novella*, meaning new.

is what drove the development of the extremely elaborate frontispiece, or title page, which eventually morphed into the blurb. And as well as unpacking the story, the first edition of *The Pilgrim's Progress* also included an illustration. In it, the slumbering everyman 'Pilgrim' is surrounded by the dream landscape that he travels through – with the 'start' and 'destination' of the journey helpfully labelled. No matter how literate you were or weren't, the basic structure of the story was there to encourage you to read on.

Other books started to follow this pattern with their frontispieces: Jonathan Swift's *A Tale of a Tub*, published in 1704, explained in his that the book was 'Written for the Universal Improvement of Mankind', and included a helpful illustration of the 'allegory' of the book for the reader to decipher. By 1719, when Daniel Defoe published *Robinson Crusoe*, the frontispiece was beginning to look a little more like modern-day cover copy.

THE

L I F E

AND

STRANGE SURPRIZING

ADVENTURES

OF

ROBINSON CRUSOE,

Of *YORK*, MARINER:

Who lived Eight and Twenty Years,
all alone in an un-inhabited Island on the
Coast of AMERICA, near the Mouth of
the Great River of OROONOQUE;

Having been cast on Shore by Shipwreck, where-
in all the Men perished but himself.

WITH

An Account how he was at last as strangely deliver'd by PYRATES.

Written by Himself.

LONDON :
Printed for W. TAYLOR at the *Ship* in *Pater-Noster-
Row*. MDCCXIX.

In roughly fifty words (if we exclude the title and subtitle), we learn that Crusoe is a mariner from York, that he lived for 'Eight and Twenty Years' alone on an uninhabited island off the coast of America, near the mouth of a great river, having been delivered there by a shipwreck that had killed all his shipmates, and then finally that he is 'deliver'd by PYRATES'. Like all good cover copy, this grabs our attention and tells us just enough about the story to leave us wanting to know more – by picking up and reading the book. Not only that, there are PYRATES. Who wouldn't want to read on?

These frontispiece 'blurbs' became more and more elaborate as the novel form developed – Samuel Richardson's frontispieces for *Pamela* and *Clarissa* tell us that his writings address 'The most important concerns of private life' and 'The distresses that may attend the Misconduct of Parents and Children' (*Clarissa*) and 'the Principles of Virtue and Religion in the Minds of the YOUTH of BOTH SEXES'. (*Pamela*).

P A M E L A:

OR,

VIRTUE Rewarded.

In a SERIES of

FAMILIAR LETTERS

FROM A

Beautiful Young DAMSEL,
To her PARENTS.

Now first Published

In order to cultivate the Principles of VIRTUE and RELIGION in the Minds of the YOUTH of BOTH SEXES.

A Narrative which has its Foundation in TRUTH and NATURE; and at the same time that it agreeably entertains, by a Variety of *curious* and *affecting* INCIDENTS, is intirely divested of all those Images, which, in too many Pieces calculated for Amusement only, tend to *inflame* the Minds they should *inform*.

In TWO VOLUMES.

The SECOND EDITION.

To which are prefixed, EXTRACTS from several curious LETTERS written to the *Editor* on the Subject.

VOL. I.

LONDON:

Printed for C. RIVINGTON, in *St. Paul's Church-Yard*; and J. OSBORN, in *Pater-noster Row.*

M DCC XLI.

So, three hundred years ago the job of the blurb was exactly as it is now: to use a small amount of space to tell us enough of what we might find inside the covers to whet our appetite, and persuade us to invest our time and money in the words inside.

Shrieking with delight

Gradually, the blurb on a book began to incorporate two elements: the cover copy describing what the story was about, and endorsements for the book from a third-party source. In 1925, when an unknown Ernest Hemingway published *In Our Time*, the book was sent out into the world with a jacket covered in endorsements from other writers: Ford Madox Ford, Gilbert Seldes, John Dos Passos, Donald Ogden Stewart, Waldo Frank and Sherwood Anderson. Anderson's blurb began: 'Mr. Hemingway is young, strong, full of laughter, and he can write.' Despite the efforts of Boni & Liveright, Hemingway was unhappy with their publicity efforts, and later that year he broke his contract with them and defected to Scribner.

But the endorsement of books by reviewers and other writers is controversial. By 1936, George Orwell was writing in 'In Defence of the Novel': 'Question any thinking person as to why he "never reads novels", and you will usually find that, at bottom, it is because of the disgusting tripe that is written by the blurb-reviewers.' Orwell then goes on to say that with novels 'being shot at you at the rate of fifteen a day, and every one of them an unforgettable masterpiece which you imperil your soul by missing . . . you must feel so guilty when you fail to shriek with delight'.* And I can see his point.

---

*Here Orwell was referring to a review in the *Sunday Times* that he had spotted a week before he wrote 'In Defence of the Novel': 'If you can

Sometimes when I go into a bookshop and look at the piles of books everywhere, the sheer volume and excitement level of the blurbs clamouring for me to pick up each and every one and read them are exhausting. Although it's now standard for most books to have quotes from other writers or experts on whatever they happen to be writing about emblazoned across the covers, no one really *knows* what their effect is. Do readers really buy a book based on the opinions of others? Or has using endorsements now become so normalised in bookselling that it's just what you do? George Orwell might not have been surprised to discover the concept of 'logrolling' – used to describe writers who trade good reviews between themselves. And sometimes blurb endorsements feel like an

---

read this book and not shriek with delight, your soul is dead.' It does seem a bit harsh on your soul if you found the novel in question just . . . mediocre.

escalating arms race: over time, they have become shorter and snappier, but the adjectives and superlatives have become increasingly heightened: 'Magisterial', 'Compelling', 'Unput-downable'. Ford Madox Ford's blurb for Hemingway began: 'The best writer in America at this moment (although for the moment he happens to be in Paris. . .)' – a luxury pedantic aside that you wouldn't get away with now in a time of short attention spans and headline-grabbing one-word blurbs. In fact, these days it would probably be condensed to 'The best writer in America', or possibly just 'THE BEST'.

A letter to a stranger

Imagine you are at a party, drink of choice in hand, and you find yourself having to introduce one friend to another. Thinking on your feet, you need to summarise the essence of each person in a short sentence, without a hint of anything that could count as a defect. In *The Art of the Publisher*, Roberto Calasso describes how in blurb-writing 'there was room for just a few effectual words . . . . and you must overcome the embarrassment that always exists in every introduction'. Parties or short stories, the stakes are the same.

As Calasso outlines, the forebear of the cover flap was the 'dedicatory epistle', whereby the author, or sometimes the printer, addressed the person who had given patronage to their work, usually a prince or person of some standing. One of the best-known patrons was Henry Wriothesley, the 3rd Earl of Southampton; he would probably have been forgotten by history if it weren't for his patronage of William Shakespeare. Shakespeare dedicated his poem *Venus and Adonis* to him in 1593, and a year later Wriothesley was the dedicatee of *The Rape of Lucrece*: 'The love I dedicate to your lordship is without end . . . What I have done is yours; what

I have to do is yours; being part in all I have, devoted yours.' The top-level purpose of the cover copy was to flatter the dedicatee, but literally reading between the lines you might also notice, as Calasso points out, 'so often and in so many books, the author (or the printer) allowed the truth – and even drops of his poison – to emerge between the lines of the opening dedication . . . the cover flap seems inevitably to be regarded as a form that kindles mistrust'.

That mistrust dates back to classical antiquity. Until well into the eighteenth century, authors were not generally paid by publishers. So the dedication, to a well-connected person or place, was an attempt to gain some kind of remuneration for the author's (and the printer's) work. Perhaps that mistrust remains, since nearly all readers and buyers of books understand that the point of cover copy is to *sell* the book to the reader. Cover copy is a paragraph of persuasion, and as Calasso says, 'For the reader, it is a text to be read with caution, for fear of it being a piece of surreptitious hype.' It is 'like a letter written to a stranger': every potential reader who engages with a book cover will be unknown to the writer of the copy – and yet somehow, with a limited number of words, they must attempt to reach each of them individually and persuade them to buy the book.

Lunch with Miss Belinda Blurb

Where I work we have a department called 'blurbs'. Actually, that's no longer true. We *used* to have a department called 'blurbs'. Now we have just one person in blurbs. We can call her Miss Belinda Blurb, to preserve her anonymity. Belinda's job is to write the copy for each book, as well as assemble the blurbs we might want to put on the cover or jacket.

'I learned how to write blurbs shut off in a little room

lined with books, where we would spend all day reading and writing, occasionally venturing out to talk to an editor or try and get hold of a manuscript. It was wonderful. My then manager had a brilliant way with words, and she would offer constructive criticism, cutting away at my copy and improving it. I also learned a lot by looking at blurbs on other books for inspiration, and at copy on anything from ad posters to packaging. It's a craft rather than an art, which can be honed by experience.'

In an increasingly hyper sped-up world, who has time to read every word of a book to write a blurb? Did you need to read every word to create one?

'It varies from book to book. If it's fiction, then I'll try and read as much of a book as possible. A copywriter friend once said he only read the first third so that he wouldn't give too much away, but I think it's important to know where the story is going to go and how it's going to end up, in order to hint at the direction. Like Harry Burns in *When Harry Met Sally*, I'm an inveterate reader of last pages. As well as reading the text itself, I'll read around it as much as time allows, especially in the case of classic fiction, reading about the author to get some kind of context. Often I'll have to write some copy before we have anything to read, in which case I need to know what the audience for a book is and what we want our pitch to be. Sometimes not having the text available can even make the process easier, but generally I think it's good to start with the book itself to get a feel for the author's tone and voice. I'll often make lots of notes and write far too much, and then keep refining and cutting (kill your darlings!) until I'm happy. I try to bear in mind George Orwell's maxims about using the simplest and clearest language possible.'

Belinda is brutal. I find it almost impossible to murder my own wordy darlings. What did she think made a blurb good or bad?

'It's so much simpler to say what a bad blurb is! One that gives too much away, or sounds generic, or reads like a Wikipedia entry packed with reams of information. The cardinal sin is something that's too long, as your eyes will have glazed over way before the end. A good blurb should show, not tell – if you're writing copy for a comic book, don't tell the reader that it's "hilarious" or "brilliantly funny", put some actual jokes and wit in your copy so that they chuckle while they're reading it. Don't tell them a book is tense or scary or dramatic – show them with your choice of vocabulary and sentence structure.'

'Show, don't tell' is used in every type of writing imaginable to nudge the reader into experiencing the story through action, words, thoughts and feelings, rather than exposition or description. Anton Chekhov wrote to his brother that 'In descriptions of Nature one must seize on small details, grouping them so that when the reader closes his eyes he gets a picture. For instance, you'll have a moonlit night if you write that on the mill dam a piece of glass from a broken bottle glittered like a bright little star, and that the black shadow of a dog or a wolf rolled past like a ball.' That's show, not tell.

'A blurb', said Belinda, 'should plunge you into the world of the book, not sound like a publisher telling you why you should read it. It's like telling an extremely short story in less than one hundred words. Recently I worked on a series of books where the blurb was just one line on the back cover, but it was actually quite liberating – the freedom of the tight brief! And the growth in sales online has meant that often the blurb will just be a few lines that you read on Amazon – how many people actually press "Read more" to get to the end? Less is always more. One of my fellow copywriters and I often have fun discussing the shape of blurbs – sometimes they're triangles, starting with something specific and broadening out, or they can be shaped like an hourglass, starting big then getting small and then broadening out again, or they can be more of a diamond. Hours of fun!'

Who knew? So, the next time you're in a bookshop, have fun identifying the shape of Belinda's blurbs.

In a 2012 article titled 'I greet you in the middle of a great career: a brief history of blurbs', Alan Levinovitz considers the art of the blurb from Roman times to the present day. As Levinovitz observes, we have now passed through the era of the blurb and we find ourselves in the middle of the age of the blurb, blap and blover. The 'blap' is apparently 'a glossy page covered in blurbs that immediately follows the front cover'. And for when that isn't enough, there is the blover – what Levinovitz calls 'a blap on steroids' – a second book cover, printed on the same cardstock as the first, and covered in endorsements. From bromides to steroids in one short century.

While I was writing this chapter, something unexpected happened that helped move the blurb front and centre of the book-buying experience. After three months of not being able to physically buy books owing to the 2020 coronavirus lockdown (part one), when bookshops finally reopened, they did so with new restrictions on how buyers could behave in a bookshop and what shops should do to keep customers safe. One of those restrictions was that any book touched by a customer and not purchased would then have to be quarantined for seventy-two hours. To encourage browsers not to pick up books unnecessarily, booksellers began to turn copies around, with the back-cover copy facing outwards, so that customers could read the blurb without having to handle the book.

What did Belinda think about this novel way of enticing in readers?

'My immediate thought was "This is my moment!" (sung in my head in the inimitable tones of Martine McCutcheon).* Then I started thinking about how front and back book covers work together. They are inextricably linked: the front cover gets your attention, and then, and only then, do you turn it over and the moment of truth arrives – do you like the blurb? But what happens if that moment of truth is sooner? Will the experience of book browsing lose something without that invitation of the front cover, and the question it poses, which is then answered, in part, by what's on the back? Will it actually put people off? And how will I know? (this time in the tones of Whitney Houston). The answer is probably never.'

'It is my rather subversive opinion that a writer's feelings of anonymity-obscurity are the second most valuable property on loan to him during his working years,' J. D. Salinger once said. (I haven't yet been able to find out what the first property was.) Salinger's book contracts from the 1950s specified that only the title and his name were to appear on his covers, and absolutely no images (he was furious that one edition of *The Catcher in the Rye* featured an illustrated approximation of Holden Caulfield), quotes, blurb or biography. He did allow some flap copy on the first edition of *Franny and Zooey*, however, which read: 'The author writes: FRANNY came out in the *New Yorker* in 1955, and was swiftly followed, in 1957, by ZOOEY.' This is perhaps taking Belinda's 'freedom of the tight brief' a little too far. But what was her favourite blurb?

'I find it quite hard to judge the things I've written over the years, and often they're not quite what I intended, after

---

*Author of *The Mistress* and *Who Does She Think She Is?: My Autobiography*.

compromises have been made with editors and authors, which is always a fine balancing act. It's far easier to judge others' copy – for example one of my favourite blurbs is the copy that's been on the back of various editions of Margaret Atwood's *The Handmaid's Tale*:

> The Republic of Gilead allows Offred only one function: to breed. If she deviates, she will, like all dissenters, be hanged at the wall or sent out to die slowly from radiation sickness. But even a repressive state cannot obliterate desire – neither Offred's nor that of the two men on which her future hangs.

'It's just over fifty words but it says so much and uses every one of its words well. It sets up a place and sense of time, it brings in a character and dramatic tension. It's got death, fear and even a love story to boot. And it's got intriguing detail, which is so important – the strange names, the phrase "hanged at the wall", which is slightly odd and arresting.'

A Tale of Three Handmaids

Once Belinda had pointed out to me the perfection of the paperback blurb on *The Handmaid's Tale*, I thought I would do some sleuthing to see if and how it had changed over time. As Belinda said, the paperback copy was a piece of spare, perfect, taut prose. The original hardback blurb, however, was very different – in fact, it was a series of overwhelming adjectives strung together. Here is the copy from the US first edition, published in 1985 by Houghton & Mifflin:

> *The Handmaid's Tale* is not only a radical and brilliant departure for Margaret Atwood, it is a novel of such

power that the reader will be unable to forget its images and its forecast. Set in the near future, it describes life in what was once the United States, now called the Republic of Gilead, a monotheocracy that has reacted to social unrest and a sharply declining birthrate by reverting to, and going beyond, the repressive intolerance of the original Puritans. The regime takes the Book of Genesis absolutely at its word, with bizarre consequences for the women and men of its population.

The story is told through the eyes of Offred, one of the unfortunate Handmaids under the new social order. In condensed but eloquent prose, by turns cool-eyed, tender, despairing, passionate and wry, she reveals to us the dark corners behind the establishment's calm façade, as certain tendencies now in existence are carried to their logical conclusions. *The Handmaid's Tale* is funny, unexpected, horrifying, and altogether convincing. It is at once scathing satire, dire warning, and tour de force. It is Margaret Atwood at her best.

This US first edition used 188 words.* The UK first edition, published by Jonathan Cape, went even further, and used 245 words:

Offred is a national resource. She is a handmaid: viable ovaries make her a precious commodity in the Republic of Gilead, where the birthrate has plummeted to dangerous levels. Assigned to a Commander whose wife cannot produce, Offred's purpose is onefold: to breed.

Dressed in red from veil to shoes, apart from the white wings which cover her face, Offred walks in silence

---

*It also expected readers to know what a 'monotheocracy' was; I had to look it up.

each day past the Guardians of the Faith, who man each barrier. She exchanges tokens for food. She visits the Wall, where gender traitors and war criminals hang for atrocities, once legal, committed in the time before.

At night in the bare room, Offred remembers quaint outdated customs such as gossiping, using paper money, jogging. Illegal things: women having jobs, reading, her real name, love. Love used to be central to everything. Now it is irrelevant.

Margaret Atwood, who has shown her formidable insights into the complexities of contemporary women in *Life Before Man* and *Bodily Harm*, now turns her vision to the future. Through the eyes of Offred we are shown the dark corners behind the calm façade of the Republic of Gilead: a regime which takes the Book of Genesis absolutely at its word, with bizarre consequences for women, and for men as well. Brilliantly conceived and executed, this powerful evocation of 21st-century America under post-feminist totalitarian rule gives full rein to Margaret Atwood's devastating irony, wit and acute perception. *The Handmaid's Tale* confirms her reputation as a major novelist.

Now, it's a bit unfair to compare these blurbs with each other. Paperback copy usually *has* to be shorter and punchier than hardback copy because there is simply less room for it, but I think it's clear the constraints of the paperback format help create a better piece of writing.*

---

*If you want more constrained writing to admire, read 'The Lottery', by Shirley Jackson. It's 3,389 words long and every single one is made use of with no spares hanging around to dilute the effect. These words of Jackson's led to the *New Yorker* (where it was first published, in 1948) taking delivery of 'the most mail the magazine had ever received about a work of fiction'.

AND IT WAS ALL YELLOW:
COVERS AND JACKETS

In Italy, *giallo* (yellow) is used to describe an entire literary genre: crime and mystery fiction, and from 1929 onwards the Italian publisher Mondadori published a series of crime novels known as 'Il Giallo Mondadori'. These cheap yellow paperbacks were so popular that *giallo* is now a synonym for a mystery novel (or, indeed, any unresolved and mysterious affair). So much for never judge a book by its cover. In fact, that's what this chapter is all about: covers, jackets, bindings and how they've each grown beyond their original prosaic purpose to protect and contain the words that lie inside. Plus, it's really weird how often yellow crops up. Seriously.

What links *Dracula*, *A Brief History of Seven Killings*, *The Spy Who Came in from the Cold*, *The Picture of Dorian Gray*, *The Yellow Book*, *Swing Time*, *Conversations with Friends* and *À rebours*? Yellow is the answer: either on the cover, or in the story. The Old English word for yellow (*geolu*) means 'bright', or 'gleaming', certainly things you might want a book cover to be. To convince people to look at words and give them their freedom, you first have to grab your reader's attention in any way possible. Colour, images, typography – the more arresting the better. 'To cry out' is precisely what writers want their covers to do.

Celestial eyes

In August 1924, F. Scott Fitzgerald wrote to his editor Maxwell Perkins from France: 'For Christs sake don't give anyone that jacket you're saving for me. I've written it into the book.' The book was *The Great Gatsby*, and the jacket was an image designed for the first edition by the Spanish artist Francis Cugat.

Usually, the artwork for a book is designed once it has been written, with the artist or designer responding to and interpreting the author's words. But here Fitzgerald was instead responding to the artwork created by Cugat and, according to his own account, had apparently incorporated elements of it into *The Great Gatsby*. In an essay in 2003 called 'Celestial Eyes: From Metamorphosis to Masterpiece', Charles Scribner III* said that the painting on the jacket is:

> the most celebrated and widely disseminated jacket art in twentieth-century literature, and perhaps of all time. After appearing on the first printing in 1925, it was revised more than a half-century later for the 'Scribner Library' paperback edition in 1979 . . . Like the novel it embellishes, this Art Deco tour de force has firmly established itself as a classic. At the same time, it represents a most unusual – in my view, unique – form of 'collaboration' between author and jacket artist.

Fitzgerald scholars continue to debate how the jacket was written 'into the book'. As Scribner reports, it has been suggested that the 'symbolic billboard eyes of Dr. T. J. Eckleburg' derive from the jacket: 'blue and gigantic – their retinas are one yard high. They look out of no face, but, instead, from a pair of enormous yellow spectacles which pass over a

---

*Fitzgerald's publishers, Scribner, was Charles Scribner III's family business, and he is an art historian.

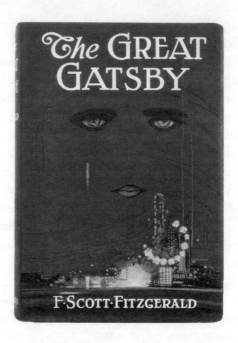

non-existent nose'. Another suggestion is that Fitzgerald was inspired by the image in Nick Carraway's description of Daisy as the 'girl whose disembodied face floated along the dark cornices and blinding signs' of the New York nights.

We might or might not agree with the description of this jacket being 'the most celebrated' of all time – there are as many jacket designs as there are books, and readers will have their own views on their favourites. Ernest Hemingway was not a fan of the jacket for *The Great Gatsby*; in *A Moveable Feast* he describes how 'A day or two after the trip Scott brought his book over. It had a garish dust jacket and I remember being embarrassed by the violence, bad taste and slippery look of it. It looked the book jacket for a book of bad science fiction. Scott told me not to be put off by it, that it had to do with a billboard along a highway in Long Island that was important in the story.'

As this suggests, anyone who loves books will have an opinion about their covers – and if one was produced with the input of the author, as with *The Great Gatsby*, it can also give us an insight direct from the author as to what the book is about. Often, for a loved book, we have an image in our mind's eye of a particular edition – we remember the covers of the books on the bookshelves we grew up with, or the artwork on the covers of the books we studied at school, and just a glimpse of that image can be enough to trigger a flood of feelings about that text and our experience of reading it. The cover artwork is (or should be) a shortcut to the message of the words inside, as well as a sophisticated marketing tool; it sets the mood of a book immediately. There are hundreds of books, blogs and articles dedicated to discussing cover artwork – what works, what doesn't, which covers and jackets are iconic.

A redesign of a book cover can even feel like an attack on 'our' version of a beloved and familiar story. 'If Sylvia Plath hadn't already killed herself, she probably would've if she saw the new cover,' wrote Jezebel in 2013 about the redesign of *The Bell Jar* for its fiftieth anniversary. I can vividly remember my copy of *The Bell Jar* – a hypnotic purple frame around a yellow-haired portrait of a woman's head, with the author's name slashed across the top in bright red, as if scrawled in lipstick. Looking at it now, it looks brilliantly 1980s, which didn't occur to me at the time, as I was living *through* the 1980s.

The fiftieth anniversary cover was described by Jezebel as featuring 'a low-rent retro wannabe pinup applying makeup. (Also, it's ugly and the colors suck.)' I have to say I agree on all counts. As is often the case, the best cover of *The Bell Jar* is the original one by Shirley Tucker: a series of understated concentric circles that draw the eye in, and perfectly reflect the claustrophobia of the heroine, trapped by society and her life choices.

Treasure bindings

The original purpose of a book's cover was to protect the words inside from wear and tear, and to project to the reader its status as a symbol of authority – particularly important when you consider that so many of the earliest bound books were of the scriptures or had religious significance. Gold, silver, jewels, ivory, silk, hand-engraved and embossed bindings, the form of the book was as precious as its contents, especially as books were in limited supply – which made them all the more valuable.

After the arrival of the printing press, books were far cheaper, more widespread and more accessible, and their bindings became more prosaic – perhaps made of leather or cloth, with metal clasps to close them and protect the edges. Book 'blocks' could also be bought with no cover (they would be wrapped in paper): the reader would then have a bespoke binding made according to their taste and budget. In the early nineteenth century, books became cheaper still and steam-powered presses and the mechanised production of paper meant that most covers were now made of cloth or paper, although without images on them. Gradually, printers took over the job of the specialist binders, and began to manufacture covers along with the book.

In 2009 the Bodleian Library in Oxford rediscovered the earliest-known book jacket, on a volume dating from 1829. The Bodleian had bought the jacket and other assorted book-trade ephemera in 1892, but it had been separated from the book it should have been attached to and had never been given its own catalogue entry. This jacket, like others of the time, enfolded the book completely, like wrapping paper. It was for a silk-covered book to be presented as a gift, called *Friendship's Offering*.

During the seventeenth and eighteenth centuries silk was often used to cover books, and the wrappers were to protect the cover and the book itself. As cover materials became more economical (fabric took over from leather), the printing and design on them became more involved, and the cover began to be used as a way to communicate to potential readers what was inside the book.

By the 1860s, advances in printing meant that more elaborate images in colour could be applied to the coverboards of books – using chromolithography, a chemical process based on the rejection of grease by water. It was still an expensive and time-consuming process – even skilled workers took months to produce the best results – but a development of cheaper variations with fewer colours and simpler images meant that more and more book covers could make use of it.

Yellowback dreadfuls

The first WHSmith to open at a railway station was at Euston in 1848, the same year as the publisher Routledge launched their 'Railway Library', cementing the enduring relationship between book buyers and railway travellers. Train travel was ideally suited to reading – the journey was smoother than by road, and oil and gas lamps meant passengers could read whatever the time of day – and with a newly mobile and more literate population, reading material was in demand. Lower production costs saw the introduction of cheap books known as 'yellowbacks' and 'penny dreadfuls'. Yellowbacks were so called because of the colour of the cheap wood pulp they were printed on, and they tended to be reprints of popular novels. Penny dreadfuls appeared in weekly instalments, with their moniker describing both their cost and their contents. These were 'sensational' stories – often rewrites of earlier Gothic thrillers, or featuring criminals, highwaymen, pirates and gypsies and supernatural entities. One of the most popular penny dreadfuls was *Varney the Vampire*, published between 1845 and 1847, and which included the first mention of sharpened teeth in connection with vampires. *Varney* was 232 chapters (roughly 667,000 words) by the time it reached its end – that's about six times as long as an average novel today, a nice earner, as authors for this type of story were paid by the line. The covers of the dreadfuls are macabre and lurid, with sketches depicting graveyards, despairing women and violence. The historian Judith Flanders quotes one publisher whose instruction to his illustrators was simply 'more blood – much more blood!'

Despite their lowbrow reputation, these cheap, widely accessible books were the forerunners of the mass-market paperback, and their front covers were the first to be used as the hook for the words inside. In a crowded and noisy market, they had to grab the attention of the potential buyer immediately, and persuade them to part with their money, before their train left the station. And gradually, the serial form was legitimised by writers like Charles Dickens* and Wilkie Collins.

Yellow nineties

As well as crying out to readers, the colour yellow evolved from a prosaic description of cheap printing in the nineteenth century to a way of signifying modernity and controversy. In *The Picture of Dorian Gray*, Lord Henry Wotton presents Dorian Gray with a copy of 'a poisonous French

---

*The Pickwick Papers was written in instalments by Dickens over two years (1836–7), but his work was also plagiarised by the penny dreadfuls. *Oliver Twiss*, *Nickelas Nicklebery* and *Martin Guzzlewit* were all real titles on sale, even if they made you sound inebriated when you asked your bookseller for a copy. Dickens successfully campaigned for reform of the law around plagiarism, but not before at least 50,000 copies of a plagiarised version of *The Pickwick Papers* had been sold.

novel', which leads to Gray's downfall. In Wilde's story, the book is yellow, and is an allusion to Joris-Karl Huysmans's novel *À rebours*.* On publication in France in 1894, *À rebours* became the ultimate symbol of decadent literature and Wilde was inspired by it when writing *Dorian Gray*. Yellow was at the time associated with this type of illicit literature – in Paris in the 1890s such books were wrapped in yellow paper to alert the reader to their lascivious content, either as warning or recommendation, depending on your point of view.

This signal was echoed in *The Yellow Book*, a quarterly literary periodical published in London from 1894 to 1897. *The Yellow Book*'s bright cloth binding in a colour that was considered to be decadent and immoral and its wide range of contributions across a number of artistic genres meant it became symbolic of the new movements of Aestheticism and Decadence. Even now it looks striking and modern.

The Yellow Book's first art editor was Aubrey Beardsley,† and it was published by John Lane of The Bodley Head (Lane's nephews, Allen, Richard and John, went on to found Penguin Books). Lane and Beardsley were often at loggerheads over Beardsley's attempts to shock public opinion through the artwork that appeared in it. Lane would carefully scrutinise the drawings supplied before they were published, but

---

*À rebours was first translated into English in 1926 with the title *Against the Grain*. The title page of that translation stated that it was 'the book that Dorian Gray loved and that inspired Oscar Wilde'. The current Penguin Classics edition uses a painting called *The Yellow Scale*, by Franz Kupka. Yes, it's very yellow.

†Beardsley died at the age of twenty-five, but along with his influential work he survives on the cover of the Beatles' album *Sgt. Pepper's Lonely Hearts Club Band* (he is at the far left of the second row from the back, next to Sir Robert Peel). The Beatles were big fans of yellow submarines.

Beardsley would conceal inappropriate details in his artwork: a game of artistic cat-and-mouse. The first volume, which appeared in April 1894, proclaimed:

> THE aim of the Publishers and Editors of THE YELLOW BOOK is to depart as far as may be from the bad old traditions of periodical literature, and to provide an Illustrated Magazine which shall be beautiful as a piece of bookmaking, modern and distinguished in its letter-press and its pictures, and withal popular in the better sense of the word. It is felt that such a Magazine, at present, is conspicuous by its absence.
>
> IN point of mechanical excellence THE YELLOW BOOK will be as nearly perfect as can be made. The present announcement shows the size and shape of the paper (now being especially woven) on which it will be printed, as well as the type that will be used, and the proportion of text and margin. It will contain 256 pages, or over, and will be bound in limp yellow cloth.

As this statement demonstrates, as well as offering a striking cover the editors were keen to break with the established

Victorian traditions of page layout, hence their emphasis on the type to be used and the proportions of text to margin. *The Yellow Book* was simple and elegant, deploying wide margins and white space to move it away from the cluttered Victorian styles that had gone before. It introduced itself in its prospectus 'as a book in form, a book in substance; a book beautiful to see and convenient to handle; a book with style, a book with finish; a book that every book-lover will love at first sight; a book that will make book-lovers of many who are now indifferent to books'.

Henry Harland, the editor, along with Aubrey Beardsley, also broke with convention by insisting that the artwork in *The Yellow Book* was not there to explain the text, but rather as something that stood alone, with value of its own. Every piece of artwork included had, like every piece of writing, its own title page – to emphasise its individual importance, quite separate from the text. So formative were these new ideas about how publications should look that even though *The Yellow Book* only appeared between 1894 and 1897 its colour gave a name to the entire decade.

The yellow future

'I have always thought it one of the worst days in the world for the British book trade when "picture jackets" began to come in,' was the view of the publisher Victor Gollancz. His publishing house was established in 1927, and Gollancz invited the innovative typographer Stanley Morison★ to work

---

★After Gollancz, Morison worked closely with Beatrice Warde (see 'Little hands and running feet') at the Monotype Corporation, and had a huge and lasting influence on modern typography. He commissioned Eric Gill's Gill Sans typeface and Times New Roman for *The Times* newspaper, first used in 1932. Gill Sans and Times New Roman are two of the most used typefaces ever.

with him on the design for his jackets. These were also bright yellow – in *Penguin Special: The Life and Times of Allen Lane* Jeremy Lewis explains that 'Gollancz . . . had decided, after exhaustive tests at a London railway bookstall, that yellow jackets were the most noticeable of all.'

Gollancz was among the first publishers to use marketing to sell his books (he would take out full-page newspaper adverts for some of them, which no other publisher had done before), and his appointment of Morison as a director at Victor Gollancz was an indication of how seriously he took the visual communication that branding and book jackets were part of. Gollancz's bright yellow jackets had bold black and purple type, stood out clearly on shelves and were immediately recognisable – he was one of the earliest proponents of branding, well before it became mainstream.

Gollancz's list was as forward-thinking and striking as his book jackets. He commissioned George Orwell to write *The Road to Wigan Pier* in 1936 and published Daphne du Maurier, Kingsley Amis and John le Carré. He published le Carré's first book, *Call for the Dead*, in 1961, and the jacket of the first edition* shows the publishing house's trademark style: on the yellow dust wrapper, the title and author's name stand out boldly in red, while instead of an image there is a boxed quote: 'Mr le Carré is a gifted new crime novelist with a rare ability to arouse excitement, interest & compassion.' The jacket of le Carré's next book, 1962's *A Murder of Quality*, builds on the advertising of the first, and reads: 'This is Mr le Carré's second thriller. His first, *"Call for the Dead"*, was more enthusiastically reviewed than probably any other first of 1961.'† Gollancz was able to use good words on a yellow

---

*There is a first edition for sale online – 'housed in a custom full morocco clamshell box' – signed on the title page, the asking price is £25,259.40.
†More enthusiastically reviewed, and in fact rarer and more valuable. A

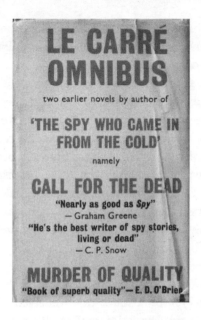

background to get the reader's attention and – and do away with artwork on his jackets altogether.

From Russia, with love, to France and England

The rise of mass advertising along with more sophisticated printing techniques led to more recognisably 'modern' cover designs from the 1920s onwards. The Russian avant-garde artist El Lissitzky claimed that 'In contrast to the old monumental art [the book] itself goes to the people, and does not stand like a cathedral in one place waiting for someone to approach . . . [The book] is the monument of the future.' Lissitzky and his fellow Russian Alexander Rodchenko heavily influenced graphic designers of the twentieth century,

---

signed first edition (no morocco clamshell box this time) is listed for sale online at £29,750.

and consequently had an impact on book design as well. Full colour, using elements of symbolism and cubism, began to be used on book jackets.

Book covers can tell us something about a country, too. Different places have their own style, and they don't necessarily translate across borders. In France, covers tend to be typographic – more restrained and intellectual than here, perhaps. They are more literal in the States, where the market is huge, and varied. What might appeal to book buyers in Florida won't necessarily work in North Dakota, and that encourages book designers in the US to be more conservative than in the UK. Sometimes, as Tom Lamont writes, the results can be baffling:

> What possible discussions took place in Germany, for instance, when publishers first received the manuscript for Martin Amis's *House of Meetings* – a novel that describes the misery of life in a Russian gulag – and set to work on a cover that featured six figures body-popping in the windows of a modern apartment block? What prompted Italian book designers to give junior wizard Harry Potter a hat shaped like a mouse, and why did the French opt against the monochrome design that jacketed Jonathan Safran Foer's *Everything is Illuminated* in the UK and the US, concocting instead a watercolour of somebody fondling a woman's breasts?

For covers, it seems, interpretation and cultural context is everything when it comes to their design.

'Good design is no more expensive than bad'

'I have never been able to understand why cheap books should not also be well designed, for good design is no more expensive than bad,' wrote Allen Lane when he established Penguin Books in 1935. Like Gollancz's editions, the earliest Penguins had no cover artwork – just text.* The original 'triband' Penguins, where the front cover was divided into three horizontal blocks, with the top and bottom ones being coloured and the middle one white, along with the Penguin logo itself, were designed by Edward Young, who became Penguin's first production manager. The earliest Penguins used the Gill Sans typeface on the cover – a strikingly modern touch – and followed Albatross Books, based in Germany, in adopting a colour-coded cover to indicate immediately to the bookshop browser what genre of book they were looking at.† As Phil Baines explains in *Penguin by Design: A Cover Story*, 'The original cover design had a tremendous impact in bookshops, appearing very fresh and modern with its directness.' The Penguin triband appeared with variations for roughly twenty-five years. Flexible and adaptable, and very clearly a 'brand', it was the base for the rapidly expanding Penguin list, as it spun off into Pelican and Penguin Special titles. In 1948 Jan Tschichold subtly redesigned the triband – giving it another lease of life. Now it lives on in a range of merchandising and in second-hand bookshops – part of our collective literary consciousness.

---

*This isn't quite correct – some early Penguins did have sketched black-and-white illustrations. And in February 1938 the first Penguins appeared carrying adverts – between then and 1944 Penguins advertised cigarettes, toothpaste, Jif and ammunition – which helped for a time to maintain the original cover price of sixpence.

†The original Penguin colours were orange for fiction, green for crime, dark blue for biography, cerise for travel and adventure, and red for plays. Yellow was for miscellaneous publications, like books of crosswords.

The return of the treasure binding

Cheaper production methods, the building of brands, the increasing importance of book marketing and mass-market reach meant that during the twentieth century the paperback cover was in the ascendant. Gollancz, Penguin and other paperback publishers used their cover designs to make books desirable, consumable, accessible, portable, collectible and recognisable, all while keeping them within the price range of the mass market. But despite this, the market for beautiful hardback books is still strong. I spoke to Coralie Bickford-Smith, author of *The Fox and the Star* and designer of the celebrated cloth-bound Classics series for Penguin, about why she thinks good book design endures, even in the face of e-readers.

'Personally I was heavily influenced by Victorian bindings, and in a move that felt slightly that it went against the ethos of Penguin (after all, the paperback Penguin was originally the cost of a packet of cigarettes), I started to play with these materials and wanted to create books that felt special and reignited the passion we feel for the printed word.

'The more elaborate art publishers have always been keyed into these ideas: the Folio Society has been doing this for seventy years. They were modelled on the private presses, like the Kelmscott Press,* and Folio began with the aim of providing handsomely illustrated books to people at prices they could afford. So this resurgence is nothing new, but it certainly was a trend that was adopted by mass-market trade publishers when it looked like the digital world was going to kill off the printed word.'

---

*The Kelmscott Press existed from 1891 to 1898 and was established and run by William Morris, printing books that he considered to be beautiful. It produced more than fifty works, and was heavily influenced by the illustrated manuscripts of Early Modern Europe.

I asked Coralie to talk to me about the constraints of book design: book formats have changed very little over the years, and cover designers are generally working in the same dimensions as two hundred years ago.

'The fact that we have been working on the same canvas for this much time says so much about the success and practicality of the book as an object. I love that book design is still steeped in its past: even the way we use point sizes to identify the type size of the font has its roots in early printmaking. We might now print differently in the age of desktop publishing, but we still use terms of measurement which point us back to the past. There are so many examples of this in a book designer's day-to-day life.'

The cover of a well-known book needs to be able to do several jobs at once: convey something fresh about a story that will speak to those who will have read it twenty times already (and who may have a strong emotional attachment to it), but also entice in new readers. In this way, redesigning a look for a classic book comes with its own particular set of challenges.

'I research everything,' said Coralie, 'the author, the time they were writing, the era they are writing about. I like to look at what was going on politically, and research graphic styles from the period. I like to delve in quite deep – I don't want to misrepresent some of the world's best-loved literature. I am giving an author's words a visual identity and I want to give them the best chance of being picked up and read. So I spend a lot of time considering all the available material, talking to editors and understanding the text. I try to find a symbolic element to adorn the cover with, then turn it into a pattern that flows around the book. I like to think of a symbol that might entice a new reader to the book because they wonder why that cover has used that particular theme. Sometimes people who have read the book before

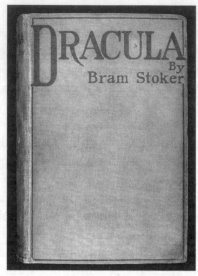

Dracula: groundbreaking in a number of
ways, including its visual impact.

understand why I might have chosen a certain symbol, and it
engages them with that book again.'

I told Coralie: One theme that has been cropping up all
throughout my research for this chapter has been the colour
yellow. From the literary quarterly *The Yellow Book* to yel-
lowback paperbacks and Victor Gollancz's bright yellow
dust jackets, I keep finding stories about yellow everywhere
I look. I know you designed the Penguin Gothic series a few
years ago – *The Dunwich Horror, The Beetle*, etc. Can you say
a little bit about why you chose yellow for it?

'I chose yellow because I felt it was a colour that defined
the horror genre convention without sacrificing the visual
impact. It was also a nod to the first edition of *Dracula* in 1897,
which had a bright yellow jacket with red type, which to this
day looks shockingly modern.'

In 2016 the *Wall Street Journal* and others reported that

yellow was the 'hot' colour for book covers once again, noting that the 2015 Man Booker Prize winner *A Brief History of Seven Killings* by Marlon James used yellow for both its UK and US editions: 'White covers in particular recede against the white backgrounds of Amazon and other online retailers. But yellow jumps off online pages and it can support both dark and bright type and graphics. Also, it carries no gender association and can signify anything from sunshine and optimism to a danger warning, making it a strong choice for a variety of genres and topics.' Politically and gender neutral, eye-catching – there's a reason airport directional signage is a heavy user of yellow, both in terminals and on runways – is a yellow background how words get good? Once our words are free, they need to compete in a crowded, noisy and competitive world – and they only have seconds in which to impress.

LITTLE HANDS AND RUNNING
FEET: TEXT DESIGN

Once we have allowed ourselves to be seduced by the prom-ise of the cover and blurb, we can embark on the adventure of reading. But before we have even read a word, we are confronted with how the very first page looks. We might not even realise what we are seeing – a good-looking page will simply encourage us to begin, and, hopefully, to keep going, without us realising that we are being led into the heart of things. What the first page of a book looks like sets the tone for the physical experience of reading it. The layout of the page, done well, plays a part in enticing us into the story.

The secret canon

In *The Secret Life of Books*, Tom Mole, the director of the Centre for the History of the Book at Edinburgh University, asserts that 'Each word occupies a particular place on the page in relation to other words and to blank spaces such as indents, paragraph breaks and margins ... This spatial dimension to the book is essential to the way we perceive it ... as we read we orient ourselves in relation to the architec-ture of the page.'

But what is this 'architecture of the page' that we orient ourselves by, and that we place our words on? Modern page layout is often based on the 'canons' of page construction – the rules that medieval- and Renaissance-era manuscripts used to divide a page up in a way that pleased the eye. Jan

Tschichold, the visionary text designer who worked at Penguin Books between 1947 and 1949, wrote: 'Though largely forgotten today, methods and rules upon which it is impossible to improve have been developed for centuries. To produce perfect books these rules have to be brought to life and applied.'

Although Tschichold only worked for Penguin for eighteen months, in that brief period he consolidated all his thoughts about standards and consistency in typesetting in a four-page leaflet called the 'Penguin Composition Rules', which was used to help elevate and standardise both the inside and outside of the Penguin list. These rules were built on by his successor, Hans Schmoller, with *Printing Review* commenting in 1956 that Schmoller 'substantially took over the main features of Tschichold's style and then brought it to a close perfection by additional subtleties and refinements'.

Schmoller's refinements to Tschichold's original style were based on how Johannes Gutenberg and other early printers composed their pages. From the very dawn of mechanised print, the *way* words looked was already of great concern to printers and compositors – who were keen to produce a harmonic visual arrangement between the parts of a page.

Tschichold was at the centre of the 'New Typography' in twentieth-century Europe. This movement wanted to break free from the conventions of existing Victorian designs, and was organised around asymmetry, the use of white space and sans serif typefaces. In his essay 'The Principles of the New Typography', Tschichold explained that 'The essence of the New Typography is clarity. This puts it into deliberate opposition to the old typography, whose aim was "beauty" . . . utmost clarity is necessary today because of the manifold claims for our attention . . .' Tschichold recognised that in an age of mass media (he would have been overwhelmed by where we are today), it was not enough for text to be ornamental: it had to be clear, so that a reader would find it easy to approach and engage with, even with other ways of communicating competing for attention.

It is interesting to note that Tschichold refers to these rules and the idea of the canons of page construction as 'largely forgotten' at the time when he was employed by Penguin Books. He was being asked to work on books that were the epitome of standardised production and design – the original mass-market paperbacks. Tschichold's skill was in recognising how to rescue from obscurity and reuse the elements of Renaissance manuscripts and apply them to the mechanised era. The 'modern typography' that Tschichold pioneered was also encouraged by the need to coordinate efficiencies in printing in the immediate post-war period – the details of his designs were in some ways shaped and forced by the regulation and mechanisation of standardised book formats and industrial printing.

Marginal gains

The layout of a page has evolved to be both useful and decorative: from the earliest days, writers understood that words needed to be organised in certain ways to make them approachable and useful – and in turn, *readable*. The running heads at the top* help us know where we are in the book, and the page numbers (also called folios) give us our location precisely.† The conventions of text design are used to help the

---

*Running heads are a useful navigational tool, and they don't have to stay at the top of the page. Sometimes they decide to sprint off and relocate to the bottom of the page, where they are then known as running feet. And yes, they can also escape to the sides, but 'running side' is not such a fun description as the other two.

†I've worked with an author who wanted the page numbering in his book

reader to know exactly what a section of text is: hence chapter titles look different from the main body of the text, and subtitles, quoted material, verses, footnotes and other text ornaments can be instantly signposted for the reader by using appropriate typefaces, emphasis and positioning – a subtle but important conversation between reader and designer that should work in harmony with what an author is trying to get their words to say.

This organisational approach to text design began in antiquity: some scrolls could reach up to 30 metres in length, so it was vital that a reader could quickly and easily orient themselves. Text was arranged in columns, running from left to right, and each column was separated by a margin, which let you know when to stop reading and move on to the next text line.

When the scroll was replaced by the codex, it became easier for readers to see where a block of text started and ended, but the margin became more important than ever, just in a different way. Previously, commentaries on a text would have been published in their own separate scroll, but the inviting white space of the margin in the codex encouraged readers to write their own thoughts and responses to the text – and that space was particularly important when paper was scarce or expensive.

Perhaps the most famous example of marginalia,* as these comments are called, was written in about 1637 by Pierre de Fermat in the margins of his copy of a book called

---

to begin at 314 and then count down (yes, a book about Pi). In another book the 'numbering' began at zero. It's like he wanted his readers to be lost in a wilderness of words.

*The word was coined by Samuel Taylor Coleridge, who turned his marginal comments into performance art, even going so far as to publish his own marginal musings. The word 'marginalia' of course gives what could be a trivial form of words a mock-pompous feel.

Arithmetica, by Diophantus of Alexandria. Fermat's marginal note read:

> It is impossible to separate a cube into two cubes, or a fourth power into two fourth powers, or in general, any power higher than the second into two like powers. I have discovered a truly marvellous proof of this, which this margin is too narrow to contain.

This piece of marginalia became known as Fermat's Last Theorem, a mathematical problem that would remain unsolved until 1995.*

Perversely, given that paper is relatively much cheaper, writing on books is disapproved of nowadays. As Leah Price highlights in *What We Talk About When We Talk About Books*, the growth of public libraries in the nineteenth century led to readers being discouraged from leaving marks in their margins: 'Good reading, once defined by what you did to a book, now became a matter of what you refrained from doing.'

But Joe Moran, a professor of English and cultural history, says that 'Books are meant to be written on'. And marginal spaces allow us to do just that. 'Marginalia allow us to see into the unguarded, uncensored thoughts of the reader,' Moran points out, 'as they respond immediately to the words on the page: a silent communion with the author or the unknown reader who might pick up the book, secondhand, a generation later. Marginalia is, by definition, something on the margins – undervalued, overlooked.'

Undervalued, that is, depending on who is doing the valuing. In 1962, while sentencing Keith Halliwell and Joe

---

* Several books have been written about the quest to prove the theorem: the margins really were too narrow to contain the whole story.

Orton to six months in prison for defacing dozens of library books, magistrate Harold Surge commented that 'Those who think they may be clever enough to write criticisms in other people's books, public library books, or to deface them or ruin them in this way' should know that this behaviour was 'disastrous'. Most of Orton and Halliwell's doctoring was to jacket art, although some of it was directed at blurbs: Dorothy L. Sayers's *Gaudy Nights* was newly described as the writer 'at her most awe inspiring. At her most queer, and needless to say, at her most crude!' 'I was enraged that there were so many rubbishy novels and rubbishy books,' said Orton, in the closest he came to an explanation. In 2019 more than £50,000 was raised for a statue of Orton in his home town of Leicester through sales of the defaced books.

Edgar Allan Poe, who called his collection of reflections and fragments *Marginalia*, wrote: 'I have always been solicitous of an ample margin; this is not so much through any love of the thing in itself, however agreeable, as for the facility it affords me of penciling in suggested thoughts, agreements, and differences of opinion, or brief critical comments in general.'

Nowadays, with electronic texts and e-readers, readers can interact with the text and with a community of other readers whenever they want to, but are these electronic marginalia the same as handwritten scrawls in a physical margin? The *New York Times* critic Sam Anderson imagines a 'readerly utopia . . . a Gutenberg-style revolution – not for writing, this time, but for reading. Book readers have never had a mechanism for massively and easily sharing their responses to a text with other readers, right inside the text itself. Now, when the Coleridge of 21st-century marginalia emerges, he should be able to mark up the books of a million friends at once.'

This 'culture of response' is what an electronic world pushes us towards, with debates on Twitter, blog posts, comments and forums allowing all of us a vast electronic marginal space. But while the electronic margin might be infinite, there is something about seeing someone articulate their immediate response to a text in their own handwriting that makes it deeply personal.*

Manuscripts and manicules

Before becoming an author, Samuel Richardson was a printer. In 1706, when he was seventeen, he was bound as an apprentice to a printer called John Wilde. Richardson worked himself up to be the compositor and corrector of Wilde's printing press, and eventually left that print shop to be an 'Overseer and Corrector of a Printing-Office'. By 1719, Richardson was running his own printing shop and, in 1722, took on the first of several apprentices of his own. Richardson was a man whose life was bound up with print: he married John Wilde's daughter Martha and obtained a contract with the House of Commons in 1733 to print the *Journals of the House*.[†]

Richardson's print background comes to the fore in *Clarissa*, his monumental novel of 1748. *Clarissa* is written in epistolary style: the story unfolds through letters sent between the main characters. In the original volumes, Richardson

---

*Although not found in the margins of a book, one of the most intriguing annotations in history is the Wow! signal. That's the name given to a narrowband radio signal that bore all the hallmarks of extraterrestrial intelligence. The signal was received in August 1977 by the Big Ear radio telescope in Ohio, and the astronomer who discovered it and noted 'Wow!' next to the data recorded was called Jerry R. Ehman.

†The *Journals of the House* are the corrected archived edition of the Votes and Proceedings of the House of Commons. Hansard is the transcripts of Parliamentary debates – it was named after a printer, Thomas Curson Hansard, who was the first official printer to Parliament.

PAPER X¹

LEAD me, where my own thoughts themselves may lose me;
Where I may doze out what I've left of life,
Forget myself; and that day's guilt!—
Cruel remembrance!—how shall I appease thee?

—Oh! you have done an act
That blots the face and blush of modesty;
    Takes off the rose
From the fair forehead of an innocent love,
And makes a blister there!—

    Then down I laid my head,
Down on cold earth, and for a while was dead;
And my freed soul to a strange somewhere fled!
    Ah! sottish soul! said I,
When back to its cage again I saw it fly,
    Fool! to resume her broken chain,
    And row the galley here again!
    Fool! to that body to return,
Where it condemn'd and destin'd is to *mourn*.

Oh my Miss Howe! if thou hast friendship, help me,
And speak the words of peace to my divided soul,
    That wars within me,
And raises ev'ry sense to my confusion.
    I'm tott'ring on the brink
Of peace; and thou art all the hold I've left!
Assist me in the pangs of my affliction!

When honour's lost, 'tis a relief to die:
Death's but a sure retreat from infamy.

Then farewel, youth,
    And all the joys that dwell
With youth and life!
    And life itself, farewel!

For life can never be sincerely blest.
Heaven punishes the *Bad*, and proves the *Best*.

sometimes used typographical features to emphasise parts of the story. Signatures at the end of letters are displayed in calligraphic handwriting, and a little hand with a pointing finger* is used to mark the furious annotations of Robert Lovelace in the margins of a letter he intercepts as part of the plot. But the most striking use of typography and page layout comes after Clarissa is drugged and raped in a London brothel. To illustrate her emotional and psychological distress, Richardson places fragments of the text – Clarissa scrawls on bits of paper which she then tears up and throws on the floor – at angles on the page, as shown above.

---

*This is called a manicule and looks like this: ☞. It's been hanging around manuscripts since the twelfth century to mark corrections or to indicate to the reader something of note on a page. By the fifteenth century in Italy it had often developed elaborate cuffs and shading and was sometimes used as the seventh footnote indicator, after the pilcrow (see 'Foot-and-note disease' for more on this).

Clarissa's emotional breakdown is represented by the literal breakdown of the typographical order. Richardson makes his words work hard in two ways – by what they say, and by how they appear. His words get good by reflecting Clarissa's distress in their placement and spatial relationship on the page; her roiling emotions can no longer be constrained by convention. Richardson asks his readers to step into the story with him – not with a gentle coax but by seizing your collar and dragging you into Clarissa's internal landscape.

The devil's dimensions and the double elephant

The largest medieval illuminated manuscript in the world is the *Codex Gigas*, which translates as 'Giant Book'. Consisting of the whole of the Christian Bible plus some other 'secular' texts, it is 92cm long, 50cm wide and 22cm thick, and it weighs 74.8kg. It also has an alternative name – the *Devil's Bible*. This is because one of the pages features nothing but a 50cm tall brightly coloured illustration of the devil, complete with forked tongue.

According to some manuscript experts, this enormous book was the work of a single scribe. Tests have demonstrated that even without the illustrations it would have taken twenty years of non-stop writing to complete it. Who has that much time on their hands? Historians think it may have been written by Herman the Recluse, a thirteenth-century Benedictine monk. According to legend, Herman had broken his monastic vows and had been sentenced to be walled up alive. To try to avert this, Herman promised to create in one night a book for the monastery that would include the sum of all human knowledge. As the night wore on and it became clear that he probably wouldn't be able to meet his deadline, he prayed not to God but to Lucifer to help him finish the book, in exchange for his soul. The

devil appeared, helped him complete the Bible, and was duly thanked by way of a portrait.

Between 1826 and 1838 John James Audubon self-published his monumental *Birds of America** – featuring hand-coloured illustrations of more than seven hundred birds. The page dimensions needed for the illustrations were so large that it had to be printed on paper known as 'double elephant'. At least the name gives you some idea of what to expect – but what about books described with the dimensions of a folio, quarto, octavo, duodecimo, sextodecimo, vicesimo-quarto or tricesimo-secundo? These unapproachable-sounding descriptions arose because historically the dimensions of hardback books were based on how many pages of a book were printed on each piece of paper, and how many times that piece of printed paper had to be folded to produce a signature of leaves that were then bound into the book. A *folio* was made by printing two pages of text on each side of a

---

*According to *The Economist*, once you adjust for inflation, five of the ten highest prices ever paid for printed books were for copies of *Birds of America*.

piece of paper, which was then folded to produce four pages. If you print eight pages on each side of a sheet and then fold the paper three times, you end up with sixteen pages – an *octavo*. To be honest, this kind of stuff is almost impossible to visualise unless you are lucky enough to have someone standing in front of you demonstrating it with a giant piece of paper.

Fortunately, most hardback black-and-white books now follow a few standardised formats. You can have A format and B format hardbacks, so they match the dimensions of the paperback version, just with stiff cover boards. The traditional larger hardback sizes we're accustomed to seeing in bookshops are known as Royal (234mm × 153mm, and often used for longer non-fiction titles) and Demy (216mm × 135mm – more likely to be used for hardback literary fiction or shorter non-fiction). In truth, you can have a book of almost any dimensions you like – and colour and illustrated titles come in a much wider variety of formats – but Royal and Demy are the most commonly found in the UK.

Readers would struggle with the dimensions of the *Devil's Bible*, and modern-day formats reflect one of the great strengths of the book: its portability.

The first Penguin paperbacks were in what is known as A format (111mm × 81mm), dimensions that meant one could be slipped into your pocket easily – indeed, in the US books of this size were often referred to as 'pocketbooks'. The A-format book became known as a 'mass-market paperback', partly because its size meant it could be conveniently sold in places that weren't bookshops – drugstores (in the US), railway stations and airports.

Although plenty of books today are still published in A format, they tend to be 'genre' fiction: romance or thrillers – books that people might read once and then dispose of. In contrast, more 'literary' works tend to find themselves published initially in hardback, before they go on to spend the rest of their lives in B-format paperback, which is roughly 129mm × 198mm.

Standardised print runs and market expectations mean that A and B formats are overwhelmingly the most common dimensions for a paperback book – they are cheap to produce, easy to carry with you and give a legible reading experience for most texts. Indeed, these page sizes provide the constraint that designers today must work within.

Say that to my typeface

Our digital times mean that we can all think of ourselves as typesetters now. We sit at our screens, click on a drop-down menu and contemplate the exotic list of options available to us. Times versus Arial. Baskerville or **Braggadocio**.*

What does it say about me that I am drawn to Cambria but not Eurostile, a font that along with its parent font Microgramma apparently had a near monopoly on science-fiction typefaces until recently? Eurostile and Microgramma have been used for the title sequences of *Alien*, *Star Trek*, *2001: A Space Odyssey*, *Back to the Future*, *The Truman Show*, *Thunderbirds*, *Red Dwarf* and 1975's *Eurovision Song Contest*. But even if graphic designers in galaxies far, far away like to work with a restrained palette, it's hard to deny there is an overwhelming amount of choice out there, each with its own distinct mood and history, quirks and benefits (and disadvantages).

How can someone with no training or background in

---

*OK, maybe not **Braggadocio**. 'Like high society in the 1920s, it should not be taken too seriously,' was one online description I found of this font. Especially as it wasn't designed until 1930. Incidentally, continuity failures in TV and films caused by using a font that wasn't in existence in the period the drama is set in are pretty common.

design possibly work out the optimal one to use? Where do you even begin? We all know that you should never, ever use **Comic Sans**,* but are there other ways of displaying words that are equally crass? I asked Tom Etherington, a designer who has created the insides and outsides of hundreds of books, to guide me round the world of typefaces. Over the years Tom has created covers for some of the world's best writers, living or dead, as well as some more peculiar design projects, including a Christmas card for Bananarama and a skin-care range for the golfer Nick Faldo.[†]

'Selecting a typeface can be overwhelming. Where I work we have access to roughly 24,000 fonts, but 23,900 of these are terrible, which helps to narrow it down a bit. There are some practical considerations to take into account – if the book has a lot of text extracts you should choose a typeface with readable italics; if the type is going to be printed small you want a typeface with a larger "X" height (the height of the lower-case letters) so that the shapes of the letters are clear. So often, the content of the text itself helps you decide on an appropriate typeface to use.

'There are also cultural factors that can point you in the right direction. If you are designing a book all about Germany in the eighteenth century you might want to find a typeface from the same period. These connections add meaning and make type sympathetic to the text, but to be honest not many readers will be conscious of these historical cues. Sometimes there are massive blunders – the British Veterinary Association should probably have looked into Eric

---

*Of course, this isn't true. **Comic Sans** is the font everyone loves to hate, but, as Simon Garfield explains in *Just My Type*, it is often used along with **Trebuchet** (both fonts come from the same developer, Vincent Connare) by those who work with people with dyslexia.

†Imagine how sad I was to discover that Nick F's skincare range was not called 'Foreskin'.

Gill's relationship with dogs before setting all their promotional material in his eponymous typeface.*

'Most important of all, though, is readability, which is different to legibility. Readability is about how easily your readers can understand what you're trying to say. Legibility is about how readers can decode the symbols you use to say it – the ability to distinguish one letter from another in a typeface, for example. It seems illogical, but serif typefaces are easier to read than sans serif. You would rarely see a long textbook set in sans serif, but of course all kinds of monstrosities exist. American books are some of the worst offenders. I once saw a whole book set in a **bold Didone** – madness. Other factors, like generous leading (the space in between lines of text, named after the bits of lead put between metal type), can help make long texts more readable.'† Back up. Set in a what? Apparently, Didone is a portmanteau of the surnames of the typefounders Firmin Didot and Giambattista Bodoni and refers to the dominant types of the nineteenth century that the two of them created. Described by Talbot Baines Reed in 1890 as 'trim, sleek, gentlemanly, somewhat dazzling', they have more recently fallen out of favour, with Stanley Morison calling types of their era 'the worst that have ever been'.

'Typesetting is a very conservative craft,' continued Tom, moving on from the offensiveness of Didones; 'one man's "characterful" typeface is another man's nightmare reading experience. Even the most well-intended flourish

---

*Let's just say that Gill's reputation has been re-evaluated in recent years, after details of his personal life (some of which involved intimate knowledge of canines) emerged in the 1990s.

†As well as leading there is kerning, which describes the process of adjusting the spacing between characters in a font so that they are visually pleasing. The word comes from the French *carne*, which means the quill of a pen or a projecting angle.

or ornamental embellishment fails as soon as it distracts the reader from the text. There are many typefaces that fit within the frame of "readable" though – you wouldn't choose the same typeface for a book of romantic poetry and an essay on quantum physics.

'There are classics that all designers will lean on: Sabon, Caslon, Plantin, Bell, Baskerville, the list goes on. And back in the days of the Arts and Crafts movement, private presses would sometimes commission a typeface specifically for their books.'

This was the case with the Doves type, used for the Doves Press. Established by T. J. Cobden-Sanderson in 1900 in partnership with Emery Walker (Walker was friends with William Morris, and Morris was inspired by him to set up the Kelmscott Press – see 'And it was all yellow' for more), Cobden-Sanderson was a bookbinder who in 1887 gave the Arts and Crafts movement its official name – the Arts and Crafts Exhibition Society.

Walker and Cobden-Sanderson were by 1909 engaged in a long-running dispute over the Doves type, which Emery had designed. It was based on types used by Nicolas Jensen in the 1470s, notably in the Doves Bible, which is considered to be one of the most beautiful examples of Bible design. When the Doves Press closed in 1916, Cobden-Sanderson began to destroy the type by throwing it into the River Thames ('bequeathed to the river', as Cobden-Sanderson described in his diary); he made 170 trips to the Thames between August 1916 and January 1917 to dispose of it. In 2015 graphic designer Robert Green worked with the Port of London Authority, and together they were able to salvage 150 pieces of the original type. Green was then able to revive and refine a new version of it. From Dove to Phoenix.

I asked Tom to tell me the difference between a typeface and a font – I know I always use the wrong word, making the designers I encounter wince on a daily basis. 'A typeface is a family of fonts, so Helvetica is a typeface and **Helvetica Bold**, *Helvetica Italic*, Helvetica Regular, etc., are fonts. Serif typefaces have additional lines or dashes at the end of strokes on the letters. Sans serif typefaces do not have these lines, hence "sans" – French for "without". Lots of typographic terminology relates to old hot-metal printing techniques, like casting, melting and carving. My favourite is upper and lower case, so called because when printing with metal type, the capital letters were stored on a case above the rest of the letters.'

The crystal goblet

In 1930 Beatrice Warde gave a speech to the British Typographers' Guild called 'The Crystal Goblet, or Printing Should Be Invisible'. Warde was an American who had moved to Europe in 1925. In 1926 she investigated the origins of Garamond type, concluding that it had been made ninety years later than previously thought – and not by Claude Garamond. She published this work under the pen name 'Paul Beaujon', and as a result was offered the position of editor at the *Monotype Recorder*, to the confusion of the Monotype Corporation executives, who assumed she was a man. She worked with Eric Gill promoting Gill Sans and with Stanley Morison pioneering modernist typefaces for the Monotype Corporation.

In her speech, Warde compared good typesetting to choosing whether to drink wine from a gold goblet or a crystal glass: 'You will choose the crystal, because everything about it is calculated to reveal rather than hide the beautiful thing which it was meant to contain.' Warde continued:

The book typographer has the job of erecting a window between the reader inside the room and that landscape which is the author's words. He may put up a stained-glass window of marvellous beauty, but a failure as a window; that is, he may use some rich superb type like text gothic that is something to be looked at, not through. Or he may work in what I call transparent or invisible typography . . . The third type of window is one in which the glass is broken into relatively small leaded panes; and this corresponds to what is called 'fine printing' today, in that you are at least conscious that there is a window there, and that someone has enjoyed building it. That is not objectionable, because of a very import-ant fact which has to do with the psychology of the subconscious mind. That is that the mental eye focuses through type and not upon it. The type which, through any arbitrary warping of design or excess of 'colour', gets in the way of the mental picture to be conveyed, is a bad type. Our subconsciousness is always afraid of blun-ders (which illogical setting, tight spacing and too-wide unleaded lines can trick us into), of boredom, and of officiousness. The running headline that keeps shouting at us, the line that looks like one long word, the capitals jammed together without hair-spaces – these mean sub-conscious squinting and loss of mental focus.

When I asked Tom about Beatrice Warde's goblet, he said that it 'perfectly encapsulates the typesetter's role. One of the main debates in graphic design theory is the role of the designer as subjective collaborator or neutral operative. It's a combination of things: the reading experience, how the lay-out references the text. How generous the size of the type can be without making a ridiculously long book. If there are pictures, do these coincide with the correct part of the text, should they be inset, or on a page of their own? If there are loads of footnotes,* how will they look? A thousand tiny decisions are taken when you are designing a book: "Will the reader understand this?" "Is this where your eye goes to first?" Context is an important factor. It goes without saying that an encyclopedia will look different to a novel; small type in a reference book is manageable (even enticing) if you are dipping in and out of the text, but it would be unreadable in a novel where you might read it through in one or two sittings.'

Warde describes how 'the mental eye focuses through type and not upon it. The type which, through any arbitrary warping of design or excess of "colour", gets in the way of the mental picture to be conveyed, is a bad type.' As Tom explained, 'Typefaces are generally most suitable for the printing methods used around the time of their release. For instance, letterpress fonts would have a thinner design to allow for the ink to spread. Digital fonts have new methods like font hinting (basically a digital instruction to allow fonts to appear sharper on a screen) . . . a way of the type getting out of the way to let the words do their work.'

I love Warde's description of the relationship between the reader and the author that the designer is there to facilitate – the pane of glass that allows the words to be clearly seen and, more importantly, to communicate easily with the reader. But the glass needs to be crystal clear for that to happen.

'It's quite amazing to think how little has changed in the canons of page design,' said Tom. 'Designers working now still rely heavily on the work of people like Jan Tschichold and Raúl Rosarivo[†] from over fifty years ago, who in turn

---

*NB to my text designer: you've probably noticed by now that this book has loads of footnotes. Sorry.

[†]Raúl Rosarivo was an Argentine typographer who analysed the golden

looked to Renaissance-era books to understand those prin-ciples. Look at the modern edition of the *Book of Common Prayer*, for the Church of England, designed by Derek Bird-sall.* It's a simple book, all set in Gill Sans, but, perhaps due to the nature of the content, it displays such craftsmanship. The book wouldn't stand out to the average churchgoer, but the consideration and craft make every page a joy to look at. It's a masterclass in beautiful, understated design. Invis-ible goblets are obviously impossible – the human hand will always be there – but it can be visible without interfering with the reading experience. Nobody wants to drink from a dirty glass.'

From dingbats to grasshoppers

We've seen with *Clarissa* that an author can use the elements of design as part of the story. This kind of experimental design can work well, especially if a writer and designer share a vision. 'Smaller publishers tend to be more daring and experimental,' said Tom. 'For example, Four Corners, a small art book publisher, have created a series called "Famil-iars", where they reprint classic novels, collaborating with an artist for each. So, for instance, *The Picture of Dorian Gray* is reimagined as a 1970s Parisian costume drama, and the text is set like a magazine from the period, accompanied by appropriate adverts and headlines.

'Actual fashion magazines are always entertaining to look at for typographers – I've seen whole magazines set in

---

ratio in Renaissance books, particularly as it was used in the Gutenberg Bibles.

*The original *BCP* was published in 1549 and redesigned by Birdsall in 2000. In England only Cambridge University Press, Oxford University Press and the Queen's Printer are entitled to print it. CUP and OUP are known as the 'privileged presses' for this reason.

monospaced typewriter fonts with line lengths so long you need an athlete's neck muscles to read them – it's like they don't want people to read it! This is actually true of an article in music magazine *Ray Gun*.* Designer David Carson[†] found an interview with Bryan Ferry[‡] so boring that he set the entire thing in Dingbats, an unreadable font made entirely of symbols.'

I'd thought that dingbats were a recent thing, but apparently you can use the word to describe a printer's ornament, and those have been around for centuries. Printer's ornaments have been used since, well, print was established, to divide text up. The proper name for these typographical devices is the charmingly pretty word *dinkus*.[§] The fleuron (✿), one of the earliest typographic ornaments (they were used in early Greek and Latin texts to divide paragraphs), was described by Robert Bringhurst in *The Elements of Typographic Style* as a 'horticultural dingbat'. Zapf Dingbats, which anyone who uses a computer will be familiar with, was dreamt up by typeface designer and calligrapher Hermann Zapf (Zapf was also the designer of the less wacky typefaces Palatino and Optima). Dingbats led to Wingdings, and eventually on to emojis, some of which use the same keyboard shortcuts as Zapf's original 'bats.

---

*Ray Gun published seventy issues between 1992 and 2000, with a focus on 1990s pop culture explored through experimental typographic design.

†Carson is apparently the most googled graphic designer ever, according to *Eye* magazine. I'd put a bit more biographical detail about him here, but maybe you want to google him yourself.

‡I did look but I couldn't find anything about Bryan Ferry worthy of a footnote.

§The word 'dingbat' was first used to describe an alcoholic drink in 1838. It has somehow morphed into one of those words like 'gizmo' and 'thingamabob' that can be used as a stand-in for anything with an unknown name.

It's hard to imagine what designers like Warde and Tschichold would have made of the digital design age. Words on a digital screen are far less beguiling than those viewed through the crystal goblet. The fixed constraint of the dimensions of the page has encouraged great creativity over the centuries. While doing away with constraint might seem positive, freeing text from the design rules that anchor it can mean we lose more than we gain. As Tom told me, the possibilities created by moving away from a 'fixed' set of page dimensions leads to other issues – there's too *much* freedom. 'There's a flexibility with digital design that means a certain amount of craft is impossible: for instance the "runt" (a single word left on a line of its own at the end of a paragraph) is a typesetter's enemy and usually you would find a way to fix it, but if the text is going to be displayed on all manner of tablets and formats, typesetters won't be able to iron them out.'

As well as runts, designers talk about widows and orphans (their language is strangely emotionally brutal for such an elegant craft). A widow is a short line (often only one word) at the end of a paragraph or column that falls at the beginning of the following page or column. An orphan is a paragraph opener that has been cruelly separated from its family by, say, the bottom of the page. How do you remember the difference? 'An orphan starts alone, a widow ends alone.'

But none of these evocative ways of talking about our words mean anything as soon as you take them away from the fixed dimensions of a page and move them onto an infinitely flexible screen.

There are advantages, however. 'I think the ebook allows for more innovation,' said Tom. 'It's in its infancy and it seems like the format hasn't properly embraced its potential yet. The opportunity for the reader to adjust the size of the type on the screen is a great invention, which must help so many readers with visual impairment. These seem like obvious improvements to me, but people's reading habits are slow to adapt, and ebooks have not been the game changer they were forecast to be. Perhaps technology has moved faster than people's reading habits: the ebook virtual page turn is evidence of that – insane skeuomorphism.'

Skeuomorphism? Apparently, a skeuomorph is defined as 'an object or feature which imitates the design of a similar artefact made from another material'. So as Tom noted, the virtual page turn of an e-reader is a skeuomorph that emulates the physical book – we seek the comfort of the familiar by any means possible, even as everything changes around us. The virtual world uses many skeuomorphs – think of the bin symbol on your desktop computer – but they've been around for centuries. The Minoans were known for producing elaborate silver cups that were then recreated in pottery for a wider market, complete with approximations of the rivets on the metal originals. Skeuomorph. What a word.

r-p-o-p-h-e-s-s-a-g-r

In this chapter we've seen how Samuel Richardson subverted typographic norms to help the reader feel and understand his protagonist's experiences. The American avant-garde poet E. E. Cummings went a step further with his 1935 poem 'r-p-o-p-h-e-s-s-a-g-r', using the subversion of linguistic convention to achieve a more oblique ambition: to put the reader directly into the life and mind of a grasshopper.

A more dynamic relationship between form and content is what Cummings is working towards. He wants us to experience the poem through the shape of it and, in doing so, bring us a little closer to understanding what it is to be a grasshopper.

Cummings doesn't so much rewrite the rules of typography, punctuation and grammar as rip up the rulebook.

```
                              r-p-o-p-n-e-s-s-a-g-r
                    who
          a)s w(e loo)k
          upnowgath
                    PPEGORHRASS
                                        eringint(o-
          aThe):l
                eA
                    !p:
          S                                              a
                         (r
          rIvInG                   .gRrEaPsPhOs)
                                             to
          rea(be)rran(com)gi(e)ngly
          ,grasshopper;
```

Take, for example, how he uses parentheses to break up words, creating syllables in places we wouldn't usually expect to find them. Cummings is trying to convey something of a grasshopper's leap into the air and return to the ground (hence the cascading components of 'leap' in the centre of the poem that connects its two halves). Our eyes skitter around the page in a series of grasshopper-like jumps. The word 'grasshopper' itself is used four times, but only as a fully formed word at the end of the poem. After its dissonant hop, skip and jump across the page, the grasshopper finally reveals itself.

Traditionalists, rejoice. There is also a decoded version of this poem.

Grasshopper,
who
as we look
up now gathering
into the
leaps
arriving to
become arrangingly,
Grasshopper

But where's the fun in that? Sometimes we need to look at words through a very different, and compound, eye.

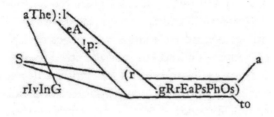

'THE MEMORY OF THE
LOSS': LOST WORDS

Words that were and then weren't

In *The Book of Lost Books: A Complete History of all the Great Books You Will Never Read*, Stuart Kelly sums up 'the entire history of literature' as also being 'the history of the loss of literature'. These 'lost' words include Shakespearean plays,* a comic play by Homer† and a novel by Sylvia Plath. Plath described the novel, called *Double Exposure*, as 'hellishly funny' and left behind 130 manuscript pages of it when she died in 1963. Although Ted Hughes admitted to burning one of her journals, he claimed that he had not destroyed the manuscript (which those who saw it said was semi-autobiographical) and that Plath's mother had stolen it. Her undiscovered words may still be out there somewhere.

Although we feel frustrated when we know that words we might value are 'lost' to us, losing words can sometimes

---

Cardenio was performed in 1613 and was attributed to William Shakespeare and John Fletcher in the Stationer's Register in 1653, but no copies of it exist. It is thought to have been based on Miguel Cervantes's *Don Quixote*, which had been translated and published in England in 1612. Shakespeare may also have written a lost play called *Love's Labour's Won*, although that might just be an alternative title to *Much Ado About Nothing* or *All's Well that Ends Well*.

†Although its authorship is disputed, the play is generally attributed to Homer. Called *Margites*, its central character is a man who according to Plato 'knew many things, but all badly'. The title character was so stupid he was even unsure which of his parents had given birth to him.

alter the trajectory of a writer's career for the better. In 2000, letters between Fanny Stevenson and W. E. Henley,* a family friend, were rediscovered. In one of them, Fanny wrote about reading the first draft of *Strange Case of Dr Jekyll and Mr Hyde*, written by her husband Robert Louis Stevenson. Describing the draft as 'full of utter nonsense', she told her correspondent, 'He said it was his greatest work. I shall burn it after I show it to you.' Fanny made good on this threat and burnt the draft. Her husband immediately reworked the story, this time with his wife's feedback in mind (Fanny apparently felt that the first draft did not emphasise the allegory of the story enough), and the revised *Jekyll and Hyde* became an immediate success. The first draft, however, is lost to history.

In December 1922, Ernest Hemingway was in Switzerland while his wife, Elizabeth Hadley Richardson (always known as 'Hadley'), was in Paris. Hemingway had met a journalist and editor called Lincoln Steffens, who was impressed with his work and asked to see more of it. Hadley, who was packing to travel to Switzerland, filled a small suitcase with all Hemingway's work in progress, his juvenile writing and all the carbon copies. Stowing the case on a train at the Gare de Lyon while she went to buy a bottle of water, Hadley returned to find the case gone. When she arrived in Switzerland she had to break the news to Hemingway, who recounts the moment in *A Moveable Feast*:

---

*Henley only had one leg and was the inspiration for Long John Silver in *Treasure Island*, and if that wasn't enough he was also the author of the poem 'Invictus', with its famous closing lines: 'I am the master of my fate: / I am the captain of my soul.' His daughter, who died at the age of five, was the inspiration for the name 'Wendy' in J. M. Barrie's *Peter Pan*. Her name was Margaret, but she referred to Barrie as her 'friendy-wendy', from which he got the name.

I had never seen anyone hurt by a thing other than death or unbearable suffering except Hadley when she told me about the things being gone. She had cried and cried and could not tell me. I told her that no matter what the dreadful thing was that had happened nothing could be that bad, and whatever it was, it was all right and not to worry. We could work it out. Then, finally, she told me. I was sure she could not have brought the carbons too and I hired someone to cover for me on my newspaper job. I was making good money then at journalism, and took the train for Paris. It was true alright and I remember what I did in the night after I let myself into the flat and found it was true.

Hemingway may have remembered what he did that night, but he never told anyone else. He later said that he would have opted for surgery 'if it might remove the memory of the loss'.

Shortly after the loss of his words, Hemingway wrote to Ezra Pound to tell him what had happened. 'You, naturally, would say, "Good" etc. But don't say it to me. I ain't yet reached that mood.' Why would Pound have said 'Good'? Hemingway may have known that Pound would in some way approve of the situation: after all, Pound claimed to have burnt 'two novels and three hundred sonnets', and maintained that he wrote a sonnet every morning and then immediately ripped it up. His 1935 collection of essays was called *Make It New*, which became something of a slogan for the modernist movement, and perhaps encapsulated his attitude towards destroying words. It was Pound's deletions from the manuscript of T. S. Eliot's *The Waste Land* that in the view of many Eliot scholars improved it. Hemingway would later write: 'The first and most important thing of all for writers today is to strip language clean, to lay it bare

down to the bone.' After the loss of the suitcase* Hemingway may have changed or enhanced his writing style to be
even leaner and sparer than it had been already; he needed
to make up for lost time and earn an income. Of course, all
this is speculation, as is the whereabouts of the suitcase,† but
it's interesting to think that its loss perhaps altered the entire
trajectory of Hemingway's writing career.

This chapter looks at the afterlife of all those works
that tumble off the printing press, but not the copies that
make their way into bookshops, homes, shelves and hearts.
Instead, it's about those that find themselves banned, lost,
burnt, pulped, censored and otherwise discarded. Ever
since Gutenberg's democratisation of printing, books and
the words they contain have been destroyed: inadvertently,
maliciously, strategically or by legal necessity. A collection of
books can be free to find an audience in one era, but banned
or driven underground in another. Most right-headed people
recoil at the idea of destroying a book (at 451°F or any other
temperature). So how and why does it happen?

---

*Now of course this physical loss of an author's words is harder to
achieve – digital backups mean that a draft can rarely now be 'lost'. I did
have one author, however, who in the course of his Acknowledgements
in his long and long-awaited book mentioned that his young son had
managed to delete the first draft of it from his computer.

†So much speculation, in fact, that a science-fiction novel by Joe Haldeman called *The Hemingway Hoax* won several awards in 1991. Haldeman
described it as 'a horror novel tinged with ghastly humor, as the apparently insane ghost of Ernest Hemingway murders a helpless scholar over
and over; the scholar slipping from one universe to the next each time he
dies, in what is apparently a rather unpleasant form of serial immortality.
The tongue-in-cheek explanations for how this could happen qualify the
book as a science fiction novel . . . It may be the most "literary" of my
books, but it also has the most explicit sex and the most gruesome violence I've ever written. Nobody will be bored by it.'

'The weeder in God's garden'

Responsible for destroying 15 tons of books, 284,000 pounds of printing plates for 'objectionable' books and 4 million pictures, Anthony Comstock styled himself 'the weeder in God's garden'. Comstock, who established the New York Society for the Suppression of Vice, was born in Connecticut in 1844, and his morality crusade culminated in him persuading Congress in 1893 to pass the Comstock Laws, which criminalised the use of the US Postal Service to send (among other things) any material determined to be 'obscene, lewd or lascivious'. Titles deemed offensive and thus banned from the US mail under the Comstock Laws include *The Decameron*, *The Canterbury Tales* and *Moll Flanders*. Aristophanes' *Lysistrata* was banned under Comstock for being 'anti-war', and again in Greece in 1967 (under the short-lived military junta) for exactly the same reason.

As Alberto Manguel describes, Comstock's methods were 'savage but superficial'. He ruthlessly censored a vast number of writers, books, words, images and pages. In fact, he pursued his moral quarry so remorselessly, he is believed to have incited at least fifteen suicides. However, it can be argued his infamy outstripped his efficacy; he was perpetually chasing down copies of books that had already appeared in print and were in wide circulation. Comstock might have longed for the power of the Catholic Church which, via its 'List of Prohibited Books', prescribed what Catholics were and were not allowed to read.

The *Index Librorum Prohibitorum*, as it was styled in Latin, was formally established in 1559 by Pope Paul IV (versions had appeared as early as 1529), and it was not abolished until 1966. (The final updated edition had appeared in 1948, still with 4,000 titles on it – one of the reasons it was abandoned was that Cardinal Alfredo Ottaviani, prefect of the Congregation of the Doctrine of the Faith, believed that by 1966 there was simply too much contemporary literature for the censors to keep up with. The words had won.)

The *Index* listed books deemed heretical or contrary to morality and was a response to the widespread dissemination of literature after the emergence of mass printing. Before that, control could be much more easily maintained over the means of production, as scriptoria were labour-intensive and slow. The words could barely get a head start before they were reined in. Johannes Kepler's astronomy book *Epitome Astronomiae Copernicanae* was put on the list in 1619 (for asserting that the sun and not the earth is the centre of the solar system) and stayed there until 1835. Surprisingly, given that his theory of evolution seemed to undermine the biblical account of creation, Charles Darwin was never placed on the *Index*, but noteworthy writers who were include Simone de Beauvoir, Jean-Paul Sartre, Voltaire, Immanuel Kant, John Milton, John Locke, Blaise Pascal, André Gide and Galileo Galilei.

The last book to be banned by the government in the United Kingdom, on obscenity grounds, was in 1991. *Lord Horror* by David Britton was apparently the first 'horror genre' Auschwitz book. The decision was overturned in 1992, but 'In answer to frequent queries', reads the book's publisher's website, there are currently 'no plans to reprint the book'.

The list of books that have been banned in the United Kingdom is short: *Areopagitica* (John Milton; banned for attacking the Licensing Order), *Rights of Man* (Thomas Paine; banned owing to Paine being charged with treason and supporting the French Revolution), *Despised and Rejected* (Rose Laure Allatini; banned under the Defence of the Realm Act for criticising Britain's involvement in the First World War, and for sympathy towards homosexuality), *Ulysses* (James Joyce; banned for obscenity), *Lady Chatterley's Lover* (D. H.

Lawrence; famously, obscenity again), *The Well of Loneliness* (Radclyffe Hall; lesbian themes), *Boy* (James Hanley; obscenity), *Lolita* (Vladimir Nabokov; yet more obscenity), *Spycatcher* (Peter Wright; banned in the UK before it was even published for revealing official secrets, although the ban was ultimately pointless as it did not cover Scotland or Australia, from where readers could still order copies) and *Lord Horror*, and all of them have now had their bans overturned, even if some are no longer in print.

In the United States, the historical list is more extensive and includes John Steinbeck's *The Grapes of Wrath* (temporarily banned in a number of states, including California, owing to the unflattering way it portrayed Californians), *Howl* by Allen Ginsberg (the first edition was seized for obscenity), Joseph Heller's *Catch-22* (banned at various times in Ohio, Texas and Washington State because it referred to women as 'whores') and *Elmer Gantry* by Sinclair Lewis.*

'Burned unread'

But what happens when it is the *author* that decides their words shouldn't be set free? In February 1862, Elizabeth Siddall, who was an artist, artist's model and poet, died of a laudanum overdose, possibly self-inflicted. Siddall had been a model for Walter Deverell, John Everett Millais and Dante Gabriel Rossetti, whom she married in 1860. When she died Rossetti was overcome with grief, and although unable to attend her funeral, he was able to hide two books in her

---

*On publication in 1927 *Elmer Gantry* created a furore: the protagonist, the Reverend Dr Elmer Gantry, leads a life of philandering, drinking and debauchery rather than saving souls. Sinclair Lewis was the first American recipient of the Nobel Prize in Literature; in his Nobel Lecture Lewis observed that 'Our American professors like their literature clear and cold and pure and very dead.'

coffin (concealed by her hair) – Siddall's own Bible and Rossetti's own manuscript book. 'I have often been writing at these poems when Lizzie was ill and suffering, and I might have been attending to her, and now they shall go,' he is reported to have said. In 1869, however, as Rossetti was attempting to prepare a volume of poems for publication, he decided to arrange the retrieval of the poems and through his agent had the coffin exhumed. Rossetti was able to do this only because the Home Secretary, Henry A. Bruce, was a friend of his. Rossetti was not present at the exhumation, but in the event, much of the book had been destroyed by damp and was illegible by the time it was dug up; Rossetti's reputation never recovered from the news that he had ordered the exhumation.

Franz Kafka left instructions with his literary executor Max Brod to destroy all his writings, both published and unpublished, on his death. Before he died of tuberculosis in 1924, Kafka wrote to Brod: 'Dearest Max, my last request: Everything I leave behind me ... in the way of diaries, manuscripts, letters (my own and others'), sketches, and so on, [is] to be burned unread.' Brod famously disobeyed this request and claimed that he told Kafka he would not do so, and that 'Franz should have appointed another executor if he had been absolutely and finally determined that his instructions should stand'; between 1925 and 1935 he published as much of Kafka's work as he could.* Other writers whose 'burning wills' were ignored include Virgil, who before his death in 19 BC directed that the manuscript of the *Aeneid* was to be burnt, and Emily Dickinson, who instructed her sister Lavinia to burn all her papers. Lavinia burnt her

---

*Kafka's lover Dora Diamant also ignored his wishes. She secretly retained twenty of his notebooks and thirty-five letters. In 1933 these were confiscated by the Gestapo and are still missing.

sister's correspondence, but interpreted the will as not referring to Emily's notebooks of some 1,800 poems; in this way they were saved and published by Lavinia in the years after Emily's death in 1886.* Most lovers of literature would agree that Brod and Lavinia Dickinson were right to act as they did, even if they were betraying the wishes of those who had asked them to do otherwise.

Into the flames (or the river)

'Where they burn books, they will, in the end, burn human beings too': this quote from Heinrich Heine is engraved on Berlin's Bebelplatz (formerly the Opernplatz), site of the most infamous book-burning event of the twentieth century – that of May 1933 soon after the Nazi seizure of power – when more than 25,000 supposedly 'un-German' books were destroyed. The line comes from Heine's 1821 play *Almansor* and refers to a much earlier book-burning – that of the Koran, copies of which were burnt during the Spanish Inquisition as part of attempts to eradicate Islamic Moorish culture from the Iberian Peninsula. The destruction of books has been carried out for thousands of years and in many cultures: it is said that the Chinese Qin Dynasty (221–206 BC) didn't just burn books, they buried 460 Confucian scholars alive, because they were perceived as a threat to Qin governing policy. In 1258 the Mongols entered Baghdad and during a week of pillage threw books from the city's Great Library ('The House of Wisdom') into the River Tigris.

Destroying books was a common response by Western

---

*Philip Larkin in his will asked his companion Monica Jones to burn his diaries when he died in 1985. Fortunately, he didn't mention his many letters, which survive.

colonisers whenever they seized control of territories where other cultures lived. In the 1560s Franciscan friars in Mexico led by Diego de Landa (later Bishop of Yucatán) burnt the codices of the pre-Colombian Mayan people. The friars found a large number of these sacred books and, 'as they contained nothing in which there was not to be seen superstition and lies of the devil, we burned them all, which they regretted to an amazing degree, and which caused them much affliction'. Consequently, there are only three Mayan codices in existence that are authenticated (and one that is not),* and the destruction means the loss of valuable insights into Mayan culture. As Michael D. Coe writes, 'Our knowledge of ancient Maya thought must represent only a tiny fraction of the whole picture, for of the thousands of books in which the full extent of their learning and ritual was recorded, only four have survived to modern times (as though all that posterity knew of ourselves were to be based upon three prayer books and *Pilgrim's Progress*).'

Alberto Manguel writes that 'the history of reading is lit by a seemingly endless line of censors' bonfires, from the earliest papyrus scrolls to the books of our time'. Manguel quotes Goethe, who after watching the burning of a book in Frankfurt compared it to an execution: 'To see an inanimate object being punished is in and of itself truly terrible.'

Redressing the balance a little, some books have famously been saved from certain destruction. The Monte Cassino archives were moved by two German officers to the Vatican (the archives contained hundreds of historic manuscripts that would have been destroyed along with the abbey during the Battle of Monte Cassino), and the Sarajevo Haggadah, a Jewish illuminated manuscript dating from about 1350, was

---

*And to add insult to injury they are known by the names of the places where they are now kept: Dresden, Madrid and Paris.

saved from the Nazis and then kept safe in the 1990s during the wars that followed the break-up of Yugoslavia.

The Nazi burning of books in 1933 is notorious both for what it symbolised and for the range of writers who had their work torched. The first books burnt were by Karl Marx and the Marxist theoretician Karl Kautsky, and the extensive list of works destroyed included writings on Communism, Marxism, Bolshevism and pacifism, pornography, any literature of Jewish authors and any written in support of the Weimar Republic or which was perceived to denigrate the German people. The 1933 burning was followed by a mass exodus from Germany of writers, artists and intellectuals, and exactly one year after the burnings had begun a group of German writers who had fled to France established the Library of the Burned Books, a collection of all those titles copies of which had been destroyed. Alfred Kantorowicz, who helped set up the library, explained:

> the real significance of the Library was not confined to its material existence. When we inaugurated it, we wanted to make that day of shame a day of glory for literature and for freedom of thought which no tyrant could kill by fire. And furthermore, by this symbolic action, we wanted to awaken Europe to the dangers which threatened its spiritual as well as its material existence.*

How do words get good? By never being forgotten.

---

*The library was eventually seized by the Nazis when they occupied Paris in 1940. But it wasn't just the Nazis that burnt books – in 1946, the Allies destroyed millions of copies of more than 30,000 titles as part of the denazification programme.

Words that weren't and then were

Sometimes words are denied their audience because they were ahead of their time, or written at a moment when it was culturally impossible for the writer to say what they wanted. E. M. Forster's *Maurice*, which deals with a homosexual love affair, was written between 1913 and 1914, but only published posthumously in 1971.* In 2019 *Le Mystérieux Correspondant*, a collection of nine 'lost' stories by Marcel Proust, was published for the first time in French – Proust had chosen not to publish them because of their 'audacity' (like *Maurice*, they touch on homosexual themes).

But sometimes books are 'lost' for simpler reasons, one of which is that the creator didn't think they were good enough. 'Nearly every novelist has a shelved novel in his or her closet or desk drawer: Trying out ideas that don't work out is how writers learn,' suggests Scott Timberg in a *Salon* piece about Harper Lee's rediscovered manuscript *Go Set a Watchman*. The question is, should these lost literary try-outs be read? After all, if an author didn't think their words were publishable while they were alive, who are we to judge any differently once they are no longer around? In 2015 alone works by Charlotte Brontë, F. Scott Fitzgerald, Edith Wharton and Dr Seuss† were 'discovered', along with *Go Set a Watchman*.

Is there a difference between a 'lost' text and one that we have perhaps known about but ignored? In a 2019 *New York Times* article, Parul Sehgal recalls her recent review of a previously unpublished short story by Sylvia Plath and remarks on how many previously neglected women writers have recently been 'rediscovered' and published – Lucia Berlin, Clarice Lispector, Pauli Murray – along with new

---

*A note attached to the manuscript read 'Publishable, but worth it?'
†It's called *What Pet Should I Get?*, and was discovered by Dr Seuss's widow in a shoebox.

biographies and appraisals of writers like Shirley Jackson and Susan Sontag. As Sehgal says, 'It's not enough to give thanks that these writers have been restored to us; we need to ask why they vanished in the first place.'

While rediscovered words can seem like a good thing, *Go Set A Watchman* shows us that there are problems. Although some readers may have picked up *Watchman* thinking it was a sequel to *To Kill a Mockingbird*, it was actually a first draft of the novel that eventually became *Mockingbird* after Lee had rewritten it at the request of her editor, Tay Hohoff. In it, Atticus Finch associates with the Ku Klux Klan – a back-story that upset many readers, who were accustomed to the *Mockingbird* version of him as a vision of justice, decency and moral values. Harper Lee described *Watchman* as a 'pretty decent effort', but her decision to rework the manuscript after Hohoff's reservations was surely the right one. As Robert McCrum writes:

> in an inexplicable creative leap that will bring hope to the world's creative writing classes, something happened. Hohoff, who recognised the true heart of *Go Set a Watchman*, asked Lee to focus on Scout's childhood, opening a secret door in her imagination. Harper Lee found her voice. A new novel, entitled 'Atticus Finch', was born, and would become *To Kill a Mockingbird*.

But was it the right decision to publish *Watchman*? After all, it was a draft version that was then subsequently revised, with a very different focus and voice. *Watchman* was apparently published with Lee's consent, but the story of how it became *Mockingbird* raises questions about whether 'lost' words should remain just that.

Pulp fictions

The physical book has straddled an uneasy line between veneration and destruction – we flinch from the idea of dismantling books, but the idea of the book as a disposable product is a chapter in its story.

The mass-market paperback appeared first in the United Kingdom when Allen Lane established Penguin Books in 1935. Lane was frustrated by the failure of booksellers to take advantage of the growing middle class, which had a bit of extra money to spare, yet found that most of what was available to read were highly priced hardback editions of new titles, or thrillers and trashy romances with poor-quality printing and gaudy covers. Lane's idea was to buy the reprint rights of quality books* from other publishers and repackage them in a paperback format for sixpence – the price of a pint of beer or a packet of cigarettes. Making money from such a list of books meant that they had to be standardised in design and format, but Lane 'aimed at making something pretty smart, a product clean and bright as two pins, modern enough not to offend the fastidious highbrow, and yet straightforward and unpretentious'.

In the United States Robert de Graff had a similar idea. By the time he launched Pocket Books in 1939, Penguin Books in the UK and Albatross Books in Germany were already established and selling millions of copies. Albatross had been founded in 1932. Their books were printed in a standardised

---

*The first ten Penguins were (in the order they were numbered on their covers): *Ariel* by André Maurois (although it took until the second print run for the author to regain the accent in his name), *A Farewell to Arms* by Ernest Hemingway, *Poet's Pub* by Eric Linklater, *Madame Claire* by Susan Ertz, *The Unpleasantness at the Bellona Club* by Dorothy L. Sayers, *The Mysterious Affair at Styles* by Agatha Christie, *Twenty-Five* by Beverley Nichols, *William* by E. H. Young, *Gone to Earth* by Mary Webb and *Carnival* by Compton Mackenzie.

size and featured colour-coded genres and typographic covers – all ideas that were copied by Allen Lane. The progress of Albatross was halted by the Second World War, but they had shown Lane and de Graff what the paperback was capable of.

De Graff knew that to sell paperback books for 25 cents a copy he would have to have high print runs. The problem he faced was low demand and poor accessibility. Relatively speaking there were few actual bookstores in the US, which meant print runs were traditionally low and prices high. De Graff's solution was to change the way books were distributed, by selling them in non-traditional outlets – news-stands, train stations, drugstores, indeed anywhere that would agree to stock them. He also offered refunds for copies that weren't sold, and covered his books in colourful, even lurid drawings, which he knew would sell better in the American market than the pared-back European style of typography and colour coordination. De Graff's Pocket Books and the publishers that soon followed, including Dell and Popular Library, were the original producers of 'pulp' fictions – they democratised books, but they also got readers used to the idea that words could be disposable.

Pulping fictions

Roughly one Mills & Boon paperback book is sold in the UK every 6.6 seconds. Its business model is very different to that of other publishers (although it would have been very familiar to Robert de Graff): they publish a set number of books every month, which are sent out to bookshops and news-stands. At the end of the month, any that haven't sold are returned to the publisher to be pulped – if you don't buy a copy within the month of sale, your only hope is to track down a second-hand copy. All this means that Mills & Boon have a lot of physical books that need pulping.* Where do all these books go? Well, one place is the M6 toll road that bypasses Birmingham. In an article on book pulping, Joe Moran explains:

> All I ask as an author is that, as I should like some say over the disposal of my bodily remains, I am consulted about what happens to my books if they are pulped. My first choice would be bitumen modifier, the pellets roadbuilders use to bind blacktop to aggregate. A mile of motorway consumes about 45,000 books: the M6 toll road used up two-and-a-half million Mills & Boon novels. There is something pleasingly melancholic about converting unread books into the wordless anonymity of a road, like having your ashes scattered in a vast ocean.

Moran notes that publishers rarely talk about the volume of books that are pulped – 'it is seen as an unnatural act, akin to literary murder' – but it is a huge part of the publishing business model. Books are cheap to make, and the financial rewards of publishing a bestseller are huge, which encourages overproduction (see 'Out of print' for more on this). But running alongside this vast industry of churning out physical copies of books is our squeamishness about what to do with unwanted and unread copies. We idealise books and reading, but fail to recognise that it is an industry based on overproduction and oversupply, and that many books will never be opened or read. Where do all these books go? Book publishing is unusual in that bookshops are allowed to return unsold books to publishers, to be disposed of at their own

---

*Although perhaps fewer than they used to: they now release more than a hundred e-books a month and sell more in electronic formats than they do in print.

expense. This is only fair when you consider that in 2013 UK publishers released more than twenty new titles an hour – 184,000* new and reissued titles a year. No bookshop has space to stock that number of new titles, alongside the millions of old books already in existence, which is why they can return old stock to make way for new. It also ensures that if a bookshop misjudges how many copies of a book they can sell, they can simply return the excess stock and make it the publisher's problem.

Judging how many copies of any one individual book to print is extremely difficult. Every market for every author is different, and even within an author's work you can find substantial variations between their most and least popular books. You can standardise formats, you can make economies of scale when buying paper or print, but you can never quite know what the market for a title might be.

I asked John, who has worked in publishing for more than fifty years, largely in inventory management (the part of publishing that determines who stays in print, with how many copies, and for how long), about returns. 'On a day-to-day level it is perhaps the most depressing aspect of trade publishing,' he said. 'The concept of a firm sale is illusory, sale or return is the basis on which we trade. Although one can raise two cheers for the lower returns rates we now see, it is worth remembering, if only wryly, one of Peter Mayer's earlier observations about Penguin. Shortly after he took over he was told of Penguin's low returns. "That's your trouble, you don't publish aggressively enough!" The Penguin returns rate then increased, which was seen as a healthy sign!' As ever in the world of words, it's a matter of

---

*In a *Guardian* piece about book sales in 2013, the literary agent Jonny Geller described this figure as 'either a sign of cultural vitality or publishing suicide'.

perception: publishers need to have a level of faith in their authors, which should encourage them to print and promote a healthy number of copies of a book. If that means that sometimes the words will return to you for pulping, at least it shows that you backed your author.

Mayer was the CEO of the Penguin Group from 1978 to 1997, during which he agreed to publish Salman Rushdie's *The Satanic Verses*; he received death threats following the book publication. He also established Overlook Press, which specialised in publishing books that had been overlooked by other, larger publishers – literally saving good words from being lost. 'The real issue ought to be, is the book readable, is it valuable, is it good?' he said. 'Who cares if it's old or new? If you haven't read the book and it's an old book, it's actually a new book. It's a new book to anyone who hasn't read it.' An old word has a new life whenever it reaches a fresh reader.

The Rock Bottom Remainders

'The Rock Bottom Remainders is a band that includes some of today's most shining literary lights. Between them, they've published more than 150 titles, sold more than 350 million books, and been translated into more than 25 languages.' So begins their history on their website. Perhaps this group of literary luminaries* find comfort in confronting, head-on, the rarely acknowledged world of remaindering books. If

---

*Who are the Rock Bottom Remainders? According to their website, the original members are: Dave Barry, Tad Bartimus, Roy Blount, Jr, Michael Dorris, Kathi Kamen Goldmark, Matt Groening, Josh Kelly, Stephen King, Barbara Kingsolver, Greil Marcus, Dave Marsh, Ridley Pearson, Joel Selvin and Amy Tan. Their website notes that 'The group burst upon the world at the 1992 American Booksellers Association convention in Anaheim. A write-up in the *Washington Post* described it as "the most heavily promoted musical debut since the Monkees".'

your book isn't pulped, it might end up being remaindered – a publisher looks at a book that hasn't sold well, and decides to sell the leftover stock at a greatly reduced price. That's because if publishers are left with a huge amount of stock that they can't shift, it's more economical to sell it on at a knockdown price than it is to either pulp it or store it for long periods. Any costs that can be recovered from the sunk costs of having produced and printed it is a win, and on top of that it does at least mean that some readers will buy a remaindered book by an author, enjoy it and then look out for any new titles to buy at full price in the future. Sometimes a book is remaindered because it's a hardback and the paperback has now been published, which means any excess hardback stock needs to go somewhere. Paperback overstock is easier to pulp, so it will often have its covers removed and sent back to the publisher as proof that the books have been recycled, rather than sold on. How do you know if a book has been sold as a remainder if you encounter it outside of a bookshop? Remaindered copies usually have a thick black felt-tip mark somewhere on the bottom of the book block, near the spine.

Midnight massacre

By their very natures, publishers are invested in transmitting stories as far and as wide as possible – blurbing away, as we've seen. Their business is sending words out into the world, setting them free. But even they occasionally put a stop to words appearing in print. 'For the first time in my life I have decided against stocking a Penguin,' ran a letter that the bookseller Una Dillon wrote to Allen Lane in 1966. Dillon's letter was only one of a number that Lane had received in response to the decision by Penguin to publish a book called *Massacre*, by the French cartoonist Siné. He was a political cartoonist whose work was noted for its fascination with the Catholic Church, hangings, amputations and toilets. Despite the controversial subject matter, *Siné Massacre* had been approved for publication by the Penguin board, which included Lane, in September 1966, although this approval came very late in the publication schedule, as copies of the book had already been printed and ordered by booksellers. 'No sooner had the book appeared than the office was deluged with correspondence from outraged clergymen and, more worryingly, indignant booksellers,' recorded Jeremy Lewis in *Penguin Special*.

Allen Lane in fact disliked the book (but had been outvoted by the rest of the board) and wondered out loud to a colleague if anyone would mind if he 'got someone on the QT to pick up the copies in the warehouse and dispose of them somewhere and report the book o/p'.* One night in December 1966 a warehouse worker was woken at midnight by a phone call and told to report to the warehouse. There he found Allen Lane (plus his chauffeur and farm manager) demanding that he be allowed to take 'those bloody Sinés'; this he then proceeded to do, having them removed from the shelves, loaded into a van and then driven off. 'Now, we'll keep this a secret, we won't tell anybody, will we?' urged Lane as he departed. No one knows for sure what happened next, although it is likely that the copies of *Massacre* were buried somewhere on Allen Lane's farm, where they presumably remain to this day.

---

*Lane meant that the book should be reported as being out of print.

PERMANENT WORDS: PRINT

'Before printing was discovered, a century
was equal to a thousand years.'

Henry David Thoreau

In October 2013, the *Hollywood Reporter* ran a story that originated in Bungay, Suffolk. Some copies of *Bridget Jones: Mad About the Boy*, the *Reporter* informed its readers, had suddenly switched from the tale of a now-widowed Bridget to the recollections of much-loved actor David Jason, as told in his autobiography *My Life*. Like a typical Del Boy knock-off, buyer beware: about forty pages of Jason's book had muscled their way into the binding of Bridget's latest exploits. While Hollywood reported on the mix-up with a completely straight face, the *Independent* found the entire situation a delicious irony: 'The mix-up, which affected some editions of Fielding's book, was apparently due to a fault in the printing process . . . Accident it may have been, but it couldn't have been better devised by the guerrilla marketing buffs. Mash-up – the joining up of two literary genres – is all the rage.'*

---

*This mashing began with 2009's *Pride and Prejudice and Zombies*, with its opening line 'It's a truth universally acknowledged that a zombie in possession of brains must be in want of more brains', and then spiralled truly out of control with *Sense and Sensibility and Sea Monsters,* and my personal favourite, *Android Karenina*.

I'm with the *Independent*. Who wouldn't prefer a Jason–Jones mash-up? *Bridget Jason: The Edge of Reason*, anyone? Like many mistakes, this one can be understood using the Swiss-cheese model in which potential failures in a complex system are imagined as holes in slices of, say, a tangy Emmental. When the holes in more than one slice align, you create a tunnel towards tragedy along which an error will inevitably find its way.

In this instance, the holes that aligned were that both books were exactly the same page count and dimensions – and that the printer's new barcode-reading system only identified individual books (not individual sections of each book). These systemic holes have, of course, since been plugged. Good news for printers, a little disappointing for fans of cross-genre literary experiments. Such is the price of progress.

This all neatly illustrates the singular risks of being a printer. As with the story of the typo, there is nothing news-worthy in the millions of perfectly printed words that roll off the presses every week. Despite the fact that the results can sometimes be splendidly comic, the tortuous truth of ink is that sometimes you immortalise your own mistakes and then distribute them round the world for everyone to see.

Nothing new under the sun

In *How to Read a Novel: A User's Guide*, John Sutherland* imagines the founder of the British print trade, William Caxton,

---

*Sutherland also discusses *The Gutenberg Galaxy*, specifically McLuhan's claim that in order to decide if you want to buy a book, you should simply turn to page 69 of whatever you are browsing, and read it. If you like it, buy it. I'm not sure how this translates to ebooks and their lack of page numbers, which McLuhan should certainly have anticipated.

transporting himself in H. G. Wells's time machine to the early twenty-first century:

> The physical book, the master printer would have been overjoyed to discover, had changed hardly a jot. He would even have found his own catalogue leader, Chaucer's *Canterbury Tales* . . . in the Classics section. Some physical aspects of the books on display would strike him as nifty improvements on the 15th-century commodity: dust jackets, indexes, covers . . . coated paper, italic print, perfect binding – all worth sticking in the boot of Mr Wells's machine for the trip back. Despite all these peripheral improvements to the book as a book, Master Caxton could, with his 15th-century technology, mock up the same product.

If Caxton pioneered printing in Britain, it was of course the Mainz printer Johannes Gutenberg who, in the 1440s, as Alberto Manguel describes, 'succeeded in devising all the essentials of printing as they were employed until the twentieth century: metal prisms for moulding the faces of the letters, a press that combined features of those used in winemaking and book-binding, and an oil-based ink – none of which had previously existed'.

It was Gutenberg's simultaneous invention of the printing press and a way of making movable type that meant that in a relatively short time span, the cost of printing material in Europe fell dramatically, which meant an enormous new readership could be reached. The first book that Gutenberg printed was the Bible, sometime between 1450 and 1455, and by 1500, European printing presses had produced more than 20 million books. Gutenberg had ushered in the era of mass communication, and ultimately turned the whole structure of society on its head. Ideas and information could circle freely across borders, literacy rose, and information (and subsequently social and political power) was no longer confined to the elites. Gutenberg's invention was the big bang for words – it truly set them free.

Widespread dissemination of printed material also changed *how* people read and encountered words, in ways that would have seismic political and religious effects. Prior to the age of mass printing, reading was done out loud. Few people could read, but most people could listen: words and the stories they made were designed to be spoken in public. But as literacy increased there was less need for public readings, and silent reading by individuals increasingly became the norm.

The first silent readers were the monk-copyists: by the ninth century there were regulations instructing them to be quiet while they worked; before then the words they were to write were dictated to them. But both reading silently (which allowed time and space for individual, uncontrolled thought) and distribution of printed material were a threat to the established order: in 1517, Martin Luther would nail his theses to the church door in Wittenberg, asserting that, contrary to Catholic teaching, every person had the right to read and interpret the word of God themselves. The words were beginning to take back control. By early 1518, the theses had been translated into German from the Latin, and a few months later – with the help of the printing press – they had circulated across the whole of Europe.

The curse of the printer

The mechanised printing press meant that words, and all the ideas they could convey, were beginning to wash across society. Naturally, those with power fought back. In England in 1529, Henry VIII issued a list of proscribed books, and in 1557 during the reign of Mary I the Stationers' Company, which had been established in 1403, received a royal charter, and that meant that they could set and enforce regulations over what could be printed. The Stationers' had the power to seize books that offended, and could bring writers before the Church authorities. By the time they received their royal charter the Stationers' were effectively a printers' guild, such was the dominance of mass production over hand-produced manuscript books. These attempts to control printing and words meant that the profession of print became a potentially dangerous one.

In January 1584, William Carter, a printer, was executed at Tyburn. He had been imprisoned in the Tower of London for two years, tortured on the rack, then sent to the Old Bailey. After being found guilty of treason he was executed the next day. Carter had printed a thousand copies of a book by Dr Gregory Martin, a noted Catholic priest, which included a paragraph expressing confidence that 'the Catholic Hope would triumph, and pious Judith would slay Holofernes'. At a time of increasing tension between Elizabeth I and Philip of Spain, this was perceived as a threat to assassinate the Queen.

Illegal presses distributed both Catholic and Puritan religious works, and in 1586 in an attempt to control the flow of printed material, a Star Chamber decree forbade all printing outside London (with the exception of the university presses at Oxford and Cambridge), to better control what was printed. Previously, there had been one official royal printer, but Elizabeth I realised that there were political and economic benefits to allowing individual printers to have a monopoly on a specific type of literature. These monopolies were felt to be unfair, however, and only encouraged unlicensed printings: one-third of all editions published during Elizabeth's reign never appeared on the Stationers' Register – meaning that they were illegal.

One way in which printers attempted to protect themselves when producing controversial religious tracts was by laying false trails in their books. Around this time a colophon began to be included in books, usually at the very end of it, which told the reader where it had been printed. Printers were in effect publishers, and this was reflected in the information that the colophon contained. In fact, colophons had been around for centuries. The word comes from the Greek word for summit, or finishing touch, which for an author or scribe was exactly what the end of a book was – an exhausting stagger to the summit. Early colophons would either say something about the scribe or author, or indicate the author's feelings about the words they had written. Some colophons exhorted the reader to carry out a task (like wash your hands to avoid smudging the text) while others (especially in medieval manuscripts) contained a curse. After all, they were the only part of a book where a scribe could express themselves after the laborious task of copying out page after page.

Before William Carter printed Gregory Martin's book, he had printed one by a Dutch Jesuit priest called Peter Canisius. In the colophon of Canisius's book, Carter called himself 'Johannem Bogardi' and claimed that the book had been printed in Douai, in France, in order to try to circumvent Elizabethan England's censorship of printers. In the end, none of this subterfuge could save his life.

In 1640 the Star Chamber was abolished by the Long Parliament, leading to an immediate increase in the number of new publications available – up to three hundred, by some accounts. Despite this apparent relaxing of censorship, Parliament's intent was to replace Royalist censorship with its own systems. The Licensing Order of 1643 reinstated almost all the censorship of the Star Chamber, and required pre-publication licensing, the registration of all publications with Stationers' Hall, the destruction of any books that were anti-government, and the arrest and imprisonment of writers, printers and publishers who contravened the law. It was this act that prompted John Milton to write *Areopagitica* in 1644, opposing censorship, and, as we have seen, allowing individual readers rather than rulers or governments to decide for themselves which words were good.

The Licensing Order stood until 1688, when William and Mary were invited to ascend the throne on the condition that they agree to the Declaration of Rights. One of the effects of the Declaration was to create a more open society, and an explosion of print that led to the free exchange of ideas and information. Thomas Carlyle described the 'three great elements of modern civilization' as 'Gun powder, printing and the Protestant religion'. Printing changed everything.

Old threats made new

As well as the profound and long-lasting effects of printing on society, the history of book production is about the old and the new responding to each other. We may make books to a different industrial and mechanised scale nowadays, but at its heart a book is still a book. As Alberto Manguel notes, Gutenberg and other early printers often attempted to make their work look like the beautiful handwritten work of the monastic scribes. But ideas travelled in the other direction as well, as Christopher de Hamel, the author of *Meetings with Remarkable Manuscripts*, describes:

> [The manuscript makers] suddenly felt threatened by printers . . . [they] started very deliberately doing things in their manuscripts that they knew the printers couldn't do. They did clever borders that looked as though real insects had landed on the page. They started doing extraordinary trompe l'oeil illusions; they really brought

colour back into their manuscripts because they knew that printers couldn't do that. It was the world of technology and the handmade struggling against each other, each striving to do things that the other couldn't match.

The manuscript makers may have felt threatened by the arrival of the printing press in the same way that traditional printers perhaps felt threatened by the end of the Gutenberg era and the dawn of the electronic one. But as de Hamel and Manguel remind us, each side changed how it worked in response to the other, and we see something similar in the resurgence today of beautifully designed physical books – a reaction to the blandness of words in a digital world. As Coralie Bickford-Smith pointed out when I spoke to her about cover design, this return to the solidity of beautifully designed hardbacks 'might have been a reaction to the rise in ebooks in the early 2000s. People were saying that print was dead, and it really felt like it might become a reality at the time. There was the start of a debate about the role books played as physical objects and it felt as if there were many people, like myself, that loved the physicality of books. But then it became a thing in its own right. Lots of people fell in love with collecting affordable beautiful editions of their favourite literature.'

As well as sharing aspects of the codex (lightness, portability) e-readers do, of course, have advantages that the codex book cannot replicate: you can store hundreds of books on them, they are usable in any light conditions, and connected to the online world, too. For studying and making notes, e-readers offer a new way of learning: highlights, tags, multiple bookmarks and instant searches.

But there are pitfalls in the electronic world of words. Imagine you are in a bookshop and, after some browsing, decide to buy a book. You take it to the till, the cashier scans the barcode, and on the till flashes up: LICENSE NOW. Or: RENT THIS TEXT UNLESS THE RIGHTS ARE TRANS- FERRED TO A DIFFERENT PUBLISHER. That's what *should* appear before you commit to buying an electronic version of a book. On an e-reader, you can only license and hire words – never own them. If the publisher you bought the words from goes bankrupt, that's it: you may lose access to any book you have paid for. So, if those words mean something important to us, then we might want to know that we own them – that we have a permanent (well, as permanent as paper can be) record of them on our shelves. After all, a book will never stop holding its charge, wipe its memory, be revoked by a bankrupt publisher, stop being supported by software, or crash just when we need to refer to it.

Like a lot of people, if I read something on an e-reader that I really love, I'll often go on to buy a physical copy, too. For whatever combination of psychology, tactility and habit, I invest more meaning and value in the printed word than I do the digital one, and so do many other readers. The words we read can come to us on a screen, but how we *feel* about them and the way they are presented to us is different from the way we feel about exactly the same words on ink and paper. It's not just a feeling, either. The mathematician and computer scientist Alan Turing was aware of this concept as early as 1947:

> One needs some form of memory with which any required entry can be reached at short notice. This dif- ficulty presumably used to worry the Egyptians when their books were written on papyrus scrolls. It must have been slow work looking up references in them, and the present arrangement of written matter in books is much to be preferred. We may say that storage on tape and

papyrus scrolls is somewhat *inaccessible*. It takes a considerable time to find a given entry. Memory in book form is a good deal better, and is certainly highly suitable when it is to be read by the human eye.*

Studies show that because books are three-dimensional, it is easier to remember words we read on paper than on an e-reader. Memories are visuospatial and thus contingent on depth perception and object composition. That's why when we think of a favourite passage in a book, we often have a visual cue: we remember the way the page looked when we encountered it. We recall the physicality of the book – the smell, feel and look – which in turn makes us remember the words inside in a certain way. This sense memory begins when we are very young and read to as children, and then progresses through the books we encounter at school and beyond. If I think of *Hamlet,* an unbidden image of the (incredibly ugly) front cover and heavy inelegant type of the Signet edition I had to study for GCSE immediately comes to mind. My A-level copy of *The Waste Land* had my grandmother's name in pencil on the inside cover – I still have it, and it provides a tangible link between us. And I can remember unwrapping a hardback copy of Edvard Radzinsky's *The Last Tsar* for Christmas in 1992 and tracing my fingers over the gold foil on the jacket – reading it was the reason I studied history at university. Our memories and emotions about books and the words inside them are intimately bound up with how we encounter them.

---

*This is from a lecture that Turing gave to the London Mathematical Society on 20 February 1947.

Printing wonderland

Printing and binding a collection of words changes and shapes our response to them. It gives them meaning, life and authority, and means we can reach millions of people with an idea. For better or worse, print gives words permanence, legitimacy and protection from the ravages of time. Originally, only the most valued of words were printed – the Bible – the literal word of God. We learn about ancient civilisations through words that have lasted, because they were transcribed or carved or written down. Print is the most efficient way of sharing complex ideas, thoughts and feelings that would struggle to be passed down through the ages in any other way. Ultimately, if we didn't have print, we wouldn't have any way of recording the most profound thoughts – to share through recorded language what it means to be human. The astonishing thing about print is that it means that words exist in a form that can be republished over centuries while still keeping a coherent and recognisable identity. A copy of *The Pilgrim's Progress* printed today is still basically true to how Bunyan imagined his text, in both shape and medium – even if how we produce a copy might have evolved. How do we get these most treasured words onto the page?

The history of print begins with woodblock printing, which originated in China as a way of printing on cloth. Gutenberg's invention of the printing press then allowed the mass production of words, which had innumerable far-reaching social consequences. In England, William Caxton was the first person to use a printing press, and the first to sell books printed on one. Caxton was motivated by his own experiences in translating books and copying them out: he explained in the Epilogue to one that his 'pen became worn, his hand weary, his eye dimmed'. All these complaints could be done away with by the wonder of mechanised printing.

Caxton would recognise some of the processes of printing today – we still print in 'signatures' of pages, which are then bound together to form a book block. But much printing now is entirely automated – and indeed done digitally. Caxton would be amazed at the speed of printing, as well as the ability to produce colour printing through digital means, though he might be reassured by the occasional old-fashioned remnant of print life that clings on – printers still hand-spray the edges of books when required, for example.

So, the story of modern-day print is one of constant reinvention allied with tradition – books and words wouldn't exist without this combination. I visited Clays to learn how print really gets words good. Clays are the biggest single-site trade printer in the UK, and have had a presence in the Suffolk town of Bungay since 1876, when the Clay family bought an existing printing firm in the town. With a mixture of conventional and digital print, they now produce an average of 3.5 million books a week – 4.5 million in a busy period. That's an unimaginable amount of words being printed, bound, loaded onto lorries and distributed to bookshops around the country and then to their readers.

I spoke to Kate McFarlan, who for many years worked at Clays and still sits on their board. She explained to me how printing incorporates the old with the new: 'Some aspects are visually unchanged – the vast rolls of paper;* the "stamping" of an embossed or foiled image onto a cover. With

---

*Like everyone I know who has ever visited a printer I was amazed at the size of the paper rolls. The most exciting bit of the entire physical printing process is the roll change, where the machine somehow automatically guillotines the paper on the roll that is about to finish, and then picks up the start of the next paper roll, with no break in the books flying off the press. It's hard to explain why it's so amazing, but it is – perhaps that feeling that nothing can stop the flow of words in their urgency to be recorded.

conventional printing, there is still the business of getting ink onto a printing plate, then the image onto the paper, then folding and cutting the paper to create a book. But the actual presses are space age and enormous compared to early machines. Conversely, digital printing has no plates:* the ink hits the paper in "droplets" so the process is entirely different.'

One of the most striking things about modern-day printing is the level of automation throughout the entire process. At Clays, that automation was partly driven by the rise of the mass-market paperback: in 1939 Allen Lane asked them to print an average of 50,000 copies of three Penguin Books every fortnight. In *Clays of Bungay*, James Moran writes that 'Printing and folding machines were to run day and night to handle 80,000 Penguins a week . . . once the continuous flow of Penguins began it was not to be stopped to allow other work to be pushed through on machines allocated to Penguins. Thus the beginnings of a highly mechanised mass book production plant were now apparent.'

While printing may now be highly mechanised, it is still a mix of the sophisticated and the manual. Errors in binding (a section of the book has been bound in upside down, for example) are picked up by both manual and electronic checks. Invisible barcodes and cameras to read them on the binding line mean that issues like misplaced sections are now mostly unheard of. But, as Kate explained, a world of tradition coupled with automation can still lead to problems.

'It's a mixture of Heath Robinson-style chaos and complete precision – it's incredible that it works at all. Machines

---

*I'm afraid it also has no soul. Unlike conventional printing, which makes you feel like you're at the centre of the Gutenberg Galaxy, with moving mechanical parts, noise, colour, glitter (well, foil) and recognisable bits of books floating about everywhere, a digital printer looks like a giant greige photocopier.

break down sometimes: with a paper jam, sections can fly into the air alarmingly and chaos briefly ensues as they are collected. But the machines are full of warnings and lights and safety devices so it's a lot calmer in a factory than it used to be. There are so many stages in the process – most of these are very clean, but there are still messy, manual bits going on.'

This really is one of the strangest things about print-ers. It's a combination of millions of pounds of technology and investment, and then occasionally someone sitting sur-rounded by a pile of just-off-the-press books spray-painting the book block edges by hand.

As books fly off the binding line, those that have gone before are moving on a conveyor belt overhead (the only place where there is any space available), for no other reason than to let the glue that holds the spine to the book block dry, something, Kate says, visitors are 'always mesmerised by'. Just like hanging your words out to air on a moving washing line.

Types of printing

There are three types of printing going on at most trade printers: print-on-demand (POD),* digital and conventional. Print-on-demand does exactly what it says on the tin: twenty years ago the lowest print run that was economically feasible would have been roughly 750 copies; now you can 'demand' one copy to be printed at a time. If you do, Clays will print

---

*Print-on-demand is particularly useful in academic publishing, where it makes it much easier to keep academic monographs available. The high retail price relative to historical low print runs in this market meant that titles would often go out of print. Now, they can go straight to print on demand to test the market before a physical print run is considered.

it, and then post it directly out to you – your own bespoke printing service. POD encourages publishers to keep books in print that might otherwise become completely unavailable; like the index of indexes and the idea of a universal catalogue of books, POD theoretically means that no words need go out of print, ever – instead, they will always be there, waiting for us in some far-flung corner of the Gutenberg Galaxy.

What's also amazing about POD is that the machine is able to produce books in different formats and lengths without a pause. No stopping and starting to reset up after each copy is printed: the data comes in from a server, the book block is produced, the barcode on the cover is scanned, and that tells the machine which size the three knives inside it should trim the book block to. At Clays, they now print roughly one thousand books a day using this method.

Digital printing is generally used when more than one but fewer than 5,000 copies of a paperback book are needed. Digital print runs used to be much smaller, because the machines were a lot slower. The big advantage is that it has no set-up costs, because you don't need to make plates for it, which means that books can be printed quickly and cheaply. It also means publishers can order smaller print runs (meaning that they are less exposed to holding excess stock, and that they can keep books, and words, in print for longer) because they know that they can reprint quickly.

Over time, the average print run at Clays has dropped – but with more separate print jobs being created, the number of books being produced overall is the same. There's now an almost 50–50 split in the UK between digital and conventional print.

Conventional printing is generally used for print runs of more than 5,000 copies – its great advantage is producing consistently high-quality results over thousands of copies.

Conventional printing is probably what we think of when we imagine a printing press – a huge roll of paper, an enormous, noisy machine and a production line of books coming off the other end. It really is something to behold – the sheet of paper fed into the machine will be wide enough to have sixteen individual pages laid out on it, but as it progresses through the machine it is folded and folded and folded again until by the end of it you have a signature of sixteen folded pages – the width of a standard book page. A mass of words starts off on one huge sheet of paper and is gradually reduced to a manageable, readable, human scale.

Inking the future

Clays, like all big printers, is about the scheduling of books to make the most efficient use of their printing presses. Their lines run all night if needed. You can print a run in one day if you are really desperate for stock (though you'll pay more for the privilege), but the usual lead times are about ten days for new books and four for reprints. Like most of publishing, printers are geared towards a big peak from late summer through to Christmas for the Christmas market. The last time I went to visit was one December and they were running at something like 104 per cent of capacity. Which didn't seem possible to me, though no one there seemed to find this at all surprising.

Printers don't just print the books, they also send them on to their next destination, and in Clays' automated loading bay pallets and pallets of books are stacked up and up, on metal frames, with no human involved, patiently awaiting their departure slot. 'Clays delivers more than half the books it produces direct into retail hubs,' Kate says. 'Amazon have twenty in the UK, and then they deliver to Waterstones, WHSmith, supermarkets and many others – they send up to twenty trucks out on a daily basis to more than 150 destinations every week.'

Earlier in this chapter I touched on the story of William Carter, executed for his work as a printer. The stakes for those involved in putting ink droplets onto paper are these days fortunately far lower, but increasingly printers are asked by publishers to operate in the shady underworld, protecting the words that everyone we have met in this book has gone to great lengths to commit to paper from being seen by the wrong eyes. Or rather, protect them from being seen at the wrong *time* by the wrong eyes. As Kate explains, 'Embargoed titles are now a regular event with serialisations to protect and with the publicity hype that goes with big names: Harry Potter, Dan Brown, Stephenie Meyer, Margaret Atwood, political biographies. From a "heads down, say nothing, get the books produced as fast as possible and stack them out of sight" approach to the "full works" that was developed during the Harry Potter years – security guards, even a dog, a ban on cameras and phones in the factory, a ban on visitors, black opaque shrink wrap used on all parcels, plastic covers over all pallets of work in progress, factory doors and windows closed and bolted (this is a nightmare in the summer heat) – there are many ways to keep words under wraps, quite literally.'

When I visited there were not one but two embargoed titles being printed and shrouded in black shrink wrap. I desperately wanted to look and see what they were, but refrained. I trusted that the words would be set free sooner or later.

WORDS IN THE WILDERNESS:
OUT OF PRINT

A book's perfect moment

THE MUST-READ NOVEL OF 2013, THE GREATEST AMERICAN NOVEL YOU'VE NEVER HEARD OF, BOOK OF A LIFETIME – these were just some of the headlines for a novel which on publication in 1965 sold fewer than two thousand copies and went out of print a year later. It wasn't published in paperback until 1972, then went out of print again, was reissued in 1998, 2003 and 2006, was translated into French in 2011, became Waterstones' Book of the Year in 2012 and saw sales triple in 2013. The book? *Stoner*, by John Williams.

Unlike other rediscovered books, *Stoner*'s sudden sales explosion was not tied to the author belatedly winning any accolades* (John Williams had in fact died in 1994) or the book being made into a film (although it has now been optioned for one), but was driven by word-of-mouth recommendations after being reissued in 2006 by New York Review Books Classics.

---

*William Faulkner's 1929 novel *The Sound and the Fury* had a similarly low-key reception on publication. Sales picked up a little in 1931 when Faulkner's sensationalist novel *Sanctuary* was published, but it was his winning of the Nobel Prize in Literature in 1949 that really drove its popularity. By 1998 it had been ranked sixth by Modern Library on its list of the 100 best English-language novels of the twentieth century. The top ten were: *Ulysses, The Great Gatsby, A Portrait of the Artist as a Young Man, Lolita, Brave New World, The Sound and the Fury, Catch-22, Darkness at Noon, Sons and Lovers* and *The Grapes of Wrath*. Other top tens are available.

In a 2013 piece about *Stoner* Sarah Hampson wrote of the book's belated success:

> Perhaps it is simply a matter of a book finding its perfect moment. We live in an era in which happiness and success are pursued ruthlessly, selfishly. We feel entitled to have them, at any cost, whether that involves divorce or questionable ethics. This is a novel that serves as an antidote to that expectation, reminding us that a life that looks like a failure from the outside, that will be quickly forgotten once it ends, can be a noble, quirky and somehow beautiful experience.

In 1963 John Williams wrote to his agent, who had just read *Stoner* for the first time:

> I suspect that I agree with you about the commercial possibilities; but I also suspect that the novel may surprise us in this respect. Oh, I have no illusions that it will be a 'bestseller' or anything like that; but if it is handled right (there's always that out) . . . it might have a respectable sale. The only thing I'm sure of is that it's a good novel; in time it may even be thought of as a substantially good one.

We've looked at how, to get words good, they need to be available for people to read – traditionally through printing them. But of course, some good words – in fact some *very* good words – go out of print. To give me an idea of how and why books go out of print, I spoke to John, whom we met earlier in 'Lost Words', about how this happens.

'Taking a book out of print is rarer than it used to be. We shouldn't get bogged down with the various definitions – there are some strange, perhaps anachronistic contractual clauses of what constitutes being out of print – but the mention of just a couple of conundrums illustrates the ambiguity: what is the status of a book which is out of print physically but available as an ebook? And how do you describe a book which hasn't been officially declared out of print, but is out of stock everywhere, and waiting to be reprinted? To keep it simple, you are likely to take a book out of print if: you no longer have the rights; there is a libel threat, or it is actually libellous; it was a stonking dud with a demand so slight it is unsustainable;* it was ephemeral or only of immediate topicality with no backlist life envisaged; it's of such lavish specifications that it is just not economically possible to keep it in print;† the publisher might be under some financial constraint and simply cannot afford to keep all their books in print.' And, John went on, with books like *Stoner*: 'Occasionally, the benefit of keeping a slow-selling book in print will be spectacular. Something unexpected will happen to transform the sales. Perversely, the thing that encouraged me about the success of *Stoner* was just how ordinary it was. I don't begrudge its success at all, but if this title, what about countless other equally deserving novels?'

If *Stoner* was simply a book ahead of its time and had to wait for the times to catch up, perhaps every collection of words could potentially find its perfect moment. A comforting thought.

---

*For example, Anthea Turner's 2000 autobiography *Fools Rush In* sold 451 copies in its first week of sales – her publishers, Little, Brown, had paid an estimated £400,000 for it.

†What counts as 'lavish'? Well, anything that isn't a standard black-and-white hardback or paperback format. Colour. Or anything decorative – ribbon markers, head-and-tail bands (these are the nice coloured cotton threads at the top and bottom of a hardback spine), cloth bindings, non-standard paper, embossing, debossing, a Pantone colour . . .

How big is your print run?

Ask an author how many copies of their book they think should be printed and the number will invariably be higher (potentially much higher) than their publisher thinks. In 2019, Nielsen BookScan, which measures the UK print-book market, published figures that showed that 190.9 million books had been sold in 2018, with a value of £1.63 billion. This was 627,000 more books than had been sold in 2017, worth £34 million more. These are huge numbers, and they don't mean that 190.9 million books found forever homes. Print runs are cheaper the bigger they are,* but storage and disposing of returns is expensive, too. Get it wrong, and it can go very wrong. In January 2000 the UK publisher Dorling Kindersley found itself £25 million in the red after it vastly overestimated the print runs of books and merchandise to tie in with the release of the film *Star Wars: The Phantom Menace*. DK printed 13 million copies of the book and sold fewer than 3 million. At one point it had £44 million worth of books (not all of them *Star Wars* titles) printed but unsold. Ultimately, this miscalculation led to the previously independent publisher being bought by Pearson Education – a sale that would never have happened were it not for the cash-flow crisis it found itself in as a result of ordering too much stock.

In my first publishing job, I worked in production. The

---

*The Guinness World Record for the biggest print run for a book was *Harry Potter and the Deathly Hallows*, which had an initial print run of 12 million copies in July 2007. Contrast this with the figures ten years earlier for the first book in the series, *Harry Potter and the Philosopher's Stone*, which had a hardback print run of 500 copies, of which 300 went to libraries. Unusually, J. K. Rowling is credited as 'Joanne Rowling' on the copyright page, instead of J. K. This same mistake happened again in *Harry Potter and the Prisoner of Azkaban* and the hardcover print run was stopped mid-printing. According to AbeBooks, a signed, pristine edition of the incorrect version can now sell for up to £8,600.

production team were responsible for telling the printer exactly how many of each book we needed them to print. At that time (the very late 1990s), we would check our pigeon-holes every morning for a computer-generated printed slip of paper that our inventory management colleagues had left there, telling us the crucial figure we needed to know for each print run. I never really thought too hard about the number – it was my job just to instruct the printer, and that was that. But of course the number of copies you printed for each reprint was a crucial part of cash flow for a publisher, and it could change the direction of your business if you got it wrong. It was John who had left those slips of paper in our pigeonholes, and, from his perspective, the data that is now available to publishers helps shape print runs more mean-ingfully than ever. For words, this might be a double-edged sword: there's no ambiguity about how many copies of a book have been sold when every copy is now tracked via its barcode. 'Publishing is a better informed, more cautious business. You used to have the very dubious, virility-driven boast of how many copies you had in print. That's all very well, but how many have you *sold*? In the shape of Nielsen BookScan there is now irrefutable evidence to answer that question. They compile point-of-sale data for book sales. The simple bit is shifting books from the distribution centres to the book-selling outlets. The ultimate measure is the actual sales from these outlets. If there is a big divergence between the number of books you have sent out and the weekly sales being recorded from these outlets you know trouble may be looming.'

Deciding how many copies of a book to print – how many words it is safe to set free – means taking account of a huge number of variables. Every book is unique: no matter how much previous data you look at for an author, genre or topic, you can't assume one book will sell as well or badly as another. How do you *know* what will sell well, or quickly, or will you misjudge things and end up with millions of words of overstock in storage? As John said: 'There are reasons for caution. It's a platitude, but you can recover from under-printing by reprinting; you can seldom, if ever, recover from over-printing. You have spent, or rather squandered the money and the value of the excess stock will have to be written off at a later date. For a straightforward black-and-white title the first print run will be fixed about ten weeks before publication. There is still some room for speculation, but you should have a strong indication of what your main customers will be taking. If the book is by an existing author, previous sales can guide you, but you should never be enslaved by them.'

On the side of twenty-first-century words, however, as John explained, is that 'modern supply chains mean that retailers now are more prudent in what they order. If they need more, they reorder on the assumption the supply chain is quick, which it usually is. And printer's reprint times are now very fast – they can be extremely responsive. You can routinely expect a reprint to be delivered in six working days, and it can be even quicker than that. It should be said it has never been as easy as it is now to keep black-and-white titles in print, and to do so economically. They can be kept in print conventionally with a print run of a thousand copies or upwards, by a short run (anything from about 30 to 900 copies), and by POD. Again, the printers have been very responsive in enabling this. Only incompetence and bad judgement makes good books unavailable.'

Too many words

'Even with these titles with short lead times things can still go wrong,' said John. 'The scope for error is even greater with titles that have to be printed abroad, especially in the Far East where the costs for colour titles are often at their cheapest. Here you can be peering into the unknown. The print run may have to be fixed four months before publication. You are unlikely to have a single order then. Experience and judiciousness are called for. You will also have to bear in mind that even a reprint might take three months to print and deliver if it has to be shipped from the Far East. Mistakes can easily be made, especially for seasonal or topical books, regardless of how easy and quick they are to reprint. There won't be a single trade publisher who hasn't rued the one-reprint-too-many.'

The long tail and the slow burn

While we assume that writers *want* their words to stay in print – to find as large and wide a readership as possible, that they will do whatever it takes to reach that readership – it's not always the case. Sometimes the author themselves decides to banish their words to the wilderness. Bestselling author Nora Roberts has over 400 million copies of her titles in print, but 1984's *Promise Me Tomorrow* is not among them. In 2009 she told the *New Yorker* that the book 'was full of clichés', and, in defiance of the romance genre, had an unhappy ending. Online there is a copy of it listed for £129, described as:

> British first edition. Softcover: paperback. This is NOT the 'stock image' shown but the rare variant edition with the alternate, photographic cover art of a young woman with her hair up, wearing a suit and tie, holding a pen touching her chin, and standing in front of a background of blurry skyscrapers. A VG+ copy: two or three moderate reading creases along the spine, old printed prices

have been scratched out at bottom corner of back panel, one rear corner tip slightly creased. Tightly bound with a firm, square spine. No store inkstamps or previous owner names, no staining or thumbing to pages, no dog-ears. A clean, bright, collectable copy of a very scarce book that the author will not allow to be reprinted.

In 1982 Martin Amis authored *Invasion of the Space Invaders: An Addict's Guide to Battle Tactics, Big Scores and the Best Machines*, which was published with an introduction by Steven Spielberg. The book was out of print for a long time, with second-hand copies selling for roughly £300 each:

> Soon out of print and expunged from his official bibliography ever since, it became a legendary text, fetching enormous second-hand prices and consulted tremblingly by an elite band of researchers in copyright libraries. Now, cheeringly, it's no longer all that embarrassing to declare an intellectual interest in video games, so the book has been reissued.*

Amis claims he didn't disown the book (which was written at the same time as he was writing *Money*), but continues to turn down interviews about it. But presumably he has got over his embarrassment and is now happy to be associated with it again, because in 2018 it was reissued by Jonathan Cape in a facsimile edition: 'While preparing this week's unexpected reissue, the publishers Jonathan Cape discovered that the original files of *Invasion of the Space Invaders* had been unlovingly lost; the book had to be scanned in and

---

*Steven Poole, 'Invasion of the Space Invaders by Martin Amis review – a swaggering ode to arcade culture', *Guardian*, 22 November 2018.

rebuilt, pixel-by-pixel.'* Which seems fitting for a reissued book about video games.

Sex, Russian electronica and arranged marriages

AbeBooks describes *Sound in Z: Experiments in Sound and Electronic Music in Early 20th Century Russia* by Andrey Smirnov as 'A very obscure book from 2013. Who knew there was electronic music in Stalin-ruled Russia? . . . Drawing on materials from Moscow archives, this book reconstructs Avraamov's "Symphony of Sirens", an open-air performance for factory whistles, foghorns and artillery fire first staged in 1922.'

BookFinder.com's annual report in 2017 on the most searched-for out-of-print books included *Sound in Z* along with works by Neal Stephenson and Dave Eggers. *Sex* by Madonna is a perennial on this list ('*Sex* has sturdy aluminium covers which makes it rather durable, and also means that this book won't rust,' says AbeBooks), as is *Rage* by Stephen King – another example of words denied their audience by the author, who decided to withdraw it from sale after it was associated with several school shootings. Number one on the list is *Arranged Marriage* by Chitra Divakaruni, a collection of stories about Indian-born women and their lives in America, last print run in 1997.

The 2017 list also includes *In the Bronx and Other Stories* by Jack Micheline (one of San Francisco's original beat poets, and an artist), first published in 1965, and described as 'a really scarce book'. Except that the enterprising Martino Fine Books brought it back into print in 2017, which means you can now pick up a copy for less than £15. That's the thing about books going in and out of print – the value placed on a writer's words can vary significantly over time

---

*Ibid.

depending on whether their work is in print, how long it has been unavailable and how difficult or easy it is to find copies of it.* As with *Stoner*, publishers never know what might come along to suddenly propel a book into the stratosphere. A film adaptation, a rediscovery of a forgotten author, a recommendation from a trusted reviewer, a new president.† But perhaps in the future none of this serendipity will matter any more. Will digital technology and print-on-demand mean that every book ever published can stay in print? And what will that mean for the second-hand book market? A 2018 survey found that in both the UK and US more than half of book buyers choose to buy more second-hand books than new books. The second-hand book market is growing by 8–10 per cent a year, driven by the online book market. And our willingness to buy second-hand has also lifted sales for second-hand bookshops, too. Now that anyone can quickly and easily find out the market value of a used book, more people are inclined to buy and sell them. Pre-loved words are easier to hunt down than ever. Even if the cost might be outlandish in some cases, the internet means that if you really want them, you can have them, and quickly. And think of second-hand books as Virginia Woolf did: 'Second hand books are wild books, homeless books; they have come together in vast flocks of variegated feather,

---

*Which books have never gone out of print? Here are a few: *The Pilgrim's Progress*, *Robinson Crusoe*, *Emma*, *The Adventures of Tom Sawyer*, *Dracula*, *Gone with the Wind*, *Rebecca*, *The Fountainhead*, *The Diary of a Young Girl*, *To Kill a Mockingbird* and *The Tiger Who Came to Tea*.

†*It Can't Happen Here*, by Sinclair Lewis, was first published in 1935. It was reissued in 2017 as a Penguin Modern Classic in response to President Trump's inauguration, and tells the story of 'A vain, outlandish, anti-immigrant, fearmongering demagogue [who] runs for President of the United States – and wins'. It went temporarily out of stock immediately after Election Day in 2016 and then again after the inauguration.

and have a charm which the domesticated volumes of the library lack.'

Quiet words

'Yes, of course, I knew all my books were out of print. The author usually does know these things. It makes it all the more fun to search for second-hand copies.' The author Barbara Pym wrote this in a letter to a friend in 1966. Between 1950 and 1962, Pym published six novels, and Philip Larkin, who was a great supporter of her work, described her as a 'chronicler of quiet lives' with 'a unique eye and ear for the small poignancies and comedies of everyday life'.

But, in 1963, when Pym submitted her seventh novel, *An Unsuitable Attachment*, to her publisher, Jonathan Cape, it was rejected. Cape's view was that her writing was too old-fashioned for a market that had moved on. Pym's novels featured the clergy, spinsters and academics, and by the 1960s she was considered out of step with the times ('I feel it [*An Unsuitable Attachment*] can hardly come up to *Catch 22*,' Pym herself acknowledged in a letter to Larkin in 1963); her books also suffered from the closing down of circulating libraries.* Although she makes light of her books being out of print, she was in fact deeply hurt by Cape's rejection, especially as they had published her for a dozen years.†

---

*Circulating libraries were particularly popular in the nineteenth century – they offered a way for readers who couldn't afford new books to access them by renting them out to readers. They lasted in England until 1966 when paperback books (which were cheaper to buy) had become commonplace – until then circulating libraries had been the natural home of middle-class, middle-brow readers.

†According to Hazel Holt in *A Lot to Ask: A Life of Barbara Pym*, Cape told her that the minimum 'economic figure' for sales was about 4000 copies, and they did not believe that *An Unsuitable Attachment* would achieve this.

Between 1963 and 1977 Pym was unable to find a publisher for any of her work. She continued to write, though, redrafting existing work and writing new novels and short stories, and submitting manuscripts to other publishers. In 1977, however, she was named in the *Times Literary Supplement* as one of the most underrated writers of the twentieth century. Indeed, she was the only living writer to be named by two people.* As a result, she was able to find a publisher (Macmillan) for a novel she had been working on in her wilderness years, *Quartet in Autumn*, and a reworked version of *The Sweet Dove Died*, which she had been refining for ten years. *Quartet in Autumn* was shortlisted for the 1977 Booker Prize, and Cape reprinted her earlier novels† as they still held the rights; she was also able to find an American publisher.

As Barbara Pym's experience shows, a writer can fall in and out of fashion, and almost overnight the words that once were perfectly publishable are unable to find an audience.

John had also mentioned to me a thriller called *Kolymsky Heights* by Lionel Davidson. ʻDavidson was a thriller writer who more easily garnered good reviews than sales. For a time, all his books were out of print. Faber acquired the rights to his backlist when they set up their print-on-demand imprint, Faber Finds. Sales were modest but there was a hint that something better could be achieved. The catalyst was Philip Pullman who declared it was "the best thriller I've ever read". He wrote an introduction for the reissue which went on to sell more than 90,000 copies. This is a vivid example of the realising of the latent demand almost all books have. A

---

*Philip Larkin and Lord David Cecil.

†When Pym sent Philip Larkin the two reprints and a copy of *Quartet in Autumn* he wrote to her: ʻIt really is a deep joy for me to contemplate them – not *unmixed* joy, because I want to set my teeth in the necks of various publishers and shake them like rats.'

book might only sell a hundred copies this year, but, if it is of sufficient quality, and you keep it in print, there is the potential for it doing dramatically better. Publishers need patience and good judgement.'

EPILOGUE: BRAVE NEW WORDS

'There is nothing to writing. All you do is
sit down at a typewriter and bleed.'

Ernest Hemingway

'It was nine-seventeen in the morning, and the house was heavy.' These are the first words of a story called 1 *the Road*. But are they good? To paraphrase another famous opening, it's neither the best of lines nor the worst of lines. I mean, it makes sense. The words are spelt correctly, and a comma before a conjunction is A-OK. The second clause even has some metaphorical heft, evoking an oppressively leaden atmosphere. But, overall, it's no *Tale of Two Cities*.

What's more interesting than the words themselves is how they came to be. 1 *the Road* was not born of human imagination or agency, but was instead the first novel written by a machine: a black Cadillac fitted with a surveillance camera, GPS, microphone and laptop. Non-standard motorcar mod cons that streamed data into a neural network fed with millions of words from thousands of books and the coordinates of hundreds of Foursquare locations. Ultimately producing, among others, the twelve words above.

Our Cadillac-author had access to twenty million words of poetry, science fiction and 'bleak' literature – no wonder the adjective it chose was 'heavy' – to help it produce AI-powered prose on a ruminative road trip from New York to

New Orleans. Intriguingly, the machine generated characters that appeared and reappeared in the story as it narrated its journey. A mysterious painter shows up in the third line, and then returns later in the narrative: 'A body of water came down from the side of the street. The painter laughed and then said, I like that and I don't want to see it.'

'I want to go away from here, the time has come,' the machine writes at one point – an unnervingly poignant sentence to emerge from an electronic chip.

The machine's inventor, Ross Goodwin, was inspired by Jack Kerouac's travel writings and driven (so to speak) by a desire to explore the future of language:

> Each sentence in this book is an independent generative process and each occurred in a point in time. They were connected by the road trip and a car that contained the sensors dictating what it was narrating, and that's what creates the art. All of it corresponded to what it was seeing . . . Coherent prose is the holy grail of natural-language generation – feeling that I had somehow solved a small part of the problem was exhilarating. And I do think it makes a point about language in time that's unexpected and interesting.

'Coherent prose is the holy grail.' That's essentially the philosophy at the heart of *How Words Get Good*. Is AI the answer? Although it might seem that 1 *the Road* signposts us to a future of words without humans, we can quickly spot a few glitches in that matrix. The examples of the machine's literary oeuvre quoted above come from an online article. That is to say, some of the machine's words had already been selected and edited by a human. No doubt our chatty Cadillac also generated sentences that made no sense, had poor structure, and neither worked grammatically nor resonated emotionally. It's just that, like all bad words that pass through an able editor, they got kicked to the kerb before arriving on the page.

Of course, there are plenty more incredibly clever people and teams working to crack this particular nut. Retiring fount of self-deprecation Elon Musk was a co-founder of OpenAI, a Silicon Valley not-for-profit that in 2019 received a $1 billion investment from Microsoft. The company's GPT-3 generator is described as the most powerful language model ever, with 175 billion parameters enabling it to happily spit out convincing examples of everything from songs and stories to technical manuals and even code.

At its best, it's scarily good. Here is GPT-3 writing in the style of Jerome K. Jerome on 'The importance of being on Twitter': 'It is a curious fact that the last remaining form of social life in which the people of London are still interested is Twitter. I was struck with this curious fact when I went on one of my periodical holidays to the sea-side, and found the whole place twittering like a starling-cage. I called it an anomaly, and it is.'

But it's also capable of terrible howlers: while incredibly smart, GPT-3 is essentially remixing existing content created by humans on the internet, without any ethical or values-based filter. This means it currently apes us at both our best and worst, frequently generating language rooted in a series of racist and sexist tropes when seeded with words like 'Jew', 'black', 'women' and 'holocaust'. Sam Altman, another OpenAI founder, tweeted this honest take: 'The GPT-3 hype is way too much. It's impressive (thanks for the nice compliments!) but it still has serious weaknesses and sometimes makes very silly mistakes. AI is going to change the world, but GPT-3 is just a very early glimpse. We have a lot still to figure out.'

The truth is, as we've seen throughout these chapters,

words are how conscious minds communicate with each other. And while technology continues to make giant leaps towards mimicking natural language, it will be unable to match it until (or unless) artificial intelligence achieves genuine sentience. Why? Because meaning is not *only* a product of authorial intent. It is a synthesis of both what the writer wishes to communicate and which tools of under-standing – critical, cultural, personal – the reader bring to it. Truly great authors are not mere stylists. They have the ineffable ability to imagine how their words will affect their readers; to inhabit the emotional sensorium of someone they have never met. Great editors have that ability to an even greater degree. They are, after all, the voice of the reader throughout the process of making a book.

Back to the start of this section: 'It was nine-seventeen in the morning, and the house was heavy.' If this sentence stirs something in you, does this tell us more about the AI's ability to write or, as I would argue, about the reader's vital collaborative role in projecting the meaning that lights up an author's words? What we might call algorithmic writing is already an engine pumping out billions of characters of questionable online advertising and 'content', fuelled by both human and bot. But it still feels like we have a long way to go before computers do good words better than us. Certainly, further than a road trip from New York to New Orleans.

The Rewrite Squad

'She could describe the whole process of composing a novel, from the general directive issued by the Planning Committee down to the final touching-up by the Rewrite Squad ... Books were just a commodity that had to be produced, like jam or bootlaces.'

In *Nineteen Eighty-Four*, Julia describes to Winston the

details of her job working on a novel-writing machine in the Fiction Department. As she explains, there are only six plots in the subsection she works in (Pornosec, it turns out), and the books are 'ghastly rubbish'.

The cynical among you may wonder how Oceania's bureaucracy managed to conjure up as many as six plots for erotic fiction. For myself, there is a certain appeal in renaming the copy-editing department the Rewrite Squad – and having to deal only with the same six plots over and over would certainly help speed things up, editing-wise.

But the point Orwell was making is that a true creative process is not linear like a factory production line, and that genuine works of literary value are not interchangeable commodities like a barrel of oil to be bought and sold by volume or weight. Instead, each is imbued with the magic of the words they contain; a spell denoted by a set of marks on a page that casts ideas, experiences, thoughts and feelings from one mind to another. That's why books have been worshipped, revered and sometimes banned, hidden and destroyed over the centuries. Books, and words, are so powerful they can be dangerous. Though the cynics among you (hello again) might point out that much of this could also be said of that barrel of oil.

What I hope *How Words Get Good* has shown you is that although there is no 'Planning Committee' issuing general directives on what we should read, there is, behind every book, a Rewrite Squad who work on words to take them from good, to better, to free. We have met them in these pages. OK, not everyone involved in getting words good actually technically rewrites them. But, be they editors, agents, indexers, typographers, printers or designers, there is a whole behind-the-scenes army of people involved in making words good, and then better. Their mission will be, in the end, never noticed by the reader who consumes the words they have turned their attention to. That hidden human factor is what *makes* words – gives them sense and meaning to be enjoyed by readers.

In the same way that the physical book has held its ground against the electronic reader, it has also held firm against automation. Attempts to write 'coherent prose' by AI or algorithm might produce sentences we can read and understand, but it would be hard for us to imbue them with a sense of meaning, when there is no meaning to be found behind how they were constructed or edited.

As Winston Smith reads *The Theory and Practice of Oligarchical Collectivism* by Emmanuel Goldstein in *Nineteen Eighty-Four*, he considers that: 'The best books . . . are those that tell you what you know already.' I don't think he means this in a literal sense, but rather that the books we enjoy are those that reflect back to us our human experiences; that free us to realise what we knew already. Herman Melville's phrase 'the shock of recognition' describes the echo that is returned to us when we read a brilliant collection of words – when they are so true to us that we feel like we have been there before. That's because the words inside have been chosen, structured, edited, nurtured, made better and set free – by fellow humans.

> 'Books were only one type of receptacle where we stored a lot of things we were afraid we might forget. There is nothing magical in them, at all. The magic is only in what books say, how they stitched the patches of the universe together into one garment for us.'
>
> Ray Bradbury, *Fahrenheit 451*

BIBLIOGRAPHY

Introduction: Welcome to the Gutenberg Galaxy
McLuhan, Marshall, *The Gutenberg Galaxy: The Making of Typographic Man*, University of Toronto Press, 1962

www.theguardian.com/science/blog/2011/jan/19/manifesto-simple-scribe-commandments-journalists

The beautiful shape of stories: Authors
Bilman, Carol, *The Secret of the Sratemeyer Syndicate: Nancy Drew, the Hardy Boys and the million dollar fiction factory*, Frederick Ungar, 1986
Blatt, Ben, *Nabokov's Favourite Word is Mauve*, Simon & Schuster, 2017
Booker, Christopher, *The Seven Basic Plots: Why We Tell Stories*, Continuum, 2005
Dexter, Gary, *Why Not Catch-21? The Stories Behind the Titles*, Frances Lincoln Limited, 2007
Druce, Robert, *This Day Our Daily Fictions: An Enquiry Into the Multi-million Bestseller Status of Enid Blyton & Ian Fleming*, 1992
Eco, Umberto, *Narrative Structures in Fleming*, 1965
Hemingway, Ernest, *A Moveable Feast: The Restored Edition*, Jonathan Cape, 2010
——, *Death in the Afternoon*, Scribner, 1932
Mangan, Lucy, *Bookworm: A Memoir of Childhood Reading*, Vintage, 2018
Moran Henderson, Jennifer, *Josephine Tey: A Life*, Sandstone Press, 2016

Stoney, Barbara, *Enid Blyton: The Biography*, Tempus Publishing, 2006

Vonnegut, Kurt, *Slaughterhouse-Five, or The Children's Crusade*, Delacorte Press, 1969

——, 'The Shape of Stories', www.youtube.com/watch?v=oP3cih8v2ZQ

www.theguardian.com/books/2011/jul/31/robert-mccrum-elizabeth-mackintosh-mystery

www.vanityfair.com/culture/2015/09/josephine-tey-mystery-novelist

www.newyorker.com/magazine/2018/01/01/the-made-up-man

www.newyorker.com/magazine/2013/01/21/women-on-the-verge

www.newyorker.com/culture/cultural-comment/the-unmasking-of-elena-ferrante

www.theatlantic.com/entertainment/archive/2017/08/men-are-pretending-to-be-women-to-write-books/535671/

www.nytimes.com/2005/03/20/books/review/ghosts-in-the-machine.html

www.washingtonpost.com/lifestyle/style/james-patterson-doesnt-write-his-books-and-his-newest-readers-dont-read/2016/06/06/88e7d3c0-28c2-11e6-ae4a-3cdd5fe74204_story.html

'Singers of stitched words': Ghostwriters

O'Hagan, Andrew, *The Secret Life: Three True Stories*, Faber & Faber, 2018

www.newyorker.com/magazine/2016/07/25/donald-trumps-ghostwriter-tells-all

www.theguardian.com/books/2020/nov/28/james-fox-keith-richards-has-a-fantastic-memory?CMP=Share_iOSApp_Other

www.spectator.co.uk/article/among-the-ghosts

www.theguardian.com/uk/1999/oct/20/johnezard

Bibliography

The secrets of agents
Archer, Jodie, and Jockers, Matthew L., *The Bestseller Code*,
Penguin Books, 2017
Cep, Casey, *Furious Hours: Murder, Fraud and the Last Trial of
Harper Lee*, Cornerstone, 2019

Stet and echt: Editors
A. Scott Berg, *Max Perkins: Editor of Genius*, New American
Library, 2016

'The writer is your natural enemy': Copy-editing
Fadiman, Anne, *Ex Libris: Confessions of a Common Reader*,
Penguin Books, 2000
Gilad, Suzanne, *Copyediting and Proofreading for Dummies*, For
Dummies, 2007
Harrison Smith, Sarah, *The Fact Checker's Bible: A Guide to Getting
it Right*, Anchor, 2007
Judd, Karen, *Copyediting: A Practical Guide*, Robert Hale, 1995
Nabokov, Vladimir, *Strong Opinions*, Penguin Classics, 2011
Phillips, Larry W., ed. *Ernest Hemingway on Writing*, Scribner, 2002

www.lrb.co.uk/the-paper/v34/n07/christian-lorentzen/
short-cuts
www.theatlantic.com/entertainment/archive/2014/09/why-books-
still-arent-fact-checked/378789/
www.vox.com/culture/2019/1/15/18182634/jill-abramson-merchants-
of-truth-fact-checking-controversy
www.theguardian.com/books/booksblog/2015/oct/06/steven-pinker-
alleged-rules-of-writing-superstitions
www.esquire.com/entertainment/books/a33577796/nonfiction-book-
fact-checking-should-be-an-industry-standard/
www.theguardian.com/books/2015/dec/06/based-on-a-true-
story-geoff-dyer-fine-line-between-fact-and-fiction-nonfiction

www.buzzfeed.com/yelenadzhanova/this-quiz-will-tell-you-if-you-can-
copyedit-a-buzzfeed-story

Specks in your text: Grammar and punctuation

Blatt, Ben, *Nabokov's Favourite Word is Mauve*, Simon & Schuster,
2017

Cowell, Philip, and Hildebrand, Caz, *This Is Me, Full Stop.*,
Particular Books, 2017

Dreyer, Benjamin, *Dreyer's English: An Utterly Correct Guide to
Clarity and Style*, Century, 2019

Garber, Marjorie, *Quotation Marks*, Routledge, 2016

Houston, Keith, *Shady Characters: Ampersands, Interrobangs and
other Typographical Curiosities*, Penguin, 2013

Marinetti, Filippo Tommaso, *Destruction of Syntax – Radio
Imagination – Words-in Freedom*, *Le Figaro*, 1909

Pinker, Steven, *The Sense of Style: The Thinking Person's Guide to
Writing in the 21st Century*, Penguin Books, 2014

Riddle, Thoby, *The Greatest Gatsby: A Visual Book of Grammar*,
Viking Australia, 2015

Truss, Lynne, *Eats, Shoots & Leaves: The Zero Tolerance Approach to
Punctuation*, Profile Books, 2003

Vonnegut, Kurt, 'How to Write with Style', from *How to Use the
Power of the Printed Word*, Anchor Books, 1985

www.theguardian.com/books/2015/oct/20/unfinished-story-how-the-
ellipsis-arrived-in-english-literature

www.theatlantic.com/technology/archive/2018/06/exclamation-
point-inflation/563774/

slate.com/human-interest/2015/01/quotation-marks-long-and-
fascinating-history-includes-arrows-diples-and-inverted-
commas.html

www.theatlantic.com/technology/archive/2016/12/
quotation-mark-wars/511766/

Fight letters from Charlotte Brontë: Spelling
Amis, Kingsley, *The King's English*, Penguin Classics, 2011
Fadiman, Anne, *Ex Libris: Confessions of a Common Reader*,
     Penguin Books, 2000
Judd, Karen, *Copy-Editing: A Practical Guide*, Robert Hale, 1995
Norris, Mary: *Between You and Me: Confessions of a Comma Queen*,
     W. W. Norton, 2015
Silverman, Craig, *Regret the Error: How Media Mistakes Pollute the
     Press and Imperil Free Speech*, Union Square Press, 2010
Toseland, Martin, *A Steroid Hit the Earth: A Celebration of
     Misprints, Typos and Other Howlers*, Portico, 2009

web.archive.org/web/20110604174926/http://www.timesonline.
     co.uk/tol/comment/article993612.ece
www.theguardian.com/film/2019/jul/27/international-incident-
     work-mistake-official-secrets-film
www.telegraph.co.uk/culture/books/3639731/Marginalia.html
www.theatlantic.com/technology/archive/2014/06/a-corrected-history-
     of-the-typo/373396/

Foot-and-note-disease: Footnotes
Amis, Martin, *Experience*, Jonathan Cape, 2000
Foster Wallace, David, *Infinite Jest*, Little, Brown, 1996
Grafton, Anthony, *The Footnote: A Curious History*, Faber & Faber,
     1997
Nabokov, Vladimir, *Pale Fire*, Penguin Classics, 2000
Zerby, Chuck, *The Devil's Details: A History of Footnotes*, Simon &
     Schuster, 2002

www.independent.co.uk/arts-entertainment/books/features/
     the-top-ten-footnotes-9428345.html
lithub.com/the-fine-art-of-the-footnote/
www.barnesandnoble.com/blog/consider-the-footnote-why-dont-more-
     authors-use-the-most-powerful-tool-in-fiction/

www.newyorker.com/culture/cultural-comment/save-footnotes

stanfordmag.org/contents/the-decline-and-fall-of-footnotes

www.nytimes.com/2007/03/16/books/16anno.html

www.theparisreview.org/blog/2012/02/29/document-
    nabokov%E2%80%99s-notes/

www.nytimes.com/1964/06/28/archives/a-nabokov-guide-
    through-the-world-of-alexander-pushkin.html

www.theguardian.com/books/2004/dec/04/classics.
    arthurconandoyle

ideas.ted.com/what-the-mysterious-symbols-made-by-early-humans-can-
    teach-us-about-how-we-evolved/

www.nytimes.com/2011/10/09/books/review/will-the-e-book-
    kill-the-footnote.html?_r=2&ref=books&pagewanted=all

Index, Missouri: Indexes

Duncan, Dennis, *Index, A History of the: A Bookish Adventure*,
    Allen Lane, 2021

Hensher, Philip, *The Fit*, Harper Perennial, 2005

Self, Will, *Feeding Frenzy*, Penguin Books, 2002

Vonnegut, Kurt, *Cat's Cradle*, Penguin Modern Classics, 2008

literaryreview.co.uk/never-too-obscure

www.theguardian.com/books/2017/mar/30/in-our-google-era-indexers-
    are-the-unsung-heroes-of-the-publishing-world

baindex.org/

amp.theguardian.com/us-news/2018/nov/21/why-doesnt-michelle-
    obamas-memoir-have-an-index-blame-trump?

www.latimes.com/archives/la-xpm-2009-oct-11-ca-j-g-ballard11-
    story.html

www.theguardian.com/theobserver/2001/nov/11/society

alanrinzler.com/2009/01/every-non-fiction-book-needs-an-index-
    heres-why/

www.independent.co.uk/arts-entertainment/books/features/
    dishonourable-mentions-552183.html

indexhistory.wordpress.com/2017/01/11/like-the-learned-pig-
virginia-woolfs-first-index/

Inspector Maigret and the pogo stick: Translation

Bellos, David, *Is That a Fish in Your Ear?: Translation and the
Meaning of Everything*, Penguin Books, 2012

Findlay, Jean, *Chasing Time: The Life of C. K. Scott Moncrieff, Soldier,
Spy and Translator*, Vintage, 2015

www.theguardian.com/books/2014/aug/15/perfect-proust-translation-
for-purists

www.thebookseller.com/news/penguin-press-celebrates-75th-maigret-
novel-translation-1096526

www.thenational.ae/arts-culture/books/literature-s-enduring-hero-the-
inspector-maigret-novels-will-soon-all-be-available-in-
english-1.913480

Blaps, blovers and blurbs

Calasso, Roberto, *The Art of the Publisher*, Penguin Books, 2015

Orwell, George, 'In Defence of the Novel' in *The Collected Essays,
Journalism and Letters of George Orwell*, 1975

themillions.com/2012/02/i-greet-you-in-the-middle-of-a-great-
career-a-brief-history-of-blurbs.html

www.independent.co.uk/arts-entertainment/books/news/
salinger-titles-to-be-re-launched-with-new-author-approved-
cover-designs-1887769.html

www.theguardian.com/books/booksblog/2009/dec/24/whats-the-
point-of-blurbs

www.theguardian.com/books/2020/jun/24/flipping-hell-book-designers-
lament-waterstones-back-to-front-displays

And it was all yellow: Covers and jackets

Baines, Phil, *Penguin By Design: A Cover Story 1935–2005*, Allen Lane, 2005

Hemingway, Ernest, *A Moveable Feast: The Restored Edition*, Jonathan Cape, 2010

Lewis, Jeremy, *Penguin Special: The Life and Times of Allen Lane*, Penguin Books, 2006

Scribner, Charles, III, 'Celestial Eyes: From Metamorphosis to Masterpiece', *Princeton University Library Chronicle*, winter 1992

Snyman, Magdaleen, 'The History of the Book Jacket in the Nineteenth and Early Twentieth Century', *The Journal of Publishing Culture*, Vol. 4, May 2015

www.mprnews.org/story/2016/06/07/books-yellow-covers-trend

www.grapheine.com/en/history-of-graphic-design/history-of-book-covers-4

jezebel.com/the-bell-jar-gets-a-hideous-makeover-5978457

www.theguardian.com/artanddesign/2010/may/09/judge-book-by-cover

Little hands and running feet: Text design

Baines, Phil, *Penguin By Design: A Cover Story 1935–2005*, Allen Lane, 2005

Garfield, Simon, *Just My Type: A Book About Fonts*, Profile Books, 2010

Mole, Tom, *The Secret Life of Books: Why They Mean More Than Words*, Elliot and Thompson, 2019

Price, Leah, *What We Talk About When We Talk About Books: The History and Future of Reading*, Basic Books, 2019

www.theguardian.com/commentisfree/2011/mar/22/notes-in-the-margin-social-networking

www.newyorker.com/books/page-turner/the-marginal-obsession-
    with-marginalia
www.nytimes.com/2011/03/06/magazine/06Riff-t.
    html?pagewanted=2&ref=magazine
veryinteractive.net/content/2-library/52-the-crystal-goblet/
    warde-thecrystalgoblet.pdf
www.atlasobscura.com/articles/joe-orton-stolen-books
www.theguardian.com/artanddesign/shortcuts/2015/jun/10/why-we-
    love-hermann-zapf
fathom.info/frankenfont/

'The memory of the loss': Lost words
Cep, Casey, *Furious Hours: Murder, Fraud and the Last Trial of
    Harper Lee*, Cornerstone, 2019
Coe, Michael D., *The Maya*, Thames and Hudson, 1987
Hemingway, Ernest, *A Moveable Feast: The Restored Edition*,
    Jonathan Cape, 2010
Kelly, Stuart, *The Book of Lost Books: An Incomplete History of all
    the Great Books You Will Never Read*, Penguin, 2006
Lewis, Jeremy, *Penguin Special: The Life and Times of Allen Lane*,
    Penguin Books, 2006
Manguel, Alberto, *A History of Reading*, HarperCollins, 1997

www.newyorker.com/magazine/2015/01/05/pulps-big-moment
www.theguardian.com/commentisfree/2008/jan/26/books.
    generalfiction
www.theguardian.com/uk/2000/oct/25/books.booksnews
www.mentalfloss.com/article/12247/how-paperbacks-transformed-
    way-americans-read
www.theguardian.com/books/2015/jul/19/go-set-watchman-harper-lee-
    review-literary-curiosity
www.nytimes.com/2018/05/11/obituaries/peter-mayer-
    publisher-of-the-incendiary-satanic-verses-dies-at-82.html

www.theguardian.com/books/2015/jul/19/go-set-watchman-harper-lee-review-literary-curiosity

www.nytimes.com/2019/01/25/reader-center/sylvia-plath-story-discovered.html

www.telegraph.co.uk/news/uknews/1449742/Toll-road-built-on-pulped-fiction.html

Permanent words: Print

Manguel, Alberto, *A History of Reading*, Flamingo, 1997

Mole, Tom, *The Secret Life of Books: Why They Mean More Than Words*, Elliott and Thompson, 2019

Moran, James, *Clays of Bungay*, Richard Clay, 1978

Sutherland, John, *How to Read a Novel: A User's Guide*, Profile Books, 2007

www.theguardian.com/books/2017/may/14/how-real-books-trumped-ebooks-publishing-revival

www.theguardian.com/books/2006/aug/12/featuresreviews.guardianreview9

www.printweek.com/news/article/clays-boss-defends-decision-to-stay-open

www.hollywoodreporter.com/news/bridget-jones-printing-gaffe-40-647149

www.independent.co.uk/voices/comment/the-great-bridget-jones-david-jason-mash-up-8872121.html

Words in the wilderness: Out of print

Anderson, Chris, *The Long Tail: How Endless Choice is Creating Unlimited Demand*, Random House Business, 2009

Holt, Hazel, *A Lot to Ask: A Life of Barbara Pym*, Sphere Books Ltd, 1992

www.theguardian.com/books/2013/dec/13/stoner-john-williams-julian-barnes

www.theguardian.com/games/2018/nov/05/martin-amis-invasion-of-the-space-invaders-1982-gaming-book-republished

www.newyorker.com/magazine/2009/06/22/real-romance-2

www.abebooks.com/books/most-searched-for-out-of-print-books-2017/index.shtml

www.theglobeandmail.com/arts/books-and-media/stoner-how-the-story-of-a-failure-became-an-all-out-publishing-success/article15803253/

www.theguardian.com/books/2014/oct/22/uk-publishes-more-books-per-capita-million-report

www.bbc.co.uk/news/business-46386557

Epilogue: Brave new words

www.technologyreview.com/2020/07/20/1005454/openai-machine-learning-language-generator-gpt-3-nlp/

www.theguardian.com/commentisfree/2020/sep/08/robot-wrote-this-article-gpt-3

ACKNOWLEDGEMENTS

If there's one truth I hope you'll take from this book, it's that publishing is a collective effort. And a book about the story of books is the ultimate collective effort.

I have benefitted from the expertise and experience of two fantastic editors over the lifespan of this project. Helen Conford originally came up with the book's idea (and title) and steered me through its initial stages. That she took me seriously as a potential author gave me the confidence to actually become one. Cecily Gayford then stepped in elegantly to help foxtrot it over the finish line. I'm extremely grateful to both for their wisdom, attention and support.

This book would be much poorer (and shorter) without my interviewees. I have been truly lucky in that all of them were entertaining, open and generous in offering up their words for me to pass on to you. Enormous thanks to Coralie Bickford-Smith, Luke Brown, Shannon Cullen, Sarah Day, Richard Duguid, Tom Etherington, Lesley Levene, Kate McFarlan, Shoaib Rokadiya, John Seaton, Karolina Sutton, Martin Toseland, David Watson, Chris Wellbelove, Hannah Westland, Louise Willder and Simon Winder.

I must also invest some ink in thanking print impresarios Paul Hulley and Ian Smith at Clays for allowing me to visit the site and patiently walking me through the complexities of modern commercial printing. I'm so pleased this book was produced there; I couldn't imagine these words being applied to paper anywhere else.

For words to get good, someone really has to read them first. My early supporters and beta testers Peter James, John Seaton and

Acknowledgements

Shoaib Rokadiya all helped chisel a more refined artifact from the lumpen shape of my first draft.

Kathy Fry had the unenviable meta task of copy-editing a book about copy-editing, and my words benefitted greatly from her rigour and insight. Anthony Hippisley's eagle-eyed proofreading saved me from plenty of embarrassing errors, and reminded me that even when you think that your words are *finally* good, there is always something bad lurking in the lines. And the adroitness and aplomb with which Graeme Hall managed a fellow managing editor merely confirmed my suspicion that he is a much more accomplished managing editor than I.

My colleagues and authors at Penguin Press (past and present) have been brilliantly supportive and encouraging, and I continue to learn from all of them every day. Richard Duguid, Ruth Pietroni and Anna Wilson are the most entertaining and patient of colleagues. Ruth kindly applied her forensic eye to the proofs,* and Richard heroically provided the index – no one else would have suited for this book.

I'm also hugely grateful to Alison Alexanian, Louisa Dunnigan, Alex Elam, Emily Frisella, Samantha Johnson, Ed Lake, Hannah Ross and the team at Profile Books for making my first experience as an author an enjoyable one. Thanks also to those readers who wrote to me with suggested corrections, nearly all of which I took on board for the paperback. No author likes to be told what they've got wrong, but all of my correspondents were unfailingly cheerful, tactful and helpful, and I am very grateful to them.

This book is dedicated to my late mother, Patricia, but love and thanks go to my father, Dave Lee. He has always supported and encouraged my enthusiasm and passions, while continuing to surprise me with the depth and breadth of his own. My wider family

---

*She found a satisfying number of errors from her point of view, and an embarrassing number from mine. I could almost hear her red pen pounce when she read 'Stephen Spielberg' instead of 'Steven.'

and friends were my cheerleaders during the tough months of writing through lockdown, not to mention thought leaders over many years of lively conversations covering the gamut of words, books, ideas and life.

As well as providing endless support, meals, snacks and patient encouragement, Grant Saunders' position as easily the best writer in our household holds firm. Every word, line or paragraph I showed him benefitted from his meticulous eye and natural ability to get words good. I couldn't have done it without him.

INDEX

Index

Index